12-14-72

REUNION

❧REUNION❧

Twenty-Five Years Out of School

ROBERT DOUGLAS MEAD

Saturday Review Press

NEW YORK

Published simultaneously in Canada by
Doubleday Canada Ltd., Toronto

Library of Congress Catalog Card Number: 72-79057

ISBN 0-8415-0194-7

Saturday Review Press
380 Madison Avenue
New York, New York 10017

PRINTED IN THE UNITED STATES OF AMERICA

Design by Tere LoPrete

To

*The Men and Women
of the Middle Generation*

Whoever cares for his own safety is lost. . . . What will a man gain by winning the whole world, at the cost of his own true self?

LUKE 9:24

Leave the dead to bury their dead.

MATTHEW 8:22

Contents

REUNION

1

Going Back

Seven o'clock. The Chevy Chase Country Club, Wheeling, Illinois, a village northwest of Chicago. I come in out of the Midwestern summer twilight of the parking lot to the windowless entrance hall and suddenly I am dazzled, not by the artificial light but by the confusion of people, the whirling mixture of time present and time past. It is a Saturday night, the twenty-sixth of June, and we have gathered, some two hundred of us, with as many more wives or husbands, for the twenty-five-year reunion, the first ever held, of the first postwar graduating class of Evanston High School. Not just any school, you never forget, but a famous and much-imitated one, then and now rated among the best in the country, maybe *the* best. And not just any high school class but the first to enter the new world that World War II brought into existence: the first over the threshold into Auden's Age of Anxiety (the poem was published the year we graduated)—aspirin age, atomic age, computer age, the age of the Cold War and of all the small wars that never end, that no one ever wins—charter members of what fashionable writers a few years back, having to say *some*thing about us, used to call the silent generation. It is, you remind yourself, twenty-five years later for all of us who grew up in Evanston, a city-suburb immediately north of Chicago. We have become middle-aged, we have children graduating from high schools ourselves, looking to us or not looking to us as we did to our own parents.

In this confusion of people, of past and present, you grasp at whatever is nearest and familiar, each moment set off by a little explosion of recognition. I find myself at the end of a line. There are two card tables, two women at the tables efficiently checking off our names on a list, like a voter checkoff. Behind the tables is a slender, bespectacled man with dark, wavy hair drawn back around a long widow's peak, the head now lightly etched with gray. He wears a cream-colored jacket, smokes a pipe. He seems more drawn-in, self-contained than I remember—he is looking over the women's shoulders, counting—but instantly name and face come together.

—Bill Eichelberg! I shout and reach across to shake his hand. I have not seen Bill since high school, but my clearest memories are earlier, of a boy I used to play with who lived two blocks from us on another street: Evanston's "Germans" were among the first groups you learned to identify, and boys with surnames like Schultz were automatically nicknamed Heinie or Dutch, though not Bill. Later someone tells me that he is an accountant, has managed the reunion's finances.

We have hardly said hello when I realize that standing in front of me in the line is a woman I'll call Julie Chasin. Our arms open, we touch each other's shoulders, and we kiss. Julie's black hair is shorter now than the style of the 40s that I remember, cut close to the head but fluffed out, her dress a long one with a pattern of big, bright flowers on a white background: a style that several other women have chosen, and like theirs her face has become both more angular and more content, more beautiful, with less of the look of—what? impatience, search?—that I remember in so many of those girls' faces. Of Julie my last clear memory seems to be of a dance I took her to at the high school in the fall of our senior year. It was our only date, at a moment when she and the boy she had been going with were out of touch; the moment—the institutional brick walls of the school auditorium, the crepe paper festoons strung from the overhead lights, the girls in their sweaters, pleated skirts, bobby socks, saddle shoes, the boys in white shirts, ties, tweed jackets, all of us smiling imperishably—was to be preserved forever in a snapshot in the pages of our senior yearbook.

As we begin to talk, someone points us toward an enormous bulletin board set up on easel legs. Pinned to it are self-adhesive name tags for all who are supposed to be coming—and for their husbands and wives. The graduates' tags give name and nickname, with, mercifully, a blow-up of the graduation picture pasted on and bordered in orange ink (one of the school colors) so that we will know each other; those without pictures are husbands or wives. Julie and I have both come by ourselves. As I attach the name tag to my lapel, a woman who has come from California, also alone, helplessly asks if I won't put hers on for her and then if she can go in to dinner with me.

—Of course! Shall I take you in? and I offer my arm.

At one side, the entrance hall opens out around a large,

oval bar leading to the ballroom where we will eat, and we start toward the bar. Before I can order drinks, I see still another old friend, one of the few in the class whom I have known as an adult: a tall, blond, high-colored man with a beaklike nose, a strikingly beautiful blond wife. For a short time twelve or thirteen years ago we and our young families were neighbors in another suburb of Chicago before we both moved on, and we still exchange Christmas cards. Allen tells me that he gave the reunion committee my address. He tries to buy me a drink but the bar is closed. It is time for us to go in to dinner. I turn away to lead my companion in.

Why are we all here, the 200 of us, the 150 or so wives and husbands? How has it come about?

The mechanics of the reunion were simple enough, though they had taken years to carry out. The idea of a class reunion had first been broached five or six years earlier, but accident, job transfers, the birth of children had intervened, and what might have been a twentieth reunion became a twenty-fifth. The first problem was simply to find the six hundred or so members of the class. Evanston High School—large, distinguished, with its own way of doing most things—is nevertheless a public school; it has no alumni association, no permanent roster of whereabouts. More than half the addresses came, in fact, from local telephone directories and the pooled Christmas-card lists of the reunion committee members, from elderly parents still living in the Chicago area, from friends of friends. The women, of course, mostly with married names, were hardest to find. By the time the first mailing went out in January of the reunion year, the list of missing members of the class was down to about 250.

This first mailing, which reached me at the end of February, was professionally gotten up (several of the men in the class are in the printing business). It consisted of a cheery letter from the chairman of the reunion committee; a short questionnaire; and the list of missing persons. Someone had designed a logotype for the letterhead and envelope, two hands clasping through the openings in the class numerals, '46. The letterhead also listed the twenty-six members of the reunion committee, including three of the seven couples married within the class, and I was pleased to discover that nearly every name recalled a face: a few were people I'd gone through the whole Evanston school system with, starting in kindergarten almost forty years ago; one, a doctor, I had gone to college with.

The questionnaire in that first mailing asked whether we'd go to the reunion, how far away we lived, how long we'd been married, how many children we had, and, with an exclamation mark, how many grandchildren we had (yes, you thought, it *is* possible—and it was)—all matters that would figure in the reunion program—and there was space for the addresses of people on the missing persons list. A second mailing came in April, a self-mailer giving the time and place and asking for a reservation with a payment of $12.50 per person.

For the reunion committee, the motive in all this was straightforward enough, and the clasped hands of the logotype said it: to bring us together again. While perhaps half the graduates were easy to find, living near Chicago, many in Evanston itself, the others were scattered around the growth cities of the 50s and 60s: Los Angeles, Miami, Washington, Dallas, a few in and around New York, half a dozen abroad (in Italy, France, England, Mexico, Japan). Finding them became a game, an end in itself, played with special intensity by Jackie, the reunion chairman. I remember a dark-haired, smiling, energetically competent girl in the modest green uniform, with full-cut shorts derived from he bloomers of a still earlier era, in which the girls of our time played field hockey and their other mysterious sports. Jackie, like a doting supernumerary aunt, became the collector of all the information about us. And for her, every refusal had a particular pain. There were indeed those who were ashamed to show themselves or who hated the place, the school, the idea of returning. And there is one group within the class that in the passage of twenty-five years has come to represent a special concern: the blacks.

Of the 588 faces in our senior year book, 29 were, in the polite expression of 1946, colored. (Twice that number had started with us in 1942.) Seventeen were actually located, but most refused to come to the reunion and none would serve on the committee that planned it. For the committee members and especially for Jackie, conditioned like all of us by the shift from the civil rights movement to black power and then to the black violence that destroyed cities, these black refusals were a source of embarrassment, pain, anxiety, anger: these hands would not be clasped. And yet, I would find, the reasons for the blacks' rejection of the reunion were as interesting and complicated as the whites' acceptance.

At the reunion, as I moved around, talked, I noticed some of the reasons that had brought people back. Several women asked for news of some man I had known particularly well and who had not come. They were, I suppose, curious to know about another kind of life they might have lived, that they had thought about through the years of looking and trying out, the years of casual or serious dating in the style of our youth in that time and place. What *might* life have been? So, many of us at the reunion came looking for—or perhaps fearing to find—one person in particular we remembered. And we were curious in a more general way, for the class is large and diverse enough to include most of the alternatives, most of the styles of life that, back in 1946, we might have chosen and did not. Only the women ask openly about this. The men look and are silent. We talk about the present, not the past, making the conversation of the middle-aged adults we have become.

And I? When the announcement of the reunion came through the mail, I was intrigued. It gave definition to the twenty-five years that had passed, reminding you that it had *been* twenty-five years, bringing into focus all that had come between. That night at dinner, I told my children about the reunion, about the high school I had gone to, the people I had known. Someone could write a book about this, I said with the reflex of twenty years of book publishing. And then: why not write it yourself?

As that question answered itself over the next few weeks in the grand phrases forming in my mind, the reunion became a lens through which to examine the twenty-five years the Class of 1946 had lived since high school and the War. We were the forward edge of the postwar generation, its obvious representatives. We had a common starting point and, among us, most of the kinds of experience people our age could have. As for Evanston, I had not been back to the town or the school, for all practical purposes, since I graduated, had not seen most of the members of my class for nearly as long—I would be a kind of *tabula rasa*, wiped clean to receive whatever new impressions were to be had. I would return and match up my boyhood impressions with the actuality. I would go back to the beginning, as in a time machine, and tell us where we were really going. I would descend through all the layers of time to the deepest level of truth, our origins. I would write the autobiography of my generation.

I take Barbara's arm and we go into the main ballroom of the country club, where dinner will be served. It is a big square room with perhaps forty long tables arranged around the dance floor, each set up for a banquet, with a white tablecloth reaching to the floor. With the bar closed, the room seems to have filled up quickly, and without looking farther we go down the steps into the room and choose a table near the entrance where there are still four empty places.

Across the dance floor on the opposite side of the room there is a stage with a huge dark-blue banner attached to the wall behind it and, in orange letters, the words " *Welcome* Class 1946." Orange and blue balloons, the colors of Evanston Township High School, are pinned to the backdrop. At each place there is a medium-size brandy glass etched with the legend "ETHS 1946–1971" and a blue or orange ribbon tied around the stem. The effect is artless, like those long-ago school-auditorium dances that I remember, and it is deliberate. One of the committee members has already told me that they have avoided the obvious trappings of a formal dinner, that there will be no high table, no elaborate program and long list of speakers. Just dinner, a few announcements, later a little music and a chance to talk.

We try to introduce ourselves to the other six people at the table, offer names, tell where we live, but the sound of four hundred voices in the room is already making it hard to hear: to our astonishment, although the faces seem familiar, we cannot say that we know each other. As we are starting the fruit cup, John Colwell arrives with his wife. A big, tanned, handsome man, his hair gone gray, he is a doctor, the son of a distinguished specialist. Now, it seems, his own career is at last beginning to open out a little. He has a new appointment in Charleston, where he will move his family later in the summer. John and I grew up within a couple of blocks of each other. We were the two from Evanston who went to Princeton that year.

At the next table there is a woman I recognize instantly: Nancy Lloyd (as I'll call her). As the roast beef arrives, I go over to speak to her. In our second year in high school we were in the same English class with a teacher—almost the only one I remember with special distinctness—who practiced an unusually relaxed style of teaching. Nancy and I seemed always to be violently on opposite sides of every argument, and one day—it was that kind of a class, that was what made it memorable—the teacher, John Husband, prophesied that if "Bob Mead and Nancy Lloyd ever stop throwing rocks at each other"—something wonderful would happen; but it never did. What set her apart was a look of wit in her expression, but at the moment the wit has been replaced by severity, she looks as if something is bothering her. We shake hands, smile, talk for a little. Her hair, unlike most of the other women's, is longer than it was, to her shoulders, the blond streaked with dark. She introduces her husband, sitting across from her at the table, and we lean across it to shake hands.

As the dinner plates are removed and a bland white pudding set before us, there appears at the microphone on the stage a portly figure in a white double-breasted jacket who reminds me of Sidney Greenstreet, a movie personage of our youth more sinister and hardly less notable than Humphrey Bogart. But Chuck Leffel, the class's last president, is benign, a political figure in the style of our time, elected not because he was political but because we trusted him. Chuck assures us that there will not be any speeches and then produces loose sheafs of notes from his pockets which he attempts to read—in the glaring stage lighting he is having trouble with his eyes. There are to be prizes, bottles of red Bordeaux: for the person who has come farthest (from Vancouver, Washington), for the person longest married (a woman, twenty-three years—it hardly sounds long enough), for the grandparents (there are four, one woman with two grandchildren who gets a bottle for each), for those most recently married (there are a man and a woman, both within the last three months, for the first time), for the woman with the youngest child (one of the grandmothers, looking trim in a pants suit, with seven children, the youngest only a few months old). As Chuck labors at the names, the people come up to the stage, receive their bottles of wine, shake hands.

And then it is my turn. I have been hoping that Chuck will forget, but he doesn't. He calls my name, mentions the book—the autobiography of our generation—and asks me to come up. I lope toward the stage, my palms sweating, and talk too fast and too briefly: our generation has been called the silent generation, but with their help I'll correct that, give our generation its voice; a lot of others have given their time and talents to this reunion—this is what I am able to do. "God bless you all!" I find myself concluding, and I walk quickly back to my table.

And now it is time for the reunion committee, and above all Jackie Wieder (the married name by which we are getting to know her), who more than anyone else over the past three years has worked to find the people and their addresses, to bring us back together—and has, Chuck tells us, found 80 percent of the roster. He produces a small box, opens it in the glaring lights, and tells us what's in it: a gold bracelet with a single pendant, engraved "ETHS Reunion 1946–1971." Jackie comes to the stage, he puts it on her wrist and they embrace—then change to a different pose as a flashbulb pops for the photograph.

The rest of the committee, Chuck says, are unimportant compared to Jackie, but he proceeds to name them: Chuck Reding (a fireman in Wilmette, the town next to Evanston), who had the idea for the brandy glasses; Bill Eichelberg, the accountant, who has managed the reunion finances so well that there's a small surplus with which they'll buy a gift for the school.

And now the program reaches its climax. Chuck calls all the athletes—the lettermen—to the stage, and they move slowly up, forming a half-circle behind him: the football players and basketball players, the sprinters and the swimmers, big men, athletic looking still. And then—at least a dozen of our teachers are alive and have been found, some quite frail, and several have come to the reunion, including three of our coaches. Chuck names them and—

—Come on up and lead your troops through the old fight song of ETHS. There were a few singers in the class, but I don't think we'll find any of them on the stage (he waves toward the assembled athletes behind him), so please help us out.

The coaches mount the stage and group themselves around the microphone, and one, Bill Bunn, takes the lead. He is a small, apple-cheeked old man with amazed eyes behind round glasses, a hugeness of voice that was legendary in those days before bullhorns and walkie-talkies. Several people around Evanston in the last few days have remembered this voice, each story a little more mythic than the last: how, when he was shouting orders to a bunch of runners, radios in houses across the street were drowned out; how people living half a mile away called up to complain of the noise. Now, as he bellows into the microphone, the voice is a parody of every pep rally he ever led.

—Now if we're gonna do this—we're gonna do it *right!* (We remember, there are shouts and applause.) When you sing that old cheer song, *every*body up and join!

In a momentary silence before we begin, as if an angel had passed among us, a woman's voice comes through clearly from a nearby table, happy with surprise (it is the grandmother with seven children and the newest baby):

—Why, I sing this to my kids all the time!

And then the song, ragged at first, then stronger as the words come back, the tune:

E–T–H–S we will fight for you
For the right to do
Everything for you.
We'll go in to play and win the game,
We will bring you fame,
Rah–rah–rah–rah. . . .

It looks silly enough on paper, without even a name of
its own that anyone can remember—the fight song, the
cheer song; it goes back, I seem to remember, to some
student right after World War I, maybe earlier. And yet the
tune has a spirit to it, the words suit it, and for a little while
as we stand up to sing it, the time is bridged—it is the fall
of 1945, the war is barely over, and we are all seventeen
again, attending a pep rally in that mediocre year for Evanston football. (The team, using the T formation for the first
time ever and still wearing the fragile leather helmets that
look like 1928, won only two of its six games, but no one
seemed to mind.) Mr. Bunn thinks the song good enough
to be worth singing again, and we do.

—You start it out there this time, he shouts. Now, let's
go! *Every*–body!

We sing:

. . . Orange and the blue
We'll proudly wear,
May our colors be bright.
Vic–to–ry comes while we sing.
Many trophies we will bring.
So Cheer!—Cheer!—Cheer, cheer, cheer!
We will win the game for Evanston High.

There is another burst of applause. The program is over.
Immediately, it seems, everyone gets up and starts to
move around the room. Everywhere people are shaking

hands, embracing, laughing, exchanging the data of jobs, children, homes. John Colwell, his wife and I wander in the direction of the stage, and a woman I remember from a French class gets up and introduces her husband, a big fair-haired man. Pat (as I've called her) too is wearing one of the lovely, long, flowered dresses, her jutting dark face framed by close-gathered hair; her expression, which I remember as one of permanent slight irritation (perhaps only great self-assurance), has softened and become, it seems to me in the enthusiasm of the moment, beautiful. Her husband has recently quit a large Chicago law firm to go into business for himself as an investment banker. This seems to be a function of our age, the early forties, and of the uncertain economic conditions we are living through in this year 1971: several of the men in the class (or the women's husbands) have recently gone off on their own.

My attention is drawn to a nearby table. Four Negroes who have actually come to the reunion, three women and a man, are sitting at a table by themselves. One of the women, I have been told, is Bennett Johnson's sister, also a member of the class, but it is Bennett I want to talk to. He still lives in Evanston and a year earlier ran unsuccessfully as the black candidate in a controversial school board election; it was the most violent political campaign Evanston had known since its settlement a little before the Civil War—there were demonstrations, torchlight processions, clashes with the police, arrests. The black man at the table does not look at all like Bennett Johnson as I remember him, but after twenty-five years it is impossible to be sure, and diffidently I ask. No, Bennett has not arrived yet but has said he will come.

Busboys are clearing the tables. A small band has set up on the stage, with a vibraphone in front of the microphone, and it begins to play. I drift down the room toward the bar, shaking hands, smiling, stopping to talk.

I say hello to Chuck Reding, the fireman.

—Nice turnout, Chuck tells me. I hear it's the most successful reunion Evanston has ever had, over four hundred people.

Several people tell me they haven't filled out a questionnaire I sent to part of the class mailing list—or complain that they haven't received one yet. I explain that it was sent to a random sample, every fourth person on the list—I wouldn't know how to cope with more data.

—Do you think we really were the silent generation? a man asks me.

—That's what they used to call us.

—I've never really thought about it before. But I think we were all conformists.

Indeed, the crowd circulating in the ballroom, crowding up to the bar, does seem uniform. The men are mostly in dark summerweight suits that do not call attention to themselves; one man, however, with a tan so dark it looks like greasepaint, is wearing an aggressively mod suit, another a red-and-gray jacket with a flower pattern. We nearly all have grown an inch or two of sideburn but the hair otherwise is as trim as it was in 1946. Three men sport moustaches; two have Vandyke beards short and neat enough to have been grown for the occasion.

The women, of course, are more diverse. About half of them are elegant in long dresses, some with yards of chiffon that reminds me of our one formal dance in high school, the Senior Prom the night before graduation, when we stayed up all night afterward to see the dawn over Lake Michigan and went to someone's house for breakfast. Most of the others wear some form of pants suit. They are well dressed, dressed up, as we say, but not so much as to excite envy. I look in vain for a woman in a really short skirt, but there are two in the latest fashion, hot pants, one of black velvet, the other of red; both are wives rather than members of the class, one the beautiful young wife of the man who won the prize for the most recent marriage. As these two go past, women comment, nudge their husbands, and the men turn to look.

We have, it seems, definite ideas about dress, formed once and for all in high school, and they have evolved since then without radical change. That evening, on my way to the reunion, I stopped for drinks at a classmate's house with another couple who had come from Michigan for the weekend. We talked about school dress codes—the present, not the past—which had just been abolished in the Michigan schools, as in many other places (until this happened, I had not known there were such things). We agreed that it was unfair of the schools to put this additional burden on the parents. Her daughters, the Michigan woman insisted, were not going to school in miniskirts, shorts, blue jeans, granny dresses, or any of the other garments the school now tolerated, but only in skirts and dresses of a seemly length. But her children are, of course, still too young to argue much about their clothes.

As I work my way toward the bar I see Chuck Head, heavy and muscular as if grown to the floor, like a monument carved in stone; he has wavy fair hair and pale eyebrows bushing over eyes that crinkle when he smiles. The son of a notable Evanston doctor, with several brothers who are doctors, he is, I know, the class's one farmer, and apparently it is no gentleman's amusement but something he really works at, his livelihood. I ask if I may pay him a visit.

Near the bar I meet two extremely tall men, both of whom had played basketball at Evanston: Frank Carlborg, blond, short-haired, very Swedish looking, and Muir Ferguson (whom someone calls Mike now), still with noticeably red hair. Both are consultants, on their own, Muir on marketing strategy, Frank on statistical matters (he had gotten his doctorate in mathematics, taught for several years, published a textbook). Both seem half a foot taller than I remember, dwarfing me now, and I decide that the image I have of them was formed in elementary and junior high school when we were all much the same size.

A little farther along the bar I see a man who seems at first sight unchanged, neither taller nor fatter. I remember him particularly in our last year of French, with a teacher whose accent, even then, we could hear as better than the others', a woman with an air of extreme good breeding. Trying to get him to talk, she asked him in French what he liked to read, and with a kind of weight lifter's muscle-blind struggle over the words he got out "romans policiers" —detective stories. The teacher expressed my own shocked amusement when she commented, *"Mais—mais ça semble plutôt propre pour un homme d'affaires fatigué."* And indeed Clark seemed even then like a tired businessman. His face still looks smooth and youthful, but beneath the surface it has aged, and under the skin little lines divide the flesh. He has lighted a cigar.

Clark buys me a drink and we talk about French. I try to remember the teacher's name and he does: Miss Cove. She got him through so well, he says, that he was exempt from French at college (I am amazed) and later, in the Air Force, was assigned to train exchange pilots from France.

He too is on his own now, as a management consultant. He does a good deal of writing himself, he tells me, in his business. Reports. Prospectuses. (A few days later over lunch, another classmate, the sales manager for a biggish electrical company, is puzzled when I tell him how many consultants the class seems to have produced. Just what is a "consultant," anyway, he wants to know. What do they do? It has never occurred to him to ask someone to tell him how to run his business.)

Glancing over my shoulder, I see that Bennett Johnson

has at last arrived, the only Negro in the class who seems positively to have wanted to come, to have made an effort —on a plane from Indianapolis, he tells me, where he has been doing something about his current job with the Department of Commerce, finding money for minority businessmen. I offer to buy him a drink.

—Hey *man*, Bennett calls across the bar, give me a *beer*, and I realize that one of the three bartenders is in fact a very pale, almost Oriental-looking Negro; Bennett has identified him.

Others drift over and join us: Jack Stauffer, a graying, elegant, witty man who was in the Navy for a while and has been involved in defense work ever since as an engineer and project manager; the man I'll call Ken Mills, a freelance writer for educational films, whom I remember as a runner and a baritone sax man in a band I played with briefly. For some reason, perhaps only Evanston's ingrained notions of courtesy, we all begin by talking about matters that we think are of mutual interest. Jack mentions a black slum rebuilding project that his company had been involved with in Washington, and we talk about the hidebound Southern Congressional committeemen who are supposed to run the city. Ken asks about the one Evanston black who had at first agreed to be on the reunion committee and then withdrew; he has not come. We ask Bennett about the bitter school board election.

—Everybody from Evanston in the *entire country* heard about that election, Ken asserts. I don't care where they were, they heard about it.

Of all the men present, only Ken seems to have changed his style drastically. He is wearing a bright-green tunic that hangs loose around his waist, open at the neck, tieless. On his chest hangs a pendant with a gaudy crystal of some kind; his straight black hair reaches nearly to his shoulders and he seems thinner, almost shrunken. "The older I get,"

Ken had written to me a few weeks ago, "the more radical I get." He repeats the phrase now.

Bennett asks what happened before he got there and we tell him about Mr. Bunn and the singing of the fight song. Ken says he didn't know what was up when they called the athletes to the stage (his letters were in cross-country, track) but when he found out he wouldn't sing.

—I swore up and down, he goes on, that I wasn't going to sing that goddamn school song.

—You didn't *sing?* Bennett asks.

—No, I didn't. I didn't sing it for four years in high school and I wasn't going to sing it here.

—But I *liked* the song, Bennett says. And there were some others we used to sing. . . .

We try to remember one of them, something slow, hymnlike, and harmonious, but we can't. Bennett is enjoying himself, he is like a politician holding court. Near us at the bar is a man we all remember as young and lithe, transformed now by corpulence and a cigar, the eyes almost closed by fat.

Bennett is amused. Rather loudly he says—I see two funny things here. One is to see the adult that you knew as a kid. And the other is that these adults don't realize they have stopped looking like kids.

We laugh.

I drift toward the dance floor, and as I do, in the entrance hall, I meet Jackie Wieder, give her a hug, and ask her to show me the bracelet. I congratulate her on the reunion, the number of people, the way they're enjoying themselves. The form the party has taken, its success, are very much hers.

—Yes, she says, but isn't it a pity that they left before Bennett even got here?

She means the four blacks at the table by themselves. She has noticed. Those who would come to the party are friends, but those who didn't are not.

I stand at the top of the steps leading down to the dance floor, surrounded by the music of the small band on the stage across the room. The music is all in the relaxed swinging tempos of our youth but I recognize none of the songs. A dark-haired woman by herself stops and we talk for a moment. The reunion, she says, is too big—it's impossible to talk to anyone—and I know what she means. Another woman comes by whom I remember all the way back to kindergarten, Charlyn Floyd, married to a man from the class. In the senior yearbook, representing music in the school, there is an unflattering picture of Charlyn behind her cello, but her, too, time has made more beautiful, smoothing away a certain sharpness that I remember in many of the girls of that day. Charlyn has been dancing. Has she, I ask, learned any of the current dances—the frug or whatever they're called? Not really, but she's starting to pick them up from her children. All the movements, she tells me, are the reverse of our dances, and with a few graceful steps she demonstrates.

There are twenty or thirty couples on the dance floor, most of them husbands and wives, dancing the smooth middle-aged fox-trots of people long accustomed to dancing together, dances we mostly learned thirty years ago in dancing classes. A few, standing side by side, are doing the one sedate little dance that we, too late for jitterbugging, made up for ourselves, the bunny hop. The set ends and Bill Olson, another who married within the Class of 1946, heads past me toward the bar. He is a big, round-faced blond man who played football, and he and his wife dance well together, eyes almost closed, oblivious of all but the dance. Nothing has changed; except for the drops of sweat beading his forehead, they might have stepped into this moment out of any of our high school dances of twenty-five years ago.

There were two ways of learning to dance in the Evanston of the 30s and 40s, both starting about the age of eleven. There were rather informal classes held every two weeks in various elementary school gymnasiums by a vivacious, black-haired Miss Little. And there were the fortnightly classes of Miss Pocock, an immemorial institution that carries on still, though she is dead. Miss Pocock's classes were held at the Evanston Women's Club, an elegant Georgian building near the center of Evanston with a beautiful high, white ballroom on the second floor (there was a balcony at one end where admiring parents could watch). The fortnightlys were "by invitation"—one's parents asked for one to be invited, and if one were acceptable (not a Negro, for example, and with a reasonably Anglo-Saxon name), one was. At Miss Pocock's, dark suits, black or navy blue, were mandatory for the boys, as were white silk gloves for all of us; some of the girls I remember in demure dark-blue velvet trimmed with white lace, but all of them in their different styles seemed both modest and quite dressed up. It is a measure of the time that it never occurred to us to question these evenings twice a month at the dancing class; but when my own children reached that age and I suggested they ought to do something of the sort, there was an immediate howl of protest—and they never have learned to dance.

For the boys, the chief attraction in these dancing classes was, of course, the chance to meet and dance with (though very properly, at arms' length) one of the notable beauties who generally went. Holding a girl's hand, being rewarded with a very mild kiss on her front doorstep, remained mysteries as significant as they had been for Scott Fitzgerald or Henry James, but by seventh or eighth grade there were parties in people's fixed-up basements where we played records and experimented with kinds of dancing not taught at dancing classes, and we were beginning to learn about what we called necking.

Going steady was not so formal an arrangement as it became a few years later. That state, with its loosely defined obligations, was signified by a heavy silver bracelet called a slave bracelet, with the girl's name engraved on the outside of the plaque, the boy's on the inside. Despite the rather feverish social activity, starting with the dancing classes or, for some of us, several years earlier, the sexes kept their mystery to each other. The really close friendships were formed within the groups that excluded the other sex—sports, clubs, the forbidden but quite active high school fraternities and sororities. The inner censor seemed to be highly developed. There were, it is true, whispers about girls who allowed themselves to be "felt up" or who were said to do things in the back seats of cars or, in the dazzlement of wartime, wait at the gates of the huge naval base a few miles north of Evanston. But I remember only one pregnancy, and that was a girl a couple of years older who became legendary by having the baby, keeping it, and wheeling it up and down in front of the junior high school, near which she lived. Her name became a synonym for promiscuity, a word that of course we did not actually know.

The system worked fairly well. There are the seven marriages within the class, mostly successful, to attest to it, others within the school of people a year or two apart. And yet there were rather a lot of people in the class, perhaps half, who remained outside, who never had a date while they were in high school: girls who stayed at home wishing that someone would ask them out; boys too shy to go through the ritual telephone call to a girl that might (or might not) lead to acceptance. For myself, I was surprised, coming back after twenty-five years, to find that I knew none of the women in the class, even those I had dated, in the easy-to-talk-to way I felt I knew the men. By the time I had finished college, I had given up on dances. A date had come to mean a weekend avoiding the big social events, going for a long walk, a picnic, sitting on the floor of someone's apartment, talking. I had pretty much concluded that if I did marry it could not be to a girl I had known in Evanston or in the Evanston way. When I did in fact marry, it was a relief, an escape, from the social exertions of adolescence; that set of anxieties, at least, was over and done with.

Although it must be after midnight by now and a few people are starting to leave, the babble of dance music and voices continues as strong as ever. I am standing near one end of the bar, trying to talk to a pale, very blond woman when a short man with a gross belly, who looks like a mechanic, interrupts. Absentmindedly tilting an already empty beer bottle to his lips, he loudly puts his arm around the woman's shoulders. I am nervous about what will come next, but nothing does. What I mistook for feminine softness—she had always looked like the consumptive heroine of a very old-fashioned novel—was really a self-assurance that has grown into impressive social skill, and she handles the situation without missing a beat.

Standing near the bar, a big, blocky woman who lives in Texas starts to tell me why she hasn't sent back my questionnaire. Your questions are no good, she tells me. I mean, she goes on, you want to know whether we think we're living better than our parents or not. Well, we travel, we go to Europe, we send our kids to private schools, maybe we've got more money, of course, but—we live the *same kind of life.*

I remember a girl with a fiercely determined expression who looked much as she does now except for short, straight pigtails that stuck out in back, tied with pink ribbons, but this massive force of character must have been hidden—I was not aware of it; Texas, perhaps, has brought it out. Now, as I say something soothing, one of the two women in hot pants passes near us and the woman from Texas makes loud noises of disapproval. (She herself is wearing a quite frilly floor-length dress that reminds me pleasantly of our Senior Prom.) What does she think of *that?* the man standing beside her asks. She launches with great emphasis into a story about something that happened to her recently when she went to the local hospital for volunteer work.

—Oh gee, she says, the other day at six a.m. in the morning on the steps of the hospital, there's this girl that's about six feet three and she's got her hair piled up on top of her —about yea high (she shows us with a gesture). And she's in boots with laces running up her legs and a fringed vest —and she's got this beige pair of *hot pants* that are so tight in the crotch you wouldn't believe it. So she comes waltzing in and . . . I *bulged my eyes. Those—* she points at the young woman, who is gazing elsewhere—*those* are pretty good, they're pretty *short.* But you know, we used to wear those *shorts* all the time. We just didn't have to call them hot pants.

The young woman in the velvet shorts has drifted away by now and the subject is closed.

—I hear you're a photographer who's putting a book together, a young woman at a table near the bar calls to me. I think that's grand!

I no longer bother to explain that the black leather case slung over my shoulder contains a tape recorder, not a camera. I sit down with the young woman and her husband, Herb, whom I remember arriving at school astride a series of motorcycles. He is now a car salesman.

—Hey Bob, Herb says, looking at the graduation picture on the reunion name tag on my lapel, you're one of the few guys that's got shorter hair now than he did before. If your kids see that picture, they'll think you were a *longhair*.

We talk about cars for a while. Herb's wife has a classic Mercedes which he endeavors to keep in shape for her ("It's too expensive to take it out and leave it to get fixed"). At the table with us is another man whom I also associate first with motorcycles and then with a Ford coupé of the classic year 1936. I remember a slender, dark, strikingly handsome youth with quiet, half-hooded eyes who went steady with one of the great beauties in our class, but twenty-five years have thickened and grayed him to unrecognizable middle age; he has not married. He has come up from Florida. His eyes, which were soft as a young fawn's, are circled with fat, they look shrewd and tired at the same time. He looks painfully around the room again, not seeing whatever it was he came to see, and he says that it is time for him to go.

It is time for me also. I say goodnight and get up. It is one o'clock. The musicians are packing up, the bar is punctually closing, and there is a late scattering of men trying to order more drinks while they wait for their wives to come back from the ladies'.

Don Lewis is standing near the end of the bar with a last drink. I remember him slender and small, his shoulders curved over the piano in the band I tried once to organize, but now all those sculptural voids have been replaced by solids, as if he had been inflated with a bicycle pump. I ask him if he still plays.

—The piano? Don says. The piano *disintegrated* about ten years ago. His wife has come back, is standing beside him, and she corrects him. —All right, *fifteen* years ago.

—We went all through *grade* school and high school together, a woman shrieks from the entrance hall adjoining the bar.

A wavy-haired man is standing near us, smiling, the hus-

band of the grandmother who won the prize for the youngest child. People are kidding him about how "bright-eyed"
he looks, telling him it won't be legal for him to drive, and
indeed he looks a little bleary. He is, it turns out, a detective
on the Evanston police force. (A few days later, though,
when I went to the police department to pick up a copy of
their annual report, he recognized me, told me my name,
and remembered the book—the eyes had remained professionally sharp, and I had become the observed, not the
observer.)

—Bob, Don asks me, do you know where the After-
Hours is? Let's all go to the After-Hours.

I think he must mean a bar somewhere, and I ask him if
he remembers one on the edge of Evanston where we used
to go for underage beer, Ma Schramm's Sharp-Corner Inn,
but it is no longer possible to get an answer from him.

—It's time to go home, a man gently tells his wife.

—I really don't *want* to, she answers in a sweet, compli-
ant voice.

There is a lull among all the voices of departure and
farewell, and then unaccountably I hear the clear, lovely
voice of a young woman, an angel's voice, quoting Frost:

—"But I have *miles* to go before I sleep."

And I—who a few hours earlier stood on the stage at the
microphone and publicly promised that I will write the
lives of them all—I have promises to keep. I look to see
where the voice has come from but cannot find the woman.
It is time to go.

Outside, after the hours of air-conditioned body heat, it
seems almost chilly. Three couples are standing under the
portico saying goodbye, and I speak to them, but in the dim
light I no longer recognize them, it is as if they have already
receded into the past. Most of the cars by now have left the

parking lot, which was crowded when I arrived. I look back, trying to fix the place in my memory: a half-timbered English-looking building that saw its best years in the 20s and has been semipublic ever since, catering to events like this one. Across the parking lot that surrounds it like the asphalt of a suburban shopping center, its white plaster shines in the darkness against the black wood.

I get into my car and start for my hotel in Evanston, driving slowly and carefully along the flat, straight, featureless roads that I no longer know, afraid that I will get lost along the way. Along these roads, where I remember empty lots with sidewalks, waiting to be built on, shading into farmland, there now are shopping centers, brightly lighted liquor stores, low, neat warehouse distribution centers and clean factory buildings spreading outward from Chicago. I feel uneasy.

Again it is twenty-five years ago and I am alone, driving and driving on these same empty roads at night in my first small car. I have left everyone else somewhere but still I do not want to go home. I am haunted. I must not sleep, I must somehow prolong this period of consciousness, go somewhere, but I do not know where. It is a feeling of desolation, of abandonment, and it floods over me now as it did then. Where did I get it, where did it come from?

I have miles to go before I sleep.

It was after two by the time I got back to my hotel. I poured myself another drink from the bottle of ready-mixed martinis in the dresser drawer, listened to the worthless tapes of the evening, poured another drink, brushed my teeth. And, finally, still feeling wide awake but wary of the dawn, I lay down at last to sleep.

2

Journey to the Past

For an Easterner driving west to Chicago, the nine-hun-
dred-mile trip is a journey through time as well as space.
If you set out, as I did, from eastern Pennsylvania, your
starting point is an eighteenth-century America where the
truths of human society and conduct seemed as fixed as the
stars in the sky (and as comprehensible) and the nation had
a talent for choosing leaders from among its philosophers,
scientists, political theorists: Philadelphia with its narrow,
harmonious streets of small Georgian houses, Chester
County with its stone barns and rolling fields shaped by
three centuries of tillage. As you travel west through land
settled only a century and a half ago in the first great

westward migration, the farm buildings thin out, the farms
are bigger and harder-working, the fences no longer neatly
painted white, and no one anymore keeps horses, for pleasure or for work. Between Pittsburgh and Chicago, you
have a choice of routes through Ohio and Indiana, but
whichever you take, you pass half a dozen capitals of early
twentieth-century industry—steel, rubber, meat packing—
until with a rush the Chicago Skyway carries you into the
present: a present of economic growth that still seems destined to continue forever, of advanced architecture constantly renewed; a present that is driving the young mad
with visions of racial hatred, random violence, and political
repression that sometimes turn into realities. No doubt, as
has been said, if you go west far enough you arrive at the
future.

For me, however, heading for a high school class reunion
with people I mostly hadn't seen for twenty-five years, the
journey through time was also in the opposite direction:
not only from past to present or future but into the past.
If I could travel far enough and intelligently enough I
would get back to the beginnings—ours, mine—and return
home with an understanding of where we have come to in
the half a lifetime which those twenty-five years represent.

To travel from present to past: it was not a present I was
sorry to leave behind, for a few weeks, at least, that summer. The present, the American reality I traveled through,
was the new Interstate highway system, a timeless double
fetter of concrete binding hills, valleys, streams, fields, cities with indifferent force. It was diesel trucks fearsome as
freight trains, prefabricated gas stations at every limited-
access crossroad, steel-and-glass truck stops surrounded by
acres of asphalt, and new-built motels of concrete block
with restaurants and indoor swimming pools—air-conditioned outposts of a remote urban empire—displacing

what had once been farmland. Above all, that summer on the big roads, the reality was the hordes of the migrant young, hairy of head and face, moving fast in their Volkswagens in both directions. Or you saw them singly, in twos and threes, beautiful and remote as statues, waiting at the entrances to the roads with signs ("West," "Pittsburgh," "L.A."!), lying in the grass beside the roads, slumped under bridges out of the sun. They were much of the reality I looked to the past to try to understand, perhaps all of it: young enough, most of them, to be our children, in a way they *were* our children, they were what in the mystery of twenty-five years we had become. To look at them was to feel the parental compound of anxiety, pity, rage, hope: where were they rushing to, what outrages plotting? What was this self-absorbed intentness? To a middle-aged traveler bound for an exercise in social piety, they could only seem disquieting.

The tramps of the 30s, who sometimes came to an Evanston kitchen door asking for work, traveled in boxcars and were middle-aged. These new hoboes mostly carried waterproof packs in bright colors on aluminum frames, rolled sleeping bags, and they wore sporty boots and new denims frayed with scissors and only a little dusty from the road. One boy I did drive two hundred miles across Ohio and Indiana. Sixteen, he told me, with an aura of golden hair surrounding his head, the features of an angel, the ardor and intelligence of a young Rimbaud. He carried no pack but a lumpy laundry bag stuffed with poetry and dirty clothes, heading for home. Expelled from Canada, he said, forbidden ever to return. He was famished for cigarettes, lighted one after the other for us both—no communicable diseases, he told me, lighting the first ones. Later he mentioned catching the clap (as we used to say) in Canada and being cured in Buffalo, and after that I prudently lighted my own.

The main route into Chicago from the east is still through Gary, as it was when I was growing up. And although it is a different road, it still takes you for miles past the plants of U.S. Steel and its subsidiaries, where at night the glow from the furnaces blooms like tropical flowers at the tops of a dozen smokestacks and by daylight changes to orange-red puffs of smoke, rusty against the June sky and gray-green lake. Presently, after the oil refineries and storage tanks around Wolf Lake—a bright yellow chemical stain floating on the dark-green water—and the deep-water port facilities in the old marshlands of Lake Calumet, you come to the first toll plaza of Chicago Skyway, one monument among the many to Chicago's mayor.

There was a time when strangers, hearing that you were from Chicago, invariably said something about gangsters. Now, they think of television images of the 1968 Democratic Convention: demonstrating youths being beaten in the streets by police, while in the hall the mayor shouts orders and curses opponents through cupped hands. But to many of those who live there, the mayor is first of all a *builder*—he builds office towers and apartments and roads, convention halls and airports, or he makes them possible, usually on a huge scale—and in the process, industry stays and the central core of the city, shaped by parkland and the lake, remains solid and livable. The toll plaza at the entrance to the Skyway is a foretaste of all this, smartly designed and built with a kind of swaggering competence, but forgetful of small, homely human needs. At the plaza, there is an efficient self-service restaurant between the lanes of traffic, with dark-red custom brick laid in vertical stacks and large panels of glass that make an architectural virtue of an ugly site—the cars flow past soundlessly in both directions, like fish in an aquarium. But in the men's room you wash your hands with soap powder from a white styrofoam cup—someone had forgotten to design a soap dispenser and there was no way to cut it through the beautiful exposed brick.

The Skyway, elevated most of the way, leads to the Outer Drive along the lakefront—parks, beaches, yacht clubs bristling with masts—and eventually to Sheridan Road and Evanston. The fifty miles from Gary to Evanston is a matter, now, of about an hour by car where once it meant nearly half a day of struggle through the dismal avenues, factories, and refineries of south Chicago—a drive that one detoured thirty miles west to avoid. The route today, a century after the Chicago Fire, is a museum of contemporary architecture: the convention center, already burned and rebuilt, named McCormick Place for the improbable alliance between the late publisher of the *Tribune* and the mayor; on the Chicago River, punctuated by aging drawbridges, the white circular towers of Marina city, sixty-five stories high and aptly named since they rise in urban complexity from an elaborate boating facility only minutes up the river from the lake; and, a little farther north, the slate-dark immensity of the Hancock Center, a building which, from the Outer Drive, is not massive and muscular as in its pictures but a tapering, soaring illusion of lightness against the cloud-flecked summer sky.

Farther north along the Outer Drive, framing Lincoln Park, the older apartment buildings I half-remember from twenty-five years ago have mostly been replaced by highrises in artificial colors and with an air of Miami Beach about them. As the Drive shades into Sheridan Road, you begin to pick up the names: the Tropicana, the Statesman, the Malibu, the Tiara, El Lago. Scattered among them still are a few old inward-looking mansions of smoke-stained brick that have become what such survivors become everywhere—schools, nursing homes, college dorms, adjuncts to fashionable synagogues and churches. The pink stucco Edgewater Beach Hotel, however, is long since gone, a

close-in lakeside resort until landfill and the Outer Drive
cut it off from its beach. It had a policy of big bands and
after-dinner floor shows almost to the end, and it was there,
on very special occasions, that one took a girl in a long dress
to dine and dance.

As you leave Chicago, Sheridan Road swings east,
through a kind of border territory between the city's most
northern cemetery and the curving shore of Lake Michigan, protected here by a breakwater made of huge blocks
of the creamy local limestone. Abruptly, a small black-and-
white enameled sign announces that you are in Evanston
and that the population is 79,283. In the old days, the figure
on the sign hovered around 65,000 and seemed immutable
—and for twenty years it was.

After so much novelty, the surprise about Evanston was
not that it had changed but that it was very nearly the same.
Almost without having to think where I was going, I followed the familiar roads: north on Sheridan Road past the
Northwestern University campus, west to pass the house
where I had lived, then back to central Evanston and my
hotel. There were perhaps a few more apartment buildings
among the big older houses of south Evanston, but it was
hard to tell—they fitted in, they were to the same scale, and
there had always been apartment buildings there. The elm
trees, whose blight I had read about in the newspaper, still
arched over Sheridan Road, diffusing the Midwestern
glare, but they were smaller now, and it was not only a
boy's recollection of size that had changed: the biggest were
gone, cut down and burned—giants planted by the first
settlers in the 1850s and 60s or saved from original forest—
but enough remained. The town, evidently, had fought the
battle of the high-rises and, so far, was winning. Along the
shopping streets, I saw the same stores and gas stations,
often with the same owners' names. The houses themselves
were unchanged, with the same deep-lawned setback from

the street, the same trees and shrubs around them, tenderly preserved as they had always been by whoever owned them now. I had heard something about a busing plan, started several years back, to distribute the town's 20 percent of black children evenly among the white elementary schools. Near my home in north Evanston, I half expected that some of the small children's faces looking up from play in their deep front yards would be black, but there were none. That too was as it had been. 1724935

By then it had begun almost eerily to seem as if you could reenter that life at the point where you left it, with hardly a ripple—as if the twenty-five years had not been. Somewhere at the edge of memory I seemed to be waiting—for what? For a familiar young face that would look out from the window of one of those silent, sunny, well-kept houses, be recognized in an open doorway? For a slight, towheaded boy with a deep, serious voice and a stutter of excitement at the world around him?

But if Evanston on that afternoon of my return seemed at first, in its private aspect, like a museum of one's past, in its people and its public life it was another matter. The hotel in central Evanston where I spent the next few weeks was the only one I had ever really been inside; my grandfather had lived there the last ten years of his life. From the outside, it looked pretty much as it had, an imposing, red-brick relic of the earliest 20s, with half-timbered parts and a courtyard, and the rooms too were unchanged except for air conditioners. But in the lobby through the weeks I stayed there they were tearing out the old dark-oak paneling to turn it into a new owner's notion of a retirement home for permanent residents—something it had been in fact if not in name for as long as I could remember. And the big, high-ceilinged dining room with its sea of round tables and stiff white tablecloths had vanished, as had the fountain, with goldfish and potted palms, in the lobby.

The hotel is a block from the intersection of three streets which is still called Fountain Square, although the fountain itself has long since departed. It had stood near the middle of the square, a cast-iron crane painted white, its beak pointed skyward and spouting a glorious jet of water that fell into a series of symmetrical iron basins. It was set on a raised plot of grass with two large trees, surrounded by a circular iron fence, also white. Beside the fence was a brass drinking fountain, constantly bubbling, with steps a child could climb to drink, in summer, as he crossed the street. The square, in fact, brought together several things that the town valued—space, light, trees, shade, leisure perhaps, pure water above all: the City of Evanston had begun as a merger of several earlier villages because one of them possessed a water plant while the others had only wells. The fountain, however, with its trees and grass, was deemed a nuisance to the buses and cars converging on the square, and after World War II it was removed. To compensate, there was now a war memorial off to one side of the barren square, a red granite monolith down which a thin stream of water trickled into a stone receptacle.

The startling change in the town, however, was the bronze-and-tinted-glass tower of the State National Bank building, just being finished when I arrived. A dozen stories high, it rose from a gray-paved plaza beside the square, a solitary exception to zoning laws which, in the past, had always put strict limits on height. Standing alone like the United Nations building in New York, it dominates the view of the town center for blocks around, a glass sheath reflecting a tapestry of sky and clouds. The bronze tower, in turn, connects with a low brick building housing a crisply designed Walgreen's self-service drugstore and restaurant. It replaced a big barn of a restaurant called Cooley's Cupboard, where, after school, battalions of girls trooped to sit for hours over Cokes and curlicues—twists of French-fried potato served in paper cups with catsup. It was also one of several places where, in the evening, one often went with parents for a dinner that cost not much more than a dollar, Evanston being a dry town, then as now.

A couple of blocks away, the library had been replaced by an equivalent structure of the same gray limestone, now air-conditioned. Across the street, in Evanston's other hotel, there was still a restaurant called The Huddle which, in the days when Northwestern occasionally sent a football team to the Rose Bowl and the fraternities vied with one another to build floats for the Homecoming Day parade, was decorated with mural-size photographs of football players. Now, there was a sidewalk café outside where, at cast-iron tables under bright parasols, one could sip a milkshake or a glass of iced tea.

One interesting change I came across repeatedly: the slow-moving body of water along the western edge of the town known as the drainage canal. As boys we told each other shivery stories about what would happen if you fell in, and occasionally you really did see a dead cat floating on its placid surface. In spring, we found the rank grass beside the canal useful for trapping snakes, and there, one fall, winter, and spring, gangs of the despised WPA workers had labored with picks, shovels, rakes, and braziers in fifty-gallon drums to make a cinder bridle path along one bank. Now the canal bank had become an arboretum. Here and there, pine trees and shrubs had been planted. There were topsoil and real grass, a few grass-covered cones of earth raised up to relieve the flatness. And along the asphalt paths there were people leading dogs or simply walking for pleasure.

Evanston's physical changes, even the bronze tower on Fountain Square, were delicate and deeply considered. That was why, at first sight, I had thought the town untouched by the passage of twenty-five years. The changes in the people were equally covert but seemed more striking the closer I came to them. They were the meaning of the subtly altered landscape.

Like Chicago, Evanston had provided early in the century that the lakefront should belong to the town, not to private owners, and in general that still holds. Where there are beaches, they are public and backed by parks. On a Sunday afternoon when the thermometer on the building across from my hotel window registered 96, I strolled along the lake. In the water, the swimming areas had been roped off with floats. Beyond, dozens of little boats swooped and darted, none venturing far out. Down the street toward the boat-landing area came a barefoot father with two small daughters in swimsuits, wheeling a Sunfish on a trailer. Where twenty-five years ago sailing in any form had been a serious and expensive matter that depended on getting past the waiting list for the crowded yacht club in Wilmette, the town to the north of Evanston, now there were racks of little boats stored on the beach and guarded by the town.

The beach itself was set off by a storm fence, but the price for season admission is nominal, as it always was, and the town now has a program to pay it for any families that can't afford it. A black father and his son entered without hesitation. Farther along, a Puerto Rican family was talking animatedly across the fence, the grandmother on one side, son, daughter-in-law and grandchildren on the other, until the grandmother said "adios" and they parted. In the old days, in the southeast corner of Evanston, there was one beach called the "free beach," as it was in fact, and it was quietly understood that that was where Negroes went—as Puerto Ricans would have also, if we had ever seen a Puerto Rican or knew what one was. In the distance, I could see a dozen men playing volleyball in the park with high leaps and much shouting and laughter, and by now, from their dark skins, I assumed they must be Negroes also. But when I got closer, they turned out to be Chinese, and the shouts I had heard were in their own language. Twenty-five years ago, the only Chinese one saw were the small, aging men who ran the hand laundries, one to a neighborhood, and a couple of chop suey places with improbable names like Joy Fun (I could never decide whether that one was in fact Chinese or was meant to be English).

Along the sandy path by the fence I stepped aside for people on bicycles, another element in the new presence of Evanston. The trim, multispeed lightweights did not yet outnumber the cars, but they were much in evidence on the streets, and the bicycle racks, judiciously placed in the blocks around Fountain Square, were usually full. And everywhere in the lakeside parks on that June afternoon there were older people, singly or in pairs, stretched out in folding chairs, reading the bulky Sunday newspapers. Altogether, it seemed a typical Sunday in an urban park as the bigger cities could wish it to be—people mingling, active, at peace, unthreatened, undestroying.

About the middle of June while I was there, a large decal, about eight by six inches, appeared in nearly every Evanston shop window: an American flag waving in a breeze with, under it, in quotation marks, the legend "Long May It Wave." It was distributed, the credit line said, by the Golden Age Club, Inc., Evanston, Ill., thus uniting two elements, patriotism and age, that give the town its special flavor. Yet, whether from a sense of privacy, tolerance or unchallenged self-assurance, Evanston's people did not wear their sentiments on their sleeves—or on their cars. The one flag decal that caught my eye on a car did so because it was upside down; the car was driven by a black woman.

A fad of that summer had driven the young barefoot, and

Evanston's response expressed the town's native propriety: handwritten notices on the doors of every supermarket positively and absolutely, with many underlinings and exclamation marks, forbidding anyone to enter in bare feet. Yet on the street near Fountain Square a deeply tanned shaggy-headed youth passed wearing only a pair of faded jeans, without a sidelong glance from anyone but me. The town still had its old knack of drawing the line—but with forbearance. On another Sunday afternoon in a park near the lake I noticed a boy and girl writhing on the grass, fully clothed, she with her legs clasped around his back, and again no one else seemed the least struck by whatever was occurring. I remembered an afternoon at another beach, almost deserted, when I kissed the girl I was with several times until finally the lifeguard put down his book and came over to tell us to stop—and we did, acutely embarrassed.

One evening during my stay, I talked at length with a city police official about how they were coping with the problems the police had in every other American city. Well, he said, for instance, they had an adult bookstore, it worried him and they kept an eye on what it was selling, but the owner was cooperative and they had a kind of understanding—as long as he didn't go too far over the line the police did no more than observe. This interested me, since the four Evanston movie theaters had all managed to find G-rated films. When I looked it up, however, the bookstore was a disappointment. It turned out to be the out-of-town newsstand, nestled under the embankment of the El, where cosmopolitan neighbors of ours used to go, late on a Sunday, to buy *The New York Times*. The stand had simply expanded into paperbacks and along with the cookbooks, health books, science fiction, mysteries and standard classics there were a couple of racks of up-to-date pornography, with symbolic cover designs and the new freedom with formerly forbidden words. In 1971, this was simply a part of the business.

Evanston, of course, like the rest of the country, had more serious things on its mind than bare feet, public sexuality, and dirty books, and it was these concerns that I wanted to find out about in the next several weeks: what they were now and what they had been over the twenty-five years since I left, what had or had not been done about them. These were the things I would be talking about, often for hours at a time, with the people I had gone to school with, whom I had grown up with and thought I knew best. It seems odd, but in an ordinary enough life—going to college, marrying, raising children, earning a living—I had never until then had a chance to talk at such length with anyone about the direction our lives had taken.

Those who had the clearest sense of Evanston's people—as they were now and as they had been—were the ones who no longer lived there but visited occasionally. Something about the place as we had known it had impelled them to leave, but they had thought about going back. We all remembered a coldness: you knew your neighbors' names, but you were careful to address them with the unrelenting Midwestern formality which in that time and place we took for courtesy; otherwise, you stayed within those well-tended houses and yards and did not intrude. That Sunday afternoon by the lake there was more than the beautiful, hot June day drawing people out: there was a new ease, a variety of life, enriching the old certainties.

On the Fourth of July, all afternoon and long after dinner in a town in northwest Illinois, I talked about all this with Frank Carlborg, a man I remembered mostly as a basketball player, a lanky, fresh-faced boy who had become a mathematician, now on his own as a statistical consultant. Groping, he told me why it would be interesting to go back.

—It's now a very cosmopolitan community . . . great numbers of Jewish people, who didn't live there then. . . . Extremely interesting, no longer a bedroom community. I wouldn't go back to it the way we knew it. It was all white—I didn't even know any *Catholics!* That was an *amazing* situation we grew up in.

The point was not so much that no Catholics, Jews, or blacks actually lived there—they did—but rather that these and all the other groups were as self-contained as tribes in the Brazilian jungle: for most of us, it was possible to grow up with the impression that there were no others in the world unlike ourselves, and that was indeed amazing. One of the ways Evanston has changed in these twenty-five years is that its people, like most other Americans, have been discovering that there are, after all, others in their world and that to be ignorant of that fact is both dangerous and wrong.

Later in the summer, as I sat over coffee in the Greenwich Village apartment of another and very different classmate, a foredestined bachelor, I heard much the same thing. (After trying Philadelphia, Baltimore, and Washington, he had decided that if he was going to live in a big city he might as well live in *the* city.) Spence was talking about a married sister who still lived near where they had grown up, in the original Evanston plat of a dozen blocks.

—My sister and her family have a very active and involved social life that *does* include their neighbors and a great many university people. It all sounds much more open and, I'd say, a good deal healthier, than it used to be.

On my first night back in Evanston, a man who had stayed, who was living it, had expressed his changed awareness more concretely and specifically. Ken Mills I could recall only as someone behind a baritone sax in a band I had once played in. Now he was a free-lance writer of film scripts. He had black neighbors. When, using the Eastern term, I asked how it had come about that he was living in a mixed neighborhood, he earnestly corrected me. "Bi-racial" was the word they used, he told me, as if to call it "mixed" were demeaning—and perhaps it is. The house Ken, his wife and their two children lived in was the result of the kind of conscious choice people have been called on to make—they had had a hard time buying the house, even getting a realtor to show them one in the area.

—The real estate dealers—this was five years ago—had decided that this neighborhood would go black. And there-fore they wouldn't show it to white families. They had mapped out the whole spread of the black community and the boundaries it was to take and everything else. . . .

Fantasy? The situation looked different to the town's leading realtor, another classmate, when I talked to him over lunch at the University Club. Practical realism? As a practical matter but from a different standpoint, Ken was acutely aware of the racial composition of all the streets around him—which formerly white streets were now black, when the last white family had moved, which were on the way. We had grown up in a town where 10 or 12 percent of the people were Negroes. The proportion, in fact, was about like the national one but it was an unac-knowledged reality: we knew it was there but not what it meant. It was intriguing that the town had managed to nurture someone like Ken.

By early July, a little more than a month after arriving in Evanston, I was tired, I was ready to leave. I thought often of an argument I had years ago with an Evanston girl I knew in Europe, after I got out of college. In that unlikely setting, the argument was about Evanston: whether you could, or should, go back. She told me about days she spent weeping when she was at home—it was impossible for her to return. I said that home, the place where you grew up, was simply a fact of life, whatever you felt about it—you had no choice but to root yourself there. But I was the one that life led elsewhere; the girl, eventually, went back to Illinois.

All that was pretty remote in July as I made some last telephone calls, paid my hotel bill, and got ready to leave. For me, apparently, it was possible to visit, talk, enjoy old friends and new places, but life was elsewhere and I was impatient. Thomas Wolfe, whom people of my generation used to look on as a great literary force, wrote that you can't go home again, but I think that is not true. You *can* go home again. It is only that you cannot stay.

On that last day, a little of the famous Midwestern weather sprang up to send me off. I woke before daylight to a thunderous pounding at the windows of my room, and when I looked out I saw lumps of ice the size of marbles beating against the sill: hail—the kind of Midwestern summer hail, punctuated by lightning and thunder, that on the plains pierces roofs and flattens fields of wheat. By noon, out on the sidewalk in front of the hotel as I loaded the car, it had all dried up, the sun was out, and a wild playful wind had come up. Before I finished, my suitcases had blown over on the sidewalk and hat, raincoat, a tobacco pouch, an entire Sunday newspaper had whirled all over the street. It was time to go.

3

Twenty-Five Years

Twenty-five years ago, in the spring of 1946, a chemistry teacher at Evanston Township High School asked his class to name the most important event of their lifetime. He paused, letting the effect of his question build dramatically. Cold spring sunlight glazed the row of big windows along one wall of the double classroom-laboratory and fell on thirty or so bright kids anxiously turning over possibilities in their minds. The silence lengthened. No one knew or was prepared to guess. Finally, with a flourish, the teacher said:

—The *atomic bomb*, of course!

I don't know now if he meant the explosions over Hiro-

shima and Nagasaki the previous August, which had ended
the war with Japan, or the "peaceful uses of atomic energy"
—atomic fission as a new source of fuel to replace the ex-
haustible minerals. Probably he meant both. Our education
up to that point had given us precise answers to clearly
stated questions. We had not yet faced, if we ever would,
those living situations in which there *are* no answers, perhaps not even any questions. Yet in the hindsight of
twenty-five years, when more immediate bogeymen people
our nightmares and the atom bomb and its descendants
seem as homely as dynamite, the prospect of transforming
the world by atomic energy is as remote as ever and the
teacher's answer no longer seems as conclusive as it did in
1946. There was, I think, at least an element of skepticism
in our silence. We had reason to be skeptical, the people of
my generation, coming of age in that first spring after the
War. We had lived through too much history already.

The members of the Class of 1946 were mostly born in
1928, the high point of the boom years of the 1920s, but also
the year the country chose to embody its idea of itself in
Herbert Hoover, a philanthropic Quaker engineer, in pref-
erence to the flamboyant big-city politician Al Smith. We
were hardly a year old when the stock market crash put a
stop to all that. By 1932 or 1933, many of our parents had lost
jobs, homes, businesses; our fathers had started the long
haul of indebtedness and constraint that in many cases
lasted till the end of their working lives. By the middle of
the decade, we began to be aware of preludes to a new
world war. The interminable conquest of China by the
Japanese seemed always to have been going on, and somewhere in Africa the Italians were conquering a country
known variously as Ethiopia and Abyssinia. There was that
most tragic and romantic of wars, the Spanish Civil War,
which we learned of through grisly photographs in the
pages of a new ten-cent weekly called *Life*, and there was

one's sense of shame at the cowardice of a civilization that in Austria and then Czechoslovakia surrendered to the Fascist bullies—but also to the millions of young men in England who had vowed never again to fight for king and country; and to Frenchmen like those who first misplanned the Maginot Line and then built it of shoddy materials. By now, for us in school, "current events" had begun to be an important subject. In the newspapers, charts compared the numbers of soldiers, tanks, airplanes, battleships in all the countries that might be involved; maps connected the progress of German expansion with the strategy outlined in *Mein Kampf.* On the radio one could hear the hysterical German of Hitler's speeches, followed by the sedate, British-accented translation.

All this was history, but the effects, in Evanston, were muted. School saw to it that even the dullest of us were fairly well informed about events, but the meaning, the passion, the terror, were remote. When a girl from Germany appeared at my school, I thought of her simply as German—I knew that her presence had something to do with Hitler but didn't know what.

Some time in the early spring of 1941, the Chicago *Tribune* conducted a poll: are you for peace or war? I remember it particularly because my mother strictly refused to answer —it depended, she said, on the circumstances. That probably placed her among the 20 percent or so whom the newspaper identified as "the fifth column," borrowing the term from Franco. About the same time, the America First Committee—that curious alliance of old-time populists, sincere pacifists, technicians dazzled by German effectiveness, and German nationalists—opened an office in one of Evanston's many vacant stores, across the street from the North Shore Hotel. The two things together—a more or less reasoned nationalism tempered by fear of what seemed a supreme evil—embodied the feelings of most of our parents.

When Pearl Harbor and the War finally did come, they resolved a dilemma that had become increasingly obvious, even in Evanston: it forced us to set aside theory and argument by showing us what had to be done.

In 1946, the great events of our lifetime, the Depression and the War, were for us not two experiences but one, a continuity. For our parents, in many cases, the War was an answer: it meant jobs, new business, an escape into the security of the Army or Navy.

What did the Depression mean for those of us who were born into it? One evening in the course of my weeks in Evanston, I was talking with Allen Kerr and his wife in their comfortable living room in another suburb of Chicago, a town that had remained much as Evanston had seemed to us when we were growing up there. Allen was telling a story of his father's about the days when the banks started to close all over the country—about March 1933, it would have been. It had been the end of the week, he had the week's receipts of his business to deposit, and he cautiously telephoned a banker friend to ask if his bank was still all right. "Solid as the Rock of Gibraltar," the friend told him—it was the sort of thing one said. Allen's father sent his secretary to the bank with the money, and while she waited placidly in line to deposit it, as she had been told, everyone else was feverishly taking money out. That day the bank closed for good.

It had grown into an elaborate family story that we could laugh about nearly forty years later, but the consequences were broader than the loss of a week's receipts. The business had obligations it could not meet. The family's home had been put up as collateral for stocks bought on margin that were now worthless.

—Then from that point, Allen concluded, he lost his home, he lost his business, and we lived with my mother's parents in Evanston. We didn't have a house of our own.

The father went away for a while to Texas, to earn money. Later he tried selling insurance. He had lied about his age to get into the Navy during the First World War. When the second one finally came, he joined again, at the age of forty-two. It was a way out.

I talked with a number of people whose parents had lost their home about the same time; back taxes had taken it, a margin account had swallowed it, large expenses and little income had forced them into one of Evanston's apartments. Families moved in with relatives as Allen's did, sometimes permanently, or the children were sent away for a while. For some, there were dozens of moves, from house to house, apartment to apartment. For many of us, the displacement was not only economic, but social as well. A man who had been a conductor on the train lost his job and after that was allowed to come in once in a while to clean out the washrooms in the little local stations. Another man I talked to remembered his father hitting bottom when he got a job in a cement factory where he shook out the empty bags and came home every night covered with cement dust. A man trained as an accountant at Northwestern lost his job early in the Depression but was able to get another as a milkman and didn't leave it until long after World War II, when an accident forced him back into accounting. An engineer with a degree from MIT found that the only job he could get was as a telephone lineman in Minnesota—his son remembers him coming in out of the thirty-degree-below-zero winter from stringing lines across the prairies. One woman's father, trained as an artist, went back to the small family farm to earn his living—and sent his daughter to live with relatives in Evanston for the sake of the education. She remembered a side of the Depression that most of us missed—the terrible droughts that turned parts of the country into desert, followed by rainstorms that washed out whatever was still growing.

—I can remember riding on a hayrack with my father and going down to a culvert and watching him pull the shocks of wheat out of the mud and put them back on the wagon. And then they were fed to the livestock. . . .

Another woman, a third-generation Scandinavian from northern Michigan, told me about her father, who had been a logger.

—The lumber mill burned. There was so much lumber piled up because it couldn't be sold that somebody decided to burn the stuff and then we'd go back to work. It was deliberate arson.

But of course there was no work, and the family moved to Chicago where the father tried his hand at selling real estate—and eventually she too wound up in an Evanston apartment and joined our class at Evanston High School.

And yet across the range of this experience, the Depression was always something happening to other people. Repeatedly, with a certain pride, people told me that their fathers had never been without work, without a job of some kind—"He never lost a day's work" was the recurring phrase. Frank Carlborg remembered the day his father came home from the bank where he worked and announced that his pay had been cut by 40 percent. John Pritzlaff, an engineer, told me about the time his father, who worked for the Chicago schools, was paid in something called scrip—a promise to pay when the city had the money; some stores would take it in exchange for goods while others would not. The people I talked to were the sons and daughters of survivors. Their parents had hung on in Evanston in spite of everything.

So the personal effects on these children of the Depression were minor. There seemed nothing odd about feeding the family for a week from the Sunday roast—first hot, then warmed over, and finally transformed to cold cuts and hash. Mothers went to Wiebolt's, an Evanston department store, and bought their daughters' dresses on Dollar Day— for a dollar—and then resewed them and added trimmings; or they made the dresses themselves, from scratch. A few of the women remembered feeling anxious about clothes. At a time when the knee-length pleated skirt topped by a sweater was the girls' uniform, having several sweaters was a sign of wealth and social power. Some of the men I talked to were surprised, thinking of their own children's succession of bicycles bought and discarded, to remember that their first had been at the age of twelve and had been a serious matter.

As a group, we accepted the situation as normal and permanent, and, on the whole, did not worry about it, whatever anxieties our parents may have felt. But if they did not talk to us about money, the cost of things, they were not very free with it either, and hence, for us, the American business of getting it began early, a penny at a time. Herb Harms recalled with pleasure the summer stratagems by which a boy could acquire the five pennies to buy a soft drink or the chocolate-covered bar of ice cream on a stick that was called a Good Humor.

—On a hot day you'd be playing, you'd want a bottle of pop but you didn't go home and ask for a nickel, you'd have to go out and hunt up old pop bottles . . . or you'd go down to the canal bank, the community golf course, and drag for golf balls. Of course we had fun doing this, too. We used to save old papers and bits of metal and sell them to the old rags and iron man. He came around with a horse and wagon, he had a scale. He'd yell "Old rags and iron"—a song. He'd short you ever chance he'd get. You'd be lucky if you'd get five cents for everything, but that would be enough to buy a bottle of pop. *That's* the Depression, to me.

The impulse to earn money was an effect of the Depression so obvious that the members of the Class of 1946 were hardly conscious of it. I talked about this at length with

Roy King, a carpenter, in the air-conditioned living room
of the house he had built largely with his own hands. He
told me how in those days, when times, as he said, were
hard, he had contributed to the family stoker, a new device
that fed coal automatically into a furnace at a uniform rate.

—You could go to the store for the lady across the street
and she'd give you a penny. . . . When we had a paper route,
I came in with nineteen dollars and my dad, he had to make
a stoker payment and he needed eight dollars, and I loaned
him eight dollars. And I asked him for it three months later
and he let me know that he was feeding me and providing
shelter and clothing. That really irritated me.

But hadn't that embarrassed his father, I asked, sympathizing even at this distance in time.

No, Roy told me, his dad wasn't embarrassed. —He
meant it, because he knew he was doing the best he could.
Now, I can understand. . . . That, Roy concluded, was
where I started my independence.

I don't believe the fact that Roy is black made a big
difference, at least in the matter of jobs and money. Others,
who are white, told me with gratitude that they had been
allowed to *keep* the money they earned (as Roy mostly was
himself)—they were conscious of others who handed it
over to their parents. Some of us had allowances; others
merely envied their friends' dime or quarter a week and
found ways of earning money themselves. By the time we
were in high school, thirteen or fourteen, many of us had
after-school or summer jobs, even the girls, and some of us
had been doing work of some kind for years. It was not in
most cases the money so much as the job itself that mattered. This hunger for a job—for the kind of independence
a job signified—was a new thing in middle-class Evanston.
Where did it come from?

Evanston was connected with Chicago by the Chicago &
North Western Rail Road—the steam train we called it, as

it still was in those days—and the electric elevated trains, which were cheaper, with battered wooden coaches painted khaki color and undersized seats covered with woven yellow straw, varnished, very hard and slippery. For a dime, a man could ride the El from Chicago to Evanston to look for work. Hence, if you lived within walking distance of the El, one of the things you learned about work was a man standing quietly at your door asking if he could do something around the house—wash windows or clean or paint, rake leaves, cut grass—for a little money or a meal. They were respectable looking men, and one met them without hostility or fear, even in apartment buildings.

—They would come to the door, Herb told me, and they would ask my mother if they could do anything around the yard, and they didn't have shabby clothes especially. They'd do some honest work for this meal.

And over coffee at my hotel, Nancy Lloyd, who had lived in an apartment, told me a similar story.

—They weren't beggars. They would just come and ring the doorbell and offer to do some work for a meal. Not every night but a fairly regular occurrence—going in the kitchen and seeing some strange man sitting in there eating dinner. In apartment buildings I suppose you can hit more people with less walking. . . .

Another man who lived in that same belt near the El remembered men sleeping in the small park in front of his house. And then there was the winter we had an unusual amount of snow even for the Midwest—

—We had a big house built out of snow in the back yard. And Dad told me that a man had come to the door asking for work and he had put him to work building this snow house for us. . . . It was a surprise.

When I was about ten, another boy and I went from door to door ourselves and finally were allowed to dig dandelions in someone's yard. We worked all morning, and when we were finished and the woman asked how much we wanted, we told her seventy-five cents apiece. She was outraged. She could, she said, hire a colored man to come over and work *all day* for a *dollar*.

There was no lack of sympathy for individuals looking for work of any kind, but the attitude toward the various relief programs—at least in the Evanston of the 30s as reflected in the memories of the middle generation—was quite another matter. Today, in a formal history of the period, the multiplicity of work-relief agencies that Mr. Roosevelt created seems imaginative and humane: such programs provided a little income for those without jobs and the dignity of more or less useful work. At the time, however, they roused the *Tribune* to flights of indignation and in its readers stirred more complicated emotions. It was hard even then to keep the agencies' initials and functions straight: the WPA (Works Progress Administration); the PWA (Public Works Administration), which bestowed bureaucrat-modern post offices on hundreds of towns and cities across the country, including Evanston; the CCC (Civilian Conservation Corps), which gathered jobless young men into rural work camps that looked like army posts without the military trappings. I did find one fatherless black family that had been "on relief" until the children were old enough to work, and someone told me of a doctor who for a time had had to rent the family house and practice in a CCC camp to keep going. Most of us, however, could be nervously thankful that such humiliations had not been visited on our fathers. One laughs at what one fears. To be able to share the *Tribune*'s contempt for the WPA, that most evident of all the measures against unemployment, was to keep it at a distance. That was why, whatever our actual circumstances, we could remember the Depression as something happening to others, not ourselves.

Pat Baldwin (as I've called her) remembered "laughing at the WPA—they were always the ones that were leaning on their shovels" (the *Tribune* ran political cartoons to that effect). Another woman reminded me of the year the WPA spent an entire winter, warmed by the omnipresent braziers, taking up the brick pavement in front of her house —and then putting it down again. There were still a good many brick streets in Evanston, and that happened all over town. Besides the brick streets, nearly every block in northwest Evanston was divided by a cinder-paved alley where garages were built and garbage was put out. One man was still indignant when he recalled what had happened:

—Two truckloads of men descended on our alley and started digging it up and then they hauled all the stuff away. And then the next day another truckload of men came with stuff they had dug up from another alley and put it right back in our alley. And then a steamroller came and —make-work! It was ridiculous.

And in the next breath came the unconscious corollary —the relief and pride that it was not *his* father doing it:

—My dad was never out of work or between engagements. He lost his business in the Depression, but right way got into the insurance business. . . .

For a few of us, the facts themselves and our feelings about them planted a seed of something like shame that in time flowered in rejection of much of that old life, that Evanston life. Frank, the mathematician, said:

—We were screened from what was really going on in the country. I grew up with a wrong slant, with the Chicago *Tribune* slant on the world—that TVA was *bad*, that WPA was *bad*, and all these social programs were all *bad*.

And he reminded me of a song that kids used to sing (there had been popular songs as well as jokes and cartoons):

—"I'm so tired, but I can't get fired, 'cause I work on the WPA."

And so we got jobs. We had newspaper routes. We delivered groceries and magazines and laundry and telegrams. And when the War finally did come, its most important effect on our generation was the one we were probably least conscious of at the time: it made jobs easier to get. There was more work and there were fewer people to do it—so much so that it was embarrassing *not* to have a job. A father or a girl friend might hint but the motive was already there.

At Christmas time, there were temporary jobs to be had at the post office. One man remembered delivering his own Christmas cards—and one day "losing" an entire sack of mail that did not seem very important. Or you could work at one of Evanston's stores, and on straight commission— no salary, no guarantee—that might add up to a couple of hundred dollars, a fabulous sum, in the course of the two-week Christmas vacation. Allen, still living in his grandparents' house, drove a laundry truck, then worked as a bellboy at an Evanston hotel, and must have been pretty much self-supporting by the time he finished high school. And more and more as the War progressed you could slide in behind a drill press or a lathe in one of the small machine shops that sprang up all over Evanston and Chicago. Herb amazed me by telling about a job in a shop near his home that started right after school and went on till ten or eleven at night (his father was dead, his mother and older brother both working too). When did he eat?

—I'd have a chance to eat before I went to work. Or else someone would bring back a sandwich and a milkshake.

How could he stand it? I had tried a similar job in Chicago for a while one summer and couldn't take it—I came home physically exhausted, emotionally dead.

—I didn't find it tough. I was running punch presses,

turret lathes. I was making bomb-bursters, we were making wrenches for tanks. . . .

Later, when he had learned more, he got another and better job, on a night shift, so that for a while when I remembered him arriving at school on his motorcycle he must have been coming straight from eight hours of work in a Chicago factory.

—That was very tiring, Herb said of the night shift, where he had worked up to operating an automatic screw machine. I would come out of there in the morning . . . your skin color would be different in the morning—you get an almost yellowish cast to your skin.

Money—of course, but mostly for short-term goals rather than long-range middle-class thrift: a car and its upkeep (for some reason it had been a war measure to cut the age for a driver's license to fifteen), clothes, dates, a PA system for a band. Chuck Heimsath, who was to become a college professor and a specialist in Indian diplomatic history, bought his French horn with the earnings from one Christmas vacation. But beyond that was the vague assertion of independence, of growing up in the expected way, of doing what was supposed to be right.

There was more to the War, for us, of course, than jobs. In its public aspects, the War did impinge on our lives in a good many ways, but for people of our age in the capital city of the Midwest, it was the private matters that remained important; perhaps, being lived against that backdrop of international violence and public certainty, they became all the more immediate.

Evanston, with its usual forethought, had a rather comprehensive Civil Defense organization, considering its remoteness from actual danger. There were air-raid wardens and auxiliary firemen and policemen who drilled on Saturdays and paraded, in their uniforms, on the Fourth of July (my father was proud to be one of them and to be allowed, occasionally, to drive the ancient fire truck set aside for their use). A surprising number of things were rationed—gasoline, meat, butter, canned goods, sugar, clothes, shoes—but at levels of about 1936. If the quantities were not large, they did not seem drastically reduced either. The only black market I was aware of was in gasoline. And if you were experimenting with cigarettes, you found that they had become unaccountably scarce. The only sure place for getting them was a drugstore near the Northwestern campus where twenty or thirty packs were sold, one to a customer, once an hour. The owner put up a long bench on the sidewalk outside and it became a place to congregate, talk, read, sit in the sun while you waited.

The high school made certain efforts. For the boys in the gym classes something like an Army obstacle course was built on one of the athletic fields—barriers to climb over, crawl under—and we went through it, competing for the best times. Prudent parents encouraged their sons to join the Military Training Corps in the hope they would be officers when the time came; corps members had a gray cadet uniform with an officer's cap, learned complicated drills with dummy rifles, and collected "scrap"—tin cans from which you peeled the labels and which you then stepped on to flatten. The girls could join the Girls' Drill Corps, where they wore a dark-blue uniform with a field cap and learned to parade with the flag and their own brass instruments and drums.

Really dutiful students could take courses in the high school's expanded summer program and graduate in three years. A few did—it was a kind of war work. There was also a flying program with, surprisingly, as many girls in it as boys; several future Navy pilots began their training there as well as the class's one airline captain. Right after the end of the War, the program was enhanced with an obsolete fighter plane (a Wildcat) which turned up in the school parking lot, a reward for a particularly successful scrap drive.

For most of us, however, it was a personal connection of some kind that made the War seem immediate—a brother, father, or slightly older friend who was actually in it. By 1944, a few of the boys in the class were finding their way into the service at what was then the minimum age. Some stayed on, such as Paul Stephens, a Marine lifer, a fine athlete with the body and good looks of an adult—the one Negro I thought I knew well, within the constraints of the time and place. Mostly, however, we were too young, repeating the experience of our fathers, who for the most part had missed World War I and were now too old for this one.

Even when brothers or fathers *were* in the service, the War seemed remote; exciting perhaps but not really dangerous. These were survivors, after all, and perhaps it was a family trait. Chuck Head told me of a brother shot down over Yugoslavia, hidden from the Germans by Partisans, months later spirited across the Adriatic to Italy. My own brother in the Navy wrote home amusingly about dozing through the famous dive-bomb attacks on the ships going into Salerno. He found D-Day even less interesting than Italy.

Apart from turning out luckily, incidents like these were reassuring precisely because they reduced the immense abstraction of the War to an intelligible scale, personal and unthreatening. If the War by any means could stir large emotion, it would enter your life, change it, tear it out of the safe familiarities of childhood. Twenty-five years later, Jack Stauffer still talked bitterly about his father's working himself to death making things for that conflict.

—Eighteen hours a day producing M-1 carbines for the Army. He machined all the metal parts for them. Physically abused himself to the point where he was in Evanston Hospital for over a year. Heart attacks. No one could quite understand how he had lived through them. . . .

It was the War and the Depression together, one experience, that killed him. In the 20s and early 30s, Jack's father had been a publicist for one of the movie companies, an exciting and well-paid job erased by the Depression. After a string of other jobs, he was able to open a small machine shop in Chicago. To a middle-aged outsider, it was obvious why government war contracts would have seemed an irresistible opportunity, even if they destroyed you: not the money, really, but the chance at forty or forty-five to show your family and yourself that you were worth something after all, that you could provide for them. But what remained for his son was the boy's resentment of being abandoned in death.

For the War as a whole to attain that kind of emotional force in one's life, there had to be some prior connection with the places where it was happening, a sense, learned from one's parents, of the great world beyond Evanston and the Midwest that was being destroyed. That was exceptional. Those of us who felt it were already moving, though we did not know it, toward a life very different from the one Evanston had designed for us.

Eunice Luccock's minister father had been a missionary in China until the Japanese occupied Shanghai in 1937, and it was the Chinese government that persuaded him to go home—so that he could urge his countrymen, in a series of lectures before he was called to Evanston, to stop selling the scrap metal the Japanese were making into bombs. (From early in the War, I remember an ironic newsreel showing the "Made in USA" label on bits of shrapnel from bombs the Japanese were dropping on *us* in the Pacific— and pictures of ships being loaded with scrap for shipment to Japan. That lunatic practice continued until 1941.)

The Heimsaths, the class's other clerical family, had a similar sense of the world that made Evanston seem limited and limiting. Chuck's mother in her youth had lived in Europe. When the preliminary wars of the 30s began—the one in China was the first—she expressed her sympathies by boycotting silk stockings, which came from Japan, and wearing funny-looking cotton instead. (Rayon was still unusual; Nylon, of course, did not exist.) The advice Chuck's father gave the young men of his flock was the reverse of what up-to-date ministers of the 60s have been offering.

—We used to recommend to young men like some of those in our church that they should go to Canada and join the Royal Air Force and go over and fight this war.

Such incidents had meaning because they were the nucleus around which one's quite abstract sense of the world at large was changed into passionate and personal concern.

—The America First people, Chuck told me, speaking of the years when the country still seemed to teeter on the brink of war in Europe, were like the Ku Klux Klan—beyond the pale of reason. Here we were, sympathizing with the Blitz going on in London and listening to Edward R. Murrow on the radio—and these people were telling us it was none of our damn business!

In the welling up of rage and grief, my own family's experience had set me apart also. My father had had some of his education in England, my parents and older brothers had lived there for a couple of years. They had gone night-clubbing in Paris in the 20s and spent vacations in Scotland and on the Riviera. We wept over the conquest of France, the bombing of England. When Hemingway's stories came out in a Modern Library edition in 1942, it was the ones about Paris in the 20s and the Civil War in Spain that moved me most. At the time, the war maps that I saw in the newspapers and studied in school showed the German armies blotting out Europe and western Russia and reaching across North Africa to Suez and the Japanese on the borders of India. It was a world, a reality, that I knew only at second hand as something precious to attain, if I could, if it still existed, but I seemed already to have lost it.

And then abruptly the War ended, as it had begun, in a thunderclap, with the atomic bombs exploding over those two unlovely Japanese industrial cities and the surrender of Japan. It was as if the four years from December 1941 to August 1945 had been enclosed in an enchantment, unreal, outside of time. Or like attaining a long-sought and no longer wholly-believed-in goal: the joy—we were stupefied by joy. It was a hot, bright day, a day for going to the beach, and we drove around aimlessly in cars with the windows open, wondering what to do. Some of us drove into Chicago or went down on the El, wandering with the crowds in the Loop. In the evening I went out to dinner with my parents and afterward noticed that my father was quietly smoking a cigarette for the first time since the start of the War, with relish. He had given them up—it was something he could do.

Eunice, with the eye of a writer, remembered it best. She had been waiting tables that summer at Lake Geneva, a summer resort in southern Wisconsin favored by Evanston.

—We heard the news and went in—I remember hitch-hiking in—and somebody—she was a Frenchwoman and talked about Vichy and she was going into town to buy a bottle of wine and she took us in. . . . And then, downtown Chicago. All I remember is this sailor kissing this woman a long, long time. Oh gosh, and the excitement!

There was another side to that date—all kinds of things began at once to end. Within days of VJ Day, government contracts were being canceled, the jobs we had grown used to were drying up, and the servicemen were starting to come home. Herb remembered the dates with particular clarity.

—The day they dropped the atomic bomb, August the sixth, nineteen forty-five—and that was the end of the job. That was *it!* We worked about one more week—nobody even had to say anything. We just all left that one morning at seven-thirty and that was the end of it . . . all over the United States. Everything just stopped.

But of course things didn't really stop. For some of us in the spring of 1946, the obvious next step, never questioned, was college. For others—nearly half the class, in fact—it was finding a job. In both cases, we began to discover that others were there first. It was the first exposure to what, for many of us, would be a lifelong experience.

Throughout the 30s and the War, the colleges and universities at all levels had been in a depressed, in-drawn condition. When I was applying for college myself, I heard tales of what it had been like—of young men arriving in the fall at some Ivy League place to sign up and being received pretty much with open arms. Now, in 1946, it was different. Quite a lot of men came out of the Army in 1945 to begin or continue their college education, and money was no longer a problem—they had the GI Bill. By the following year, when *we* were trying to get in, the flow of veterans into college had become a flood. Enrollments that had been considered normal for twenty years suddenly doubled. Some of us applied to a dozen places in the hope that one would take us—and were not successful. Or we settled for the state university where the high school diploma was enough to get us in. And when we at length arrived, we discovered that most of the things we had expected—from older brothers or sisters, parents—no longer applied. Classes had become enormous, the professors remote. We stood in long lines to buy books and eat meals. There was no dormitory space and we found ourselves sleeping and trying to study in Army-surplus double-decker bunks set up in hockey rinks, gymnasiums, Quonset huts planted on college lawns. It was the beginning of a condition that has remained constant in the country's education ever since, fed by successive waves of veterans of succeeding wars: getting into college, if that was what you expected for yourself, became a matter of years-long strategy stretching far back into school. It is no wonder, I suppose, that the new generation—our own children now—has turned destructive, has begun to rebel against the very idea of college. But the condition began with us: we were the advance guard.

In a number of ways, however, the benefits which a grateful nation conferred on its defenders rubbed off onto our generation as well. Some of us who had never considered college as a possibility discovered it was attainable. In the fall of 1946, to accommodate the veterans, Evanston opened a two-year community college in several unused rooms of the high school. For Ken Mills, whose mind was on music and the bands he was playing in, the community college was a casual expedient—with the result that a door was still open for him ten years later when he went back to Northwestern for the bachelor's and master's degrees that led him finally to his career as a script writer. Olga Daniel (as I've called her), the daughter of Danish immigrants, never thought of college as something she could afford. She had taken a secretarial course in high school and had a succession of part-time jobs. The summer after graduation, she got a job in the separation center at Great Lakes, the huge inland naval base north of Evanston, working evenings, Saturdays, Sundays—and saved enough money so that when the community college opened in the fall she decided to try.

—I felt that I wanted to go to college but I didn't see how—I knew that my parents wouldn't be able to send me. And then I realized I would be able to work my way through school. . . . I had to make up some math, geometry, which

I had never done, but I never regretted the fact that I had taken these courses in typing and shorthand. Had I not done that, I wouldn't have been able to make it because I wouldn't have had the jobs. I really never had trouble getting jobs—I was a very good typist. . . .

She worked her way through, went on to Northwestern with a secretarial job, and ultimately got her master's there. For more than twenty years now she has been teaching in Evanston, at schools we both went to as children.

Even at expensive colleges in the East, tuition in 1946 was still only four or five hundred dollars a year, as it had been since the 20s, but for some of us this seemed an insuperable barrier. One way around it was the college officer-training programs that for a couple of years survived the war. Half a dozen boys took that route to college and what turned out to be a career in the Navy, most of them as fliers. There was also the reserve officer program—tuition and expenses at any college you could get into in exchange for three years of active duty afterward. For Allen, driving a laundry truck to get through high school, the NROTC had made it possible to go to Brown and had sent him, when he graduated, to Guantanamo in Cuba. For John Pritzlaff, an impressively competent and resourceful design engineer, the NROTC had been, he said, one of the three crucial decisions of his life. It had made him, in effect, independent from the age of eighteen and placed him in a responsible job, as chief engineer on a destroyer off Korea, at the start of his career. John remembered on his ship another man with a similar background and a master's degree who was a second-class seaman:

—Because he had been drafted. And I often wondered whether a fellow that was so willing to work below his capabilities would ever amount to anything in life. Even though it meant that I would be in service an extra year, I was able to maximize my time.

The service—usually the Army—provided another kind of solution to the problem of paying for college. Although the War was over, the GI Bill lingered for more than a year. By joining the Army, with the unfearsome prospect of being sent to occupation duty in Germany or Japan, you could assure your tuition and living expenses at college a couple of years later, and several people did just that. Those who came out of high school ready to look for a job also found an answer of sorts in the Army: other jobs were scarce for high school graduates in 1946—the veterans, everyone told us, were there first. Jim Crandall, for example, who became a crane operator, left school half a credit shy of his diploma, disgusted with going to classes, and bursting with the need for independence. In that dawn of the postwar era, the idea of new prospects, the chance for a different kind of life, had been implanted. Why not seize it?

—The year we got out of school, Jim told me, another fellow and I hitchhiked to California and spent some time out there. When we got there, we found that you couldn't get a job—or do anything—unless you were a veteran. . . .

Someone was there first: it was a circumstance we were to face repeatedly. In the end there was nothing for the two boys to do but hitchhike back to Chicago—with the idea of signing up and becoming veterans themselves, if they could.

For those of us who went to college, jobs were again scarce by the time we graduated. Jack Dailey (as I've called him) came back from Germany in 1948, fluent in the language, the college education he'd not really expected provided for. That was also the beginning of the boom days of testing—the aptitude tests, intelligence tests, personality inventories that have been so pervasive in American education and business ever since. Jack's adviser told him the tests showed he should be a teacher, and during the next four years that was what he prepared himself for, only to find at the end that no one needed what he knew how to teach.

—One of the things the adviser forgot to tell me was that German is a cyclical subject and I would be graduating at the bottom of the cycle. There were fellows with master's degrees who didn't have jobs. . . .

Dan Magen (I'll call him) had gotten a job with a Chicago stockbroker—it had seemed a great opportunity.

—None of the young guys had gone in that business since 1928. I was a customers' man, but I saw that guys who had been there twenty or thirty years were still sitting by the phone answering customers. . . .

That, of course, was what we had learned to expect in 1946, that was the way the world had been: twenty years of hard work and waiting and then, maybe, a chance. Dan caught on quickly and left the brokerage business: some people seem to be born knowing their way around the world. Some of us took longer; some of us never did learn. One way of assessing our generation—any generation—is to notice how its members succeed in matching their expectations of the world to what actually is. But that question was not in our minds on that June day in 1946 when we stepped smartly across the platform erected in the school gymnasium to receive our diplomas and the superintendent's handshake. The world was welcoming us into its midst. There might be problems—finding a job, getting through college, enduring the continuing draft—but they looked like ones we were equipped to solve. The great threats, the Depression, the War, whatever they meant to each of us, were all safely in the past.

All through the War the newspapers carried homely predictions of what life would be like when the War was finally over. Our homes would be prefabricated, cheap, and much enhanced by imaginative technology. They would be "radiantly" heated by electric wires implanted in poured-concrete floors, air-conditioned, kept clean by central vacuum systems. Molded plastics as strong as steel would be used for furniture and suitcases and indestructible dishes. A new, clear material called Nylon would be used for everything from window screens to clothing, and clothes themselves would be permanently pressed and never need ironing. Cars would be made of new materials like magnesium and the plastics and would somehow be sleeker and better than anything we could imagine. Paints and insecticides would be sprayed from aerosol cans. Gigantic double-decker cargo and passenger planes would carry as many as a hundred passengers (a plane the size of the current 747s would have been beyond the reach of public credibility—in 1946, except for the handful actually learning to fly, virtually none of us had even been inside a plane).

Today, twenty-five years later, many of these details of everyday living, and others like them, have become commonplace. A few of them (prefabricated building techniques, aerosol cans) were in fact wartime innovations, but most were products that were just reaching the market when the War broke out. I remember, for example, in what must have been 1940 watching bits of the World Series on prototype television sets being demonstrated at the Marshall Field department store in Chicago. It was from such bits and pieces that we had built up a kind of Sunday-supplement vision of the world we were entering in 1946: a world of towering glass, steel, and plastic cities with clouds of flying vehicles darting through the air like insects. Today, if you stand back from almost any of the big American cities and use your eyes, you can see that that rotogravure world has pretty largely come to pass: the image of it, planted in our consciousness twenty-five years ago, has been clumsily shaping the reality ever since.

That shimmering vision was the outer skin of a future we believed was being born, a world where reason informed by knowledge would put an end once and for all to the human destructiveness of war and economic depression. We thought, of course, that we would correct the errors of our parents' and grandparents' generations—the divisions, the isolationism, the inhuman, self-serving irrationality, the ignorant disregard of others' needs, whether individuals, classes or nations—and we put our trust in reason expressed through collective action and mutually agreed upon institutions. Hence in the high school weekly newspaper, *The Evanstonian*, the editors of the Class of 1946 could write with what now seems touching assurance about the United Nations, brought into being in San Francisco in the summer of 1945, while the war with Japan was still on.

—The United Nations, the editorialist informed us, planned a policy of education for everybody, to be promoted by an organization called the United Nations Educational, Scientific, and Cultural Organization. The job of this organization is to use "propaganda" for peace, for brotherhood, for the advancement of research, to inform the world what people in the opposite hemisphere are doing, to prevent war by exposing to world censure the activities of evil-wishers. . . .

—It was lack of thought which brought us to the last world crisis, the writer exhorted us in conclusion. Let UNESCO teach us to think, and war will be forgotten, because to think is to be truly educated, and to be educated is to realize the futility of war.

Wasn't *that* what the four years at high school were all about? The alternative was annihilation, symbolized by the atomic bomb, and that was unthinkable. Hence, we faced the world with an optimism larger than youth, founded, as it seemed, on a self-evident truth. The inherent paradox— that the supremely irrational and indiscriminate weapon was a product of human reason—occurred to no one, to us no more than to the leaders we listened to.

Within the class, those who retained that optimistic sense of the kind of world we could make for ourselves had done something concrete over the twenty-five years about creating it. There weren't many. Interestingly, the two who remembered and expressed it best were women.

Evy Cullander had gone in the very early 50s with her minister husband to a church on the West Side of Chicago, in what we would now call a black ghetto—and straightaway she found herself, years before it became a kind of liberal conformity to do so, involved in protest demonstrations, political campaigns against the Daley organization, sending her children to schools where they might be the solitary whites. Why hadn't they chosen a comfortable parish in a place like Evanston or one of the exciting clean new suburbs already springing up on the periphery of the city?

—The war was over and we graduated from high school —in a sense, it looked like a very rosy world. Why was it that we went to the inner city? It wasn't a wave of altruism, it was a wave of more mature guys who went to seminary. . . . It seems as if there were some of them who recognized early the implications of what was happening. They just looked and they saw and they realized that there was a need for a ministry. . . .

About the same time, Janet Warren (as I'll call her) went south as a union organizer, working with the still legally segregated blacks and whites, standing in their picket lines, being kidnapped by their police.

—It seemed that the world was really going to be a peaceful place. That the war was over and was going to stay over. . . . That everything was going to be better now, we were going to be rational now—as a society we were going to devote our attention to a rich full life for all people. . . . I think probably young people in general are optimistic and idealistic and that a war tends to bring out the optimism and idealism in all people and that the combination of being young at a time when a war has just finished tends to make one think that—we're just going to go off and do all kinds of good things. . . .

As we talked, we sat in her rather worn, utilitarian union office looking out on Union Square in New York—Janet's life, in the perspective of twenty-five years, seemed to have gone in a straight line. The self-righteous certitude of the young had been irritating me more than usual. Had we at eighteen been perhaps just as provoking?

—I think we *were* self-assured, Janet said carefully, after a pause. I don't know that it was in any way different from what I think is natural for young people. I have the feeling, from the young people whom I see, there is much more pessimism than we and our contemporaries had. . . .

Among the men, those who had chosen a service career felt that outflowing idealism most strongly. For the fliers, the Navy meant several things: the joy of flying, a hand in righting the evils we had grown up with—and security. Fritz Rubins, for example, had taken his first flying lessons at the age of sixteen, in the midst of the War.

—Hitler marching all over Europe. The Japanese marching all over China. The Spanish Civil War before that. I think that's probably one thought I had when I thought about the Navy as a career. . . . "That's going to be a steady job." And as it's turned out, it *has* been a pretty steady job. . . .

We were sitting on the back porch of his house on Long Island, drinking beer and eating delicatessen sandwiches. As it happened, it was one of the days the latest crew of astronauts were making their televised exploration of the moon—and the anniversary of his retirement from the Navy.

—My father fought World War I, he was fighting World

War II at the time, and if I spent a career in the service perhaps I could prevent my sons from being drafted. . . .

If security—"a steady job"—seemed important, it was also something we expected one way or another to have. Curiously, if that was one effect of the Depression, fears about money—about not having money—were not. There seemed to be no misers among the middle-aged members of the Class of 1946. Ginny Murphy and her husband had come close to bankruptcy starting an automobile dealership in a small Midwestern town but without ever feeling deeply threatened by it. Money?

—Having thought of money constantly as a child and as a student, now I think of it as little as possible and refuse to worry about it. I just assume that there will always be a way for us to make a living.

And like most of us, Ginny felt perplexed by her children's lack of money sense, without knowing what to do about it.

—Our children don't realize the value of money. Kids think nothing of paying three or four or five dollars to go to a concert and hear someone. They always figure that the basic things will be there—house, clothing, food. . . .

And of course that was the difference the Depression did make—in the way we used money for our children, the kind of home we tried to provide. Another mother, Bobbie Collins, keyed up from going back to college to work toward an advanced degree in archaeology, was conscious of the feeling.

—I can see it coming out in the way we rear our children. I never went to summer camp, so we sort of extend ourselves to make sure our kids go to camp—or whatever else we think we missed.

Perhaps the Depression did inoculate us against the tyranny of money, but the good times since 1946 have on the whole confirmed the immunity. There was, for many of us, a marvelous fresh hopefulness about the public world, and that view extended to the private world as well. Over a good lunch at a restaurant near Evanston, Mike Ferguson thought back to how things had looked to him:

—In 1946 I just figured I had the world by the tail! I would be out there making a *million dollars*—by the time I was fifty, certainly, and probably wouldn't take that long. Money was just going to come along. And actually, there *was* quite a boom after the price controls were relaxed, and then we started having these successive breakthroughs coming through—television, air travel. I've covered almost a million miles since then.

Mike was not a millionaire yet—but in a few more years he might be. A tall, spare, red-headed man with an open Gaelic face, he had recently joined the dozen or so men of the class who had gone into business for themselves, in his case as a marketing consultant. The business, started in the midst of the recession, had, he told me, lost forty or fifty thousand dollars the first year, but he was untroubled—he had survived, he was paying it off, it was going to work out.

As I write this—in the lurid glow of the Vietnam War —one can only wonder at the sense of unity and clear-cut purpose that filled us in that first year after the War.

—I was very unaware, Jack Dailey told me, that World War Two was peculiar in the unanimity that the country seemed to feel for the rightness of it. I took this to be the natural way for a country to feel.

The world out there was clearly defined. It had a spot for you somewhere—all you had to do was find it and fit in. Jack Dailey's father was a working man who had finished sixth grade in school and drove a milk truck.

—This set a pattern for me, Jack told me. Work hard and don't ask too many questions and don't try to be a big shot. I wasn't conscious of how much I was being guided by ideas that were being fed to me by my parents. From the

time I was a little boy I was told that all you have to do is
work hard and work smart, and you will be recognized.

That was the way of the 30s in which we grew up. But
the world we were entering was not like that, and it took
time to find that out. Jack, after discovering that there was
no room for German teachers, went to work for a photo
laboratory and eventually found his way into the training
program of a giant insurance company. It took him a while,
but he learned.

—I spent six years—only to find out that when you want
it, baby, you've gotta *grab* it. If you wait for someone to
recognize you he'll *use* you. You've got to be just as much
of a businessman about merchandising yourself as you are
about merchandising the ideas that you want to get ahead.
... It's only been the last five or six years that I've realized
that a person has to very carefully plan his career.

Hard work and application? The United Nations and all
those other institutions to prevent war? Atomic power and
the other products of human reason, human ingenuity, that
would create a new world? That was what our teachers
were telling us in the spring of 1946, that was what we
expected. But it worked out rather differently.

The future was on its way to meet us, bearing all the old
griefs in new and unimagined forms: there was not going
to be much that human reason—not the hopeful institutions, not the new technology—or mere work could change
or deflect, but that was where our hopes lay. The Depression and the War had prepared us, like an army destined
for defeat, for the past, not the future. So when the new
violence again came clamoring across the world, and again,
we could only wonder that we had not expected it.

—Those things when we grew up, Frank said, trying to
express what had happened—that was the end of the time
when the great masses of people in the world would take
all this crap that the few people with power were giving

them. This is what's changed in the world now. . . .

Whatever it was that was beginning, Evanston, with the worthiest of intentions, seemed to have prevented us from experiencing it. But even Evanston was changing, if we had noticed.

4

The Middle Generation

—If you look at what was happening when we got out of high school, Evy said, there were tremendous consumer demands and demand for service that had been curtailed during the War. The technological development in industry after World War Two was tremendous and tremendously exciting.

We were sitting on the screened back porch of her home in Evanston, a couple of blocks from the junior high school I had gone to. It was one of those solid frame houses that abound in Evanston and the small towns of the Midwest, mostly built in the decades before World War I, with an air of functional farmhouse comfort and cloudless summer days: the basement raised so that you climbed a flight of steps to reach the broad front porch where in the old days you sat on summer evenings, looking out and down the street.

It was a Saturday morning in early June, a beautiful warm day, almost summer. We were talking, twenty-five years after our graduation, about leadership. Where were the men and women of the Class of 1946 who had seemed to us like the leaders when we were in high school—the future heads of companies, the scholars, scientists, artists, political figures—who came out of Evanston and its education so apparently well equipped for whatever goals they set themselves?

—If you were to say, Evy continued, what would be the reasonable aspiration for a young man in 1946 or 1947—if you found young men who had done exciting things, I would think those exciting young men would have been involved in the redesign—of U.S. Steel.

And the women? Were they all housewives?

—For the women, this was a generation that was farther behind professionally than it had been twenty years before. We were in high school at the time when women were deprived of their husbands or deprived of their marriage. . . .

Evy herself was an exception, a widow who was putting four children through school and college and in the process had become a notably creative teacher, but the observation was accurate: for the women, a career or profession in any formal sense, the drive to *have* a career, was rare compared with an earlier generation, in the flush of discovering that such a thing was possible, or with the generation that followed, assuming it was normal. And the reason she suggested for this made sense too: the War, the lesser wars that followed. For the women of our age, being without the men, the husbands, had given marriage and family a special urgency and made the alternatives seem provisional. For all of us, men and women, the times had defined our aspirations and Evanston itself had specified the ways in which it was possible to fulfill them. Our choices—and our awareness of what there was to choose—had been limited.

Several of the men had in fact been drawn into areas of advancing technology, though not to torpid basic industries like steel. Rather a lot had felt the excitement of the general economic growth of the period and had had something to do with it. Both the scientists and the businessmen, however, had followed a technical route, carrying out assignments decided by others rather than making the decisions themselves. Even the scattering of men who in the last few years, in their early forties, had gone into business for themselves were in most cases providing a technical service of some kind rather than creating anything. It was a generation of technocrats, of functionaries, rather than of entrepreneurs.

It seems as natural for someone of my generation to think in statistical terms as it was for a slightly earlier generation to think in Freudian terms. We have grown to maturity in the age of the computer, when numerical data have been generated on a heretofore unthought-of scale. Hence, when I wanted to compare Evanston's Class of 1946 with our generation at large, to find out how representative we really were, I constructed a questionnaire and sent it to a sampling of the class. From the replies, it is possible to describe the group in profile. It remains, of course, a rough sketch, weighted toward those who were reasonably satisfied with what their lives had become. Those who were not satisfied withdrew into privacy and did not reply.

For those who were married, the average number of children was fairly high, more than three for both men and women (more of the women had three children, more of the men four). One woman had nine children, one woman eight, and there was beginning to be a sprinkling of grand-children. Only about 5 percent of the couples were child-less (compared with a national figure of more than 10 per-cent for people of this age). The women had married on the average at the age of twenty-four, the men three years later (nearly all had served during the Korean War and half a dozen died there, though few who served were actually in combat); several women and a few men had married at the age of twenty, fresh out of college or a bit earlier, but there were also a couple of marriages for the first time within months of the reunion itself.

Although both the men and the women, typically, had married fairly young and produced the middle-class large families of the 50s, there were also enough divorces and variously unhappy marriages to cause distressed comment from several people I talked to. Indeed, both the number of divorced men and women and the number who were not married at all were rather high—around 10 percent in each category(in contrast, among whites this age in the nation as a whole, fewer than 5 percent are divorced and not remarried, while the figures for those never married are 7.7 percent for men, 5 percent for women).To turn it around, leaving out the unmarried, the divorced, and the newly married, the proportion of apparently stable marriages was 77 percent for the men, about 83 percent for the women (nationally, about 90 percent of the white men and women of this age are married—i.e., not divorced and not unmar-ried). It is customary to attribute the number of divorces to affluence: as a group, the class was well enough off to afford that middle-class luxury of the postwar era. But how was it that so many had resisted the pressures to marry, which had been quite real, if unstated, in that time and place. Bachelors and maiden aunts had been as scarce in my par-ents' generation as divorces; now they were almost com-monplace. The two facts together were something to brood

over. Was there something about Evanston that had somehow short-circuited the relations of a fifth of the men and
women in the class? Or something about the times we had
lived through?

I also asked my sampling to assess a random list of public
and private concerns. Not surprisingly for a group in their
forties, the area of greatest concern turned out to be their
children, their relations with them, their education: the
oldest had reached late adolescence, they were part of that
puzzling and rebellious new generation, and their parents
were girding themselves for the inflated costs of current-
day colleges—or engaged in running argument with the
young who rejected the very idea of education. Related
concerns about getting along with husbands or wives, with
other people generally, were also high on the list: altogether, it was private rather than public matters that
stirred this group. It was a rather private generation.

Indeed in that summer of 1971 the only public issue that
approached these private matters in the depth of feeling it
aroused was Vietnam: people were sick of it; they had always thought it unwise; or it filled them with shame and
loathing; or in a few cases, they felt that it had been mis-
managed by politicians, that in some way the nation had
been betrayed. Apart from Vietnam, the kinds of public
issues that newspaper editorialists and news magazines exercise themselves about stirred only a decent, moderate
interest: the whole bundle of concerns that, with their racial overtones, have to do with the viability of large cities
—public housing, welfare, crime, drugs—and relatively abstract issues like the national economy.

The areas of minimal concern were likewise striking. If
the generation of 1946 worried modestly about things like
air pollution and violence that they were told to worry
about, they felt remarkably unthreatened at either the public or the personal level. Communism at home or abroad,

which had given earnest men nightmares in the 50s, had pretty largely died out of consciousness along with any strong sense of danger from foreign powers, and neither the blowing up of banks by romantic ex-college students nor an increasingly potent Russian military strength had been sufficient to revive it. Nor were we in middle age, as a group, much concerned about money or personal achievement. Typically, when we were starting out, we had not wanted or expected to be rich, and on the whole, what had been needed had come. And perhaps too, for men and women of forty-two or forty-three, mothers and businessmen, what could be hoped for in the way of ambitions had already been achieved—or what was possible had been settled for. Those who still set a high value on achieving some ambition were exceptional in other ways—a scholar at a turning point in his career, for example, at an age when the possibility of great achievement and the possibility of failure both take on a special poignance.

This was, after all, the group that in the early 50s had been christened "the silent generation." To me at the time —a writer trying to persuade middle-aged editors to notice what he was writing, a writer who was not read—the term seemed ironic. we were not silent, it was just that no one would listen to us. Or, I thought, we were pragmatists, intent on accomplishment rather than ideology, intent on mastering the skills to rectify the failures of our elders, the Depression, the War. The postponements caused by military service and the Korean War, the anxieties of the Cold War competition with Russia, gave that sense of purpose a peculiar urgency. And yet, twenty years later, what I found was the kind of feeling the liberal journalists of the 50s had been talking about: the decently moderate concern for public issues, the deep attachment to home and family, the untroubled sense of personal and national security.

If those were the obvious characteristics of our genera-

tion in the middle of their lives, it was Evanston that gave
them their distinctive shape—an Evanston that, despite its
particular history, was simply a rather successful instance
of American life at large. Evanston, when we were growing up there, was a moderate sort of place, avoiding extremes. To the south was the teeming immensity of
Chicago; to the north, the North Shore proper, of which
Evanston considered itself a part—the string of wealthy
villages stretching along the Chicago & North Western
Rail Road almost to the Wisconsin line. The North Shore:
where the tree-lined streets were gracefully curved, and big
houses shaded into still bigger ones with Tudor or baronial
or French château references; where there were no apartment buildings, no Negroes and no poor, unless they were
comfortably secure maids, gardeners, butlers, chauffeurs,
whose children might well grow up to graduate from college and live on the North Shore themselves.

But Evanston was neither wholly North Shore nor
wholly Chicago: both suburb and, since the 90s, city in its
own right. Although many of our fathers did in fact make
their livings in the Loop, Evanston was also home for a
good many small factories and the people with German,
Bohemian and Polish names—and the Negroes—who
worked in them. And there were substantial branches of
several of the big Chicago department stores, so that for
many of the people in the farther reaches of the North
Shore, going into the city to shop meant going to Evanston.
Finally—though Evanston had grown too big to have the
feel of a college town—there was Northwestern, which had
laid out and incorporated the town and supplied its name
(John Evans, a doctor and a Methodist, was the first chairman of its board of trustees) and whose real estate holdings
still fan out across Evanston.

Being neither wholly urban nor wholly suburban, Evanston reflected a fairly complete social spectrum. In the

Class of 1946, children of well-off company vice presidents were balanced by the sons and daughters of milkmen. And if there were no families poor enough to be set apart by the marks of poverty, the small number who were actually rich blended in almost unnoticeably at the opposite end of the scale. For us this meant a considerable freedom. There were restrictions, prejudices—some of them spectacularly archaic-sounding today—but money and social class were not among them. It was one of the things that Jack Stauffer, for instance, whose father had gone in the Depression from movie publicity to a machine shop, recalled with gratitude.

—I remember many people who had nothing. And probably an equal number who had everything. And this was one of the astounding things about Evanston to me, that it really didn't make any difference. . . .

It was not simply that Evanston's people could nearly all be placed somewhere along the spectrum of the middle class. Something about the place and the time produced in us a set of characteristics as distinctive of our generation as a regional manner of speech. And really these characteristics were all one quality, differently shaped to different persons and circumstances, but present whether we were conscious of it or not, whether we rebelled or accepted: not silence but a special kind of quietness, a readiness to accept, almost without reflection, the limited and realizable goals and the moderate means defined by our parents and the Evanston way of doing things. For some of us it came out as a virtue, for others, in the world we grew into, as a weakness. In one form, for instance, it was something called duty.

John Colwell, one of the three doctors in the Class of 1946, who had followed his father and older brother into medicine, had reflected on this quality in himself and the people of our age. He asked me about it in medical terms. What was it? What was I finding?

—Do you find, John asked, groping for words a layman would understand, a sort of devotion to duty, a hard-work ethic, a kind of hard-core Methodism—a sort of *rigid* approach to life? A fair amount of depression?

I had no answers. Is trying to do well what you have been taught to do, being realistically content with what is possible—is that also to be depressed? What did *he* think?

—I never knew whether that was family. . . . Thinking back, I think that—at least the people I knew from Evanston—the strain of devotion to duty for whatever reason is going to be there: we were good little boys that were taught to do it certain ways and we just kept doing it the way we were told. We believed it for some reason, I really don't know why.

Perhaps that had made us a little slow in outgrowing boyhood, which in some cases had stretched into middle age. Chuck Heimsath, who twenty-five years later had begun to achieve several forms of recognition as a scholar, remembered how strongly he had felt pointed toward his father's university. (Although our own sons were just beginning to reach college age, the men seem to be more diffident about insisting on that sort of thing. With the women and their daughters, it is different.)

—There just didn't seem to be any alternative for me, Chuck said. I either went to Yale or nothing happened—the rest of life was a total blank. I was being groomed for something and I knew it and I couldn't escape it. I remember nightmares that I would have when I was much younger—about not getting accepted. There was nothing that I expected from life except to go to Yale, and then . . . everything would open up to me. . . . And once I had achieved that, nobody was going to ask me any more questions about what you were going to do after that. . . .

The parental questions, always the questions: looking back now, I can admire the gentle skill with which our parents moved us in the directions they intended. Ada Garrett (as I'll call her) seems to have noticed at the time how this was done, perhaps because hers was one of the really remarkable minds (she was also, as we politely said, colored). For her too there had been the questions, and then:

—What did I want to do? I still didn't really know. When you're growing up, people ask you what do you want to do. This was something so I could really shut them up: O.K., so I'm going to be a doctor!

Parents, of course, did more than ask carefully weighted questions. Barbara Corbett, for example, had transferred from a small college where she had been completely happy to a large university where she was not.

—I found myself in the wrong curriculum, leading to the wrong kind of degree for me, because I had done what my folks wanted me to do instead of what I wanted to do. My daddy said if he was going to spend this money for my education I must be able to support myself when I came out. And he thought that a degree in home economics would make this possible. . . .

This dutifulness, this sense of doing what was expected of us, what was proper, came out in other ways—for example, in the discomfort one felt from a quite early age at displeasing others, people in general as well as parents and teachers. The quality is, of course, one of the lubricants of an orderly and civilized life, but it can also make it hard to find out what one really thinks. You anticipate and suppress what others will not like until the reaction becomes automatic and it is mostly *their* thoughts that you have, vicariously. Nancy Lloyd discovered the trait in herself at the time of Joe McCarthy's Communist counting in the early 50s.

—It really forced me to examine a lot of this stuff that I had earlier—of not wanting to offend people, not wanting people to dislike me, not wanting to get into trouble. I think this was when I first began to think about all these. . . .

That was a beginning of wisdom, but for many of us it took longer. Bobbie Collins, an eager, earnest girl who had grown into a woman with energy to spare from her family to work toward an advanced degree in archaeology, had in the process discovered a whole new impatience and assertiveness in herself.

—I was more middle-aged and middle-class at eighteen than I am now. I didn't have any great ambitions or anything. I was always very uncomfortable when we would get an English composition assignment about what are your life values or this kind of thing—because it was all kind of blank. . . .

A little later Bobbie remarked that she and her husband didn't even go to a movie simply for fun (all right, she admitted with a laugh, maybe a concert).

—I think my whole life has been influenced by a sense of duty, I think if any generalization is true about our generation—we don't do too many things for pleasure in the sense that the younger generation really makes a point of it. The Protestant ethic, the work ethic that we're so involved in, we don't realize it. . . .

There was a certain restiveness in that dutiful atmosphere, but the town, which provided for so many possibilities, provided for—or at any rate tolerated—that too. That was the purpose of the trips to the bars beyond the reach of Evanston's local-option prohibition. And that was the function of the several high school fraternities and sororities, prohibited in theory but flourishing in fact, which organized dances, secret initiations, beer parties, and the only interracial fights (between a black champion and a white champion) that anyone I talked to could remember. Chuck Head, a man from a remarkable family of doctors who had become our one working farmer, remembered his fraternity that way.

—They had the fraternities and I was in one of those—much against my parents' wishes, but I went anyway, it was our way of rebelling. So our social life centered around that—you'd have your parties and dances. . . .

Chuck was exceptional both in becoming a farmer and in *not* becoming a doctor. Twenty-five years later, the men in the class, the successful ones, had more often than not chosen careers like their fathers', and where they had not it was the Depression that made the difference. At eighteen, Bill Jennings, for instance, had seemed headed for some kind of esoteric research rather than his father's real estate business. A quiet, repressed boy who was good at science and mathematics, he had graduated at the head of the class and was going to college with the precursor of a National Merit Foundation scholarship (fewer than a hundred were awarded in the country that first year). Apart from the bent of his particular talents, real estate in the 30s and 40s had not been an appealing business.

—It was a lousy way to make a living, Bill remembered. My father was working seven days a week, I never saw him. Buildings were fifty percent vacant—you just couldn't shove people in the front door faster than they'd fall out the back. Houses weren't selling and the cashier went to the penitentiary for embezzling money. . . .

But even Bill, eventually, had acquiesced. He had gotten the engineering degree, commuted to Korea for a couple of years as a technical troubleshooter for the Army, gone to graduate school, and gotten a job he thought would be in research. But more and more, he was making sales calls and finding that he liked it, was pretty good at it. By the mid-60s, when real estate prices in Evanston were at last getting back to their 1928 levels, his father's business had grown to the point where it needed the combination of things he knew how to do, and, finally, he found himself in it after all.

Duty, a nervous desire to please, acceptance of realistic goals, following in one's parents' footsteps—something in ourselves or in the times was preventing us from transmitting these qualities to the next generation. The sense of difference from their children came up repeatedly in my talks with the people in the class. For Herb Harms, it had to do with patriotism—one's perception of and identification with the nation and the nation's goals.

—I think we as a group are more responsible people than the young people today. I think patriotism is a little on the wane—I speak for myself, I'm not just blindly patriotic, but . . . I really feel as though our country is right and our foreign involvements are necessary, and if people would examine these things. . . .

Jack King and his wife could feel the difference without seeming troubled by it. (She had been in the same year at New Trier, Evanston's affluent rival high school a little farther up the North Shore, and it was in that area that they still lived.) We were talking about his first summer job —an amusing one, in recollection, cleaning cages in a zoo, feeding the animals; the money had gone into his first car. Why had he wanted a job?

—I don't think I had any special feeling about having a job, Jack said, outside of a desire to please.

And Julie, with a wife's quick perception of what her husband meant, said:

—This desire to please is a very strong element in the lives of our age group. It's gone out. My whole desire was to do well in school and please my parents—right through graduation from college.

If one felt guilty, somehow, about one's parents, one felt uneasy about one's children. For Jack Stauffer, whom the weapons business had led from New Mexico to Cleveland to an apparently idyllic life on the coast of Maryland, his anxieties as a parent centered on drugs—but for the accessibility of the marketplace in Baltimore or Washington, it would have been a paradise. Had our parents been so cruelly tested?

—I think it was probably difficult all along being a parent, Jack said. I think we're trying to do a better job. Because I thought I pulled the wool over my parents' eyes—things have come out in the ensuing years that they never realized were going on.

For us it had been not drugs but the lure of the West Campus bars, the adventurous, high-speed drives to Wisconsin and back, far into the night—hadn't our parents managed to cope with problems like ours now?

—You don't learn from the mistakes of others. We continue to make the same mistakes our parents made. I don't know how to handle them. But neglecting it is not the way out.

Again, we faced these conflicts with our children dutifully, with the helpless feeling that you had to do something even if action was no better than inaction. Duty—impersonal, the same for everyone—is not the most winning of virtues, but it was at the heart of the Midwestern proprieties that shaped the Evanston of our youth.

The Midwesterner possesses a limited repertory of courtesies and is uncomfortable when he gets beyond them. Even today, an observant Easterner is likely to be struck and even offended by the apparent coolness of his counterparts in the medium-size Midwestern towns (the smaller places and the big cities are another matter). When I went to have a look at Evanston Hospital, the two officials I talked to (after an elaborate making of appointments) carefully addressed and referred to each other as "mister," and it was not only that they were in the presence of a stranger with some kind of connection with "The Press."

A woman I had interviewed met me later on the street near Fountain Square and did the same thing: she addressed me as "mister."

These conscious but limited courtesies had a serious side. They were a source of the kind of tolerance that existed in Evanston in 1946, but they were also a technique for taking account of others' feelings without having to feel anything, the seed of that impersonal, mechanical coldness which in our lifetime has spread across the nation like a fungus. Thus, it was predictable that neighbors in most cases knew each other only in the most formal ways, even though their children played together and went to school together. Standing in front of my own house, for example, with a little turning of the head, you could see a dozen other houses, and in most of them the families had lived for the same twenty years or more, but with one exception the relationship never went beyond a rare greeting if it went that far. Spencer Beach remembered this odd situation without rancor, but it was one of the things that led him to New York.

—We knew who the neighbors were, but whether we were friendly with them depended on whether we knew them in some other way. You didn't, I think in Evanston, become close friends with your neighbors: you were polite and friendly. . . .

For Ken, the scriptwriter, his sense of personal relationships was one of the things that set him apart, a conscious liberal; it involved him, eventually, in the demonstrations and sit-ins that led, a few years ago, to Evanston's open housing ordinance. At some point, he told me, he had run into Bill Jennings at a party and argued about what the town's real estate brokers could or should be doing. The two positions were not communicable. Where Ken saw individual black families with a need for some place to live, Bill saw credit risks, potential property damage, and the agent's obligation to the client who paid his fee.

—Real estate's a very pragmatic sort of field, Bill told me later. It's very hard to explain just what your considerations are for selecting somebody for a housing unit. In most cases, it's some sort of judgment on a credit rating. And the other thing, whether the kids will tear up the place because nobody's around after school. These are problems beyond the ability of the real estate broker working within his own sphere to solve. You can go out and organize a day-care center but you can't get your tenants to agree to patronize it.

The two viewpoints were irreconcilable *because* they were both true, but it was the impersonal one, rooted in the hard common sense of Midwestern propriety, that was more characteristic of Evanston. Reconciling these two poles of civilized society—the impersonal and the personal, the public and the private, the urge to communicate and the right to be left alone—is one of the things a city exists for, but for our generation the emphasis was on the impersonal and the private. In the spring of 1946 there was a prophetic confrontation between a teacher named Clara Murphy and the students of her home room at Evanston High School. (The school then was organized in large home rooms of two or three hundred students and the home room head had many of the functions of a school principal.) When Miss Murphy called the home room together that spring, she had gone over what the graduating seniors had said about their college and vocational plans. She was *shocked*, she told them, that not one in that large group had shown any inclination toward some form of social service. It was a remarkably self-centered generation, and the contrast with her own, coming of age before World War I— or with the one that was to come after, in the 60s—was striking. There were exceptions, but by and large that was how the class as a whole turned out: limited and specific social responsibilities might thrust themselves upon us and be accepted, but we did not seek them out. Our interests were private.

The times reinforced whatever it was about Evanston that set such a high value on privacy. It was necessary to get on.

—The first thing you did, Walker Davies (as I'll call him) told me, was to go to college. And then you kind of anchored yourself to a job.

Walker, who is black and still lives in Evanston, had worked for a large utility since leaving high school, now in one of the exquisitely designed new towers in the Loop. Was that why the class had produced so little social or political leadership?

—At that time I don't think that any of us thought politics was too secure. Even now—

Unavoidably, Walker had served on the board of the Evanston branch of the NAACP, but now he was "just a member." Why?

—It takes a lot of time. . . .

The avoidance of political activity is a trait Walker shares with most other members of the class. Strong political views were not lacking, but when it came to action, the aversion to politics was generally stronger. Even those who had taken an active role—running for office, managing a campaign—had been drawn to it by a specific need, such as helping a friend or solving a specific technical problem like town drainage or traffic, and they had withdrawn when the need was past.

There were practical reasons for this general abstention from politics, but they reflected an underlying emotional stance. For example, if your work was deeply absorbing, you were probably short of time for any other commitment —the hours in a week for outside meetings, the years that holding public office would subtract from a career—but you also felt a kind of righteous disdain for those who could find personal satisfaction in such things. Ralph Mann, the financial vice president of an advertising agency, found the company's day-by-day operation consumingly exciting—providing a suitable environment for "professional and creative types" who "don't like a lot of administrative nitty-gritty." Suppose he were asked to put those skills to work on a school board or the town council?

—People who seem to get aggressive in politics are people who have a need to fill personally or have an axe to grind. . . .

It was late afternoon in the study he had built onto his delightful house—the air conditioner whirring in a window in the corner, a time to relax over the evening drink. Ralph leaned back deep in a comfortable chair, drink in hand, one side of his face touched at moments by a slight nervous tic. Well, I pursued, what if an issue came along that he felt really strongly about?

—I have strong political views—but I don't feel the need to go out and espouse them on a platform. I couldn't devote the time. . . . Running a business is to me—the way I get my jollies.

I had found working for large companies fairly political myself. Was that what he meant—the factions that formed and re-formed in a company's management, compelling one to take sides, the tension . . .? Again the tic. No, some people had had to do that but he had not. I let it go at that.

Nancy Lloyd also connected politics with aggressiveness. As a mother, she had thought about the qualities one's children must be equipped with to survive.

—Coaches and teachers always say that suburban kids don't like contact sports—they do quite well in tennis and swimming and track. I wonder if it's just part of the whole idea of being too polite to interfere with other people or be pushy. . . .

Her feeling about politics followed naturally. On the one hand, she was driven by that Evanston sense of duty—but—

—I've always joined the League of Women Voters wherever we lived. I enjoy it. . . . A lot of my friends who are active in party politics feel it's an evasion, but I just have this idea that I *am* thin-skinned and I don't—you can make a contribution without being active in your party.

Frank, a mathematician, whose life had been a series of strenuous goals defined and achieved, had also thought deeply about this and found the same kinds of feelings in himself—and it was a part of himself and of the Evanston past that he rejected.

—Life was so well organized when we grew up—all your free time was guaranteed—that nobody really got tough, mean and nasty and hard-driving. We were raised to work within the system and plod along—and things will be all right. . . . It wasn't till a lot later that I learned to really stand on my own and get a little bit aggressive and get kind of nasty now and then. . . .

Janet Warren's work first as a union organizer and now as an international union's general counsel had brought her closer to the great social and political movements of the time than anyone else in the group. It was a deep and practical commitment, but her work itself was only indirectly political. In her private life, she had worked for candidates who expressed her views when the work had to be done, but—

—It's not something that I aesthetically enjoy *at all*. It's a terrible thing for a lawyer to admit, but I dislike quarrels. I just find the whole business—I think many people get less displeasure from them than I do. . . .

And Jack Dailey, who had served a term as alderman in one of Chicago's suburbs and been good enough to be urged to run again unopposed, still served his party but could not see himself working his way up the political ladder. Why on earth not? He'd had a taste of it, and the talent, as I remembered him in high school, had been there all along. He mentioned several obvious reasons—job, family—and one that at the time surprised me—

—I don't like people all that much as individuals. I love them as a group, but as individuals I have trouble getting along with them. I don't *enjoy* the business of running for office.

It was the Evanston view of life again, aloof, proper, impersonal. One of the characteristics of American life in our time has been the new emphasis, under the name of "management," on group action and decision, in science, business, government. To that extent, Evanston had taught us the things we would have to know; in almost every field, we had had to learn the delicate art of working in groups, where leadership suppresses itself, ideas circulate without distinctions, and decisions are "arrived at," not made. John's work in medicine—teaching and research—was a specialized version of the prevailing pattern. In medicine as in other fields, research and development meant clearly defined teams—with assistants, technicians, clerical help— working on specific long-term projects that would have been inconceivable without the large capital provided by government, by foundations, by big corporations. What did that mean for a scientist of our generation?

—There's so much group action, group decision, group authority involved in practically any major endeavors that I think the era of the large leader, the one-man leader, is gradually disappearing. Maybe our age group is going to be able to accept that—whereas the people in the generation older than ours had to be the number one man. Most of us are trained—certainly I'm trained that way medically— towards a team approach to high-level problems. . . .

For Bill, still new enough at the real estate business to be systematically studying and mastering it, part of his impatience with government was precisely its inability to take purposeful action. He talked wittily about his disillusion with government leaders who claimed to be leading him somewhere: it was like being at the head of a parade or a demonstration—it seemed to be going somewhere but it wasn't. Underlying this feeling was another that, it seemed to me, we had all shared: the anxiety, as we found our way into the adult world, to gain the knowledge, master the techniques, that would make us effective; merely being perceptive, being right, was not enough. Bill told me about a trip to San Francisco when the Haight-Ashbury district was still flourishing. What was it all about? It was something one had to learn about, part of the world.

—Nobody threatened me. . . . I found an awful lot of people who wanted to bend my arm—conversationally. All kinds of problems: I listened to some problems and found that some of these individuals really had something to say —it was just that the whole process somehow seemed futile. As I get older, I acquire a prejudice against people who are right but ineffective. If you don't convert your rightness to effectiveness, you haven't done anything. . . .

Effectiveness: it was a common trait. There were exceptions, of course, in a group of nearly six hundred people, and the failures were not only economic. There were those who had entered the darkness of mental disease and apparently would never come out again. There were instances of alcoholism at all stages from incipient to long since cured. And against the generally early, happy, and enduring marriages could be set some others that were the reverse. But by and large, the people I talked to or heard about in the course of the summer *had* found ways of converting their rightness into effectiveness.

I have been describing what in an older psychology would have been called the character of the middle generation, the traits and attitudes that by 1946 were largely formed. What had we made of it since then? For an observer looking in, it seemed a generally happy and honorable life. The outlines are those of middle-class life everywhere in the country in the past twenty-five years, refined and humanized by Evanston's particular brand of effectiveness.

As a rule, marriages were with persons of nearly identical background. Seven were actually within the class, and there were as many between people a year or two apart at Evanston High School. Most of these had grown out of steady dating, that peculiar institution of our high school years; with one exception, they had lasted. Although the average age at marriage was not so young, a few people, influenced by the number of married veterans, got married while they were still in college. It was the beginning of a practice that by the 60s had become commonplace—and the beginning, also, of the colleges' surrender of authority over the lives of their students (at my own college, getting married, unless one were a veteran, remained grounds for expulsion until after I graduated). Eunice, for example, who became a writer, apparently had no qualms about marrying in her senior year, when her husband still had medical school to get through.

—We married between semesters. There was a trailer camp—they weren't mobile, but they were that small and they looked like trailers. . . . Everybody else was married too, you had that model, and a lot of older people on campus—vets. . . .

"Everybody else"—it is what the young have always told their parents, as if it were a comfort. By the time we had finished college, the Korean War was providing a more persuasive justification, and before it was over about 80 percent of the men had gone into service (another 10 percent were in before or after). Against the uncertainty of war and the prospect of the draft, it seemed important to seize whatever time one could.

It was Eunice also who had the clearest memory for our feelings about having children—that mysterious tide of babies that swept through our whole generation and now is receding.

—When I was in college, so many of us talked in terms of large families. This was the healthy thing to do—the Gilbreth thing, *Cheaper by the Dozen*. A whole generation decided to have lots rather than fewer. . . .

It seems odd indeed that in the depressed 30s and 40s books about the huge Victorian families of our parents' generation should have been so enormously popular (*Life with Father*, with its three thousand performances as a play and universal assignment in schools, was another). Characteristically, though, it was not the fun of a big family that we thought of (the books never mentioned the difficulties) but some form of duty—it seemed healthier for the children, it would spread a little wider whatever advantages we thought we had. It was often said a few years ago that the big families of the 50s were a reaction against the earlier view of parental duty that produced the one- and two-child families of the late 20s, but in Evanston, at least, three or four children was not uncommon, and those in the Class of 1946 who had grown up in such families were just as likely to have large families themselves as those who had not.

The feelings about children went deeper than the half-formed thought that having several was somehow a good thing. They sprang from the same roots that made the home a matter of central importance. Perhaps it had to do with those memories from early childhood, of our parents' lost jobs and ruined businesses, the lost or threatened homes, but for us—not all but enough to set us apart, consciously, as a group—the physical home was not simply a commodity, a housing unit bought in order to be traded off periodically in an age of mobility. It was a final goal—the first call on whatever money one could earn or borrow— and the children were a functioning part of that home, its main purpose though not its only one.

Not many of us could build our home with our own hands as Roy, the black carpenter, had done, but we would understand the act and admire it. When I saw Barbara Corbett, it was with an odd sense of going back in time— her house in north Evanston was one I had known and envied when another member of the class lived there. Being built of stone, unusual in the Midwest, made it look expensive, but that was not the point.

—Money is important to me only to spend. I enjoy spending. I enjoy giving. We don't have a lot of money— we're here by the skin of our teeth because we were willing to sacrifice other things in order to have a lovely home to be in. . . . We love to entertain. . . .

Lou Joyce (I'll call him), the outstanding athlete in the class, had twice made the same kind of supreme effort, designing and then building his own house. The first one, in northern New Jersey, they had had to leave behind when his work as an engineer took him to the Midwest: "a heartrending experience"—but when they came back to New York they made the effort again—

—A year of sacrifice. We lived apart for a year while the house was being built and we had not sold the house in Illinois. I stayed here and lived in motels and YMCAs—and did all the painting myself on evenings and so on. . . . We seem to gather every nickel and dime we can find, every time, and build the biggest, most beautiful house we can. . . .

For us, the physical home had remained the symbol for that body of deeply felt concerns that have to do with family, children, the structure of life itself. Chuck Head put it best.

—Getting married—and raising a family—that's the biggest concern—from day to day. You go from there to your friends and your involvement in your church and the community, county government and state government and federal government. But it starts there. . . .

If, typically, marriage, family, home came first, and often early in life as well, making a living assumed a double urgency, and its importance was engraved in our childhood. What did the men do for a living? There were more salesmen than anything else—twice as many as in any other category. Those who were in business of some kind, from salesmen to managers, accounted for nearly half the class's occupations. The second biggest category turned out to be engineers (about 9 percent), and there were others, like Bill, whose engineering background was concealed by another kind of work. There were also sizable groups in various trades (auto mechanics, a crane operator, a milkman), the half-dozen management consultants mentioned earlier, and a few lawyers, schoolteachers, college professors, coaches. Surprisingly, considering that we had grown up in Evanston and that Northwestern is probably the dominant medical school in the region as Harvard is in the East, there were only three doctors.

Unless you were an engineer, starting out in the early 50s had been a struggle: we got there ahead of the great economic expansion with its elaborate recruitment programs and high starting salaries. A young man wanting to get into business might try dozens of companies before finding one that would take him on—at $50 or $60 a week—and the doctors, lawyers, and teachers had the same kind of experience. We accepted the situation: it was what we had grown up expecting. Typically—though sometimes after a false start or two—in this period when changing jobs has been fairly easy, we had stayed put, like our fathers; the men who had worked for the same company for ten or fifteen or more years were commoner than those who had worked for several.

For the women, as Evy had observed, commitment to a profession was almost nonexistent. Fully three-quarters of the women identified themselves simply as housewives, often with a satisfied self-characterization like "loving wife and mother." Nearly all the rest were teachers, with as many women at the college level as there were men. Interestingly, among the women there were also as many engaged in the arts in some form (music, painting, writing) as there were men—nearly a dozen altogether.

Both the men and women had remained Midwesterners, despite the much-publicized American mobility of the 50s and 60s. Fully 70 percent lived somewhere in the Midwest, more than half in Illinois. Although 15 percent of the class was still to be found in Evanston—like the home itself, a center from which we had spread outward in diminishing circles—twice as many had moved to other, more affluent and homogeneous North Shore suburbs and still others to Chicago suburbs like those but not actually part of the North Shore. Of these, nearly all, when I asked them what it was like, said that the town they live in was the way Evanston had been when we lived there—Evanston had become a place with too many big-city problems and impossible taxes. Typically, too, their feelings about the place they had chosen instead of Evanston were divided: their children's experience was incomplete, there were no blacks to speak of, no poor; but where Evanston had racial tensions, demonstrations, sit-ins, student strikes, their fears were about drugs.

The feeling about drugs was not entirely a matter of fearing the unknown. Our children's exposure was repeating, in a more extreme form, our own. Several men reminded me that marijuana had been not so uncommon when we were in high school and college. Soon after the war, a number of entertainment celebrities were jailed for it—Benny Goodman's awesome drummer Gene Krupa, a young movie actor with heavy-lidded eyes named Robert Mitchum—and it was prevalent enough in the music world so that *Downbeat*, the weekly Bible of swing, felt obliged to warn its younger readers that marijuana really didn't do anything for your playing. (One woman told me of a rebellious older brother who had gone to New York about that time to work as a trumpeter and progressed from marijuana to heroin and alcohol; she had had to live with the twenty-year tragedy of his addiction and was now raising his child.) We encountered the drug casually, if we did, as a reefer passed around in a locker room or at a party; one man had tried it in the form that gave it its other name, tea —brewed in hot water to a bitter infusion that was drunk. Only two men that I interviewed claimed any experience with marijuana as adults. No one who had tried the drug remembered any special effect, yet nearly all were afraid of it—it meant a step toward addiction, unknown dangers, loss of will, control. Drugs in general had become the focus for whatever anxieties one had for one's children as they approached adulthood.

This generation's cultivation of its privacy draws a veil over what can be said of its children, yet typically the relationships struck me as serene. We had had no more program, as parents, than to do a little better what our own had done—to grant a little more reasonable autonomy, to provide a little more firmness. Where we were conscious of mistakes, typically it was the mistake of having pushed the older children too hard, trying to be too skillful, and the difference showed in the younger ones. As Frank, the mathematician, had discovered of the world at large, it was no longer an age in which people—even our children—

would respond to discipline imposed by others. Where we did try to impose it, the result might be an eldest son, destined for college, who refused to go and ran off to join the Marines or work in a gas station; or who simply retreated into apathy. I did not, however, find any real horror stories—runaway children, serious drug addiction, unintended pregnancies. Characteristically, by seventeen or eighteen the older children already seemed to be living quite separate lives, sometimes with the house itself divided into clearly defined zones for that purpose; because the older children had become remote, the younger ones seemed closer to their parents, the relationship easier, warmer. One had learned.

People living in the various North Shore suburbs told me very circumstantially about the drug situation in the high schools their children attended: the young pushers, the children who came to school high, the random smashing of plumbing and school equipment—nearly everyone had some personal knowledge of a boy or girl who had died or been hospitalized because of an overdose. But these were not things that were happening to *their* children. One woman quoted her older daughter—I will call her Lee—at length on the estrangement of the friends who had begun using drugs.

—To them, it's not affecting them at all, and yet, you see, Lee's not on, so she can see what it's doing to them. It's like a person who would all night long not have a single drink and watch all the rest of the people drinking and see them all get—this is the *same thing*.

Others knew which of their children had sampled marijuana and which had not. They responded with information—pamphlets, family discussions, programs at school and church that put demands on their time and energy. The children had to know and then decide for themselves: we had learned.

John took the same kind of approach, but as a doctor he saw the problem in its medical context—the explosive production of new drugs of all kinds since the war, the erosion of the scruples that had been instilled by his own medical training.

—In the old days, we were taught to select drugs extremely carefully, usually based on just what their physiological actions are. Now—the tremendous proliferation of drugs—the physician finds himself prescribing large numbers to one patient . . . one drug to offset the deleterious effects of another. . . . That feeds into the drug problem with the kids. . . . Tranquilizers? I've never felt particularly happy with these drugs. . . . I almost never have prescribed energizers.

John associated the drugs, in this sense, with the other thing that had altered the way life is lived—

—Television. You see the whole world unfold before you, you get a visual input where all we had was the books and the radio. . . . Quick change, quick solution: I'm sure that's responsible for a lot of the behavioral patterns that the adolescents have now.

Our feelings about the gray lights and flashes on the television screen and our children's response to them are peculiarly intense. It was not simply that television confirmed the technological hopes of our wartime adolescence or that we were the first generation of parents to submit anxiously to our children's twenty or thirty hours a week of infatuation. Our consciousness had been seared by a long weekend of television that came in November 1963, at the midpoint in our lives: the one man who seemed to represent our generation was shot in the back of the head like a steer in a slaughterhouse—his murder and his murderer's murder—and we had to *watch* it happen, drawn back, repelled, drawn back. For us—not all, but many—the grief, after years, remained beyond expressing except in tiny details of recollection. But for our children it was not a ritual of grief and mourning but only another, more elaborate show: a *wonder*.

There were other things that set us apart, from our parents, from our children: nearly all of us remembered from youth running arguments with parents about what was then called prejudice. It was one of the things we had set out to change in our own lives. The feelings we observed in the older generation were not limited to blacks—indeed, in Evanston at least, the possibility of any drastic change in that set of relationships probably seemed too remote to be seriously threatening. But—Catholics, Jews, Germans, Poles, Swedes: it was not so much prejudice, perhaps, as anxiety, for us, the children. It was the other reason, for instance, why Barbara's parents had persuaded her to transfer from a college she liked to one she did not: she had been dating a boy who happened to be Roman Catholic. Others married Catholics or Jews and found themselves more or less estranged from their parents.

Our own children were raised in careful freedom from such attitudes. The success of that undertaking, probably, was part of the reason why so few of the people I surveyed regarded civil rights and race relations as a primary concern. We felt rewarded when a child brought home a black friend from school unannounced and it was merely a friend from school, not a significant event requiring self-conscious explanation. Several women mentioned in passing that their daughters' dates included blacks, but they did not take it seriously, it had become, in some schools and colleges in the twenty-five years, almost a fad. If they felt any anxiety, it was not over the possibility of dark-skinned grandchildren but over the new feelings of black separatism and exclusiveness that were in the air in that summer of 1971: the voices persuading reasonable black men and

women that they were somehow traitors if they had white
friends.

Lou, after giving up the home in New Jersey and going
back to Chicago, had lived for a while in one of the North
Shore suburbs that became notorious several years ago for
its success in thwarting a middle-class housing development that refused to exclude blacks. Being there had made
Lou and his wife react by starting practical church programs, getting involved in the local politics. They had invited the fiery black Chicago leader Jesse Jackson to address
Deerfield's timid citizenry, had organized outlets for the
new black businesses starting in Chicago. Lou's feelings
about all this, like Jack Dailey's about being an alderman
in another Chicago suburb, had to do with duty—the jobs,
the people, were not something he especially enjoyed.

—Not out of any great love of people or . . . self-esteem.
It was just—somebody had to do it, why not do what I
know how to do well?

Like the rest of us, Lou remembered his parents' views,
which he had resisted and which remained a point of difference.

—We can't understand our parents' attitudes . . . although I can't think it was ever made an influence in my
life—that people of certain nationalities, races, there was
some barrier. We tell my parents please not to make any
comments when our children are present. . . .

If there was still a rivalry between our generation and
the earlier one, conflict with the one after us was also forc-
ing itself on us now. For the men, in their jobs, there had
been all along an older generation that was there first and
now there was another clamoring behind us, pushing; we
were in the middle. It was all the more surprising, then,
how readily the people I talked to, still in their early forties,
accepted the idea of being displaced. One man mentioned
his dislike of the *style* of the young—the loud music, the

flouting of elementary courtesies—"but obviously they're the wave of the future . . . and I'm not." Others were positively aggressive in their acceptance of what they felt was happening to them ("The young guys *ought* to come along and push old farts like you and me. . . .").

Eunice had felt the pressure of disregard as far back as college—from those slightly older undergraduates who were ahead of us, years older in the experience of their war —as something happening not just to her but to our generation; in part, at least, it had made a writer of her. Now it was happening again.

—You constantly deferred. . . . And now of course with the kids, we're the ones that always ought to shut up and listen to somebody else. . . . And you listened to them. . . . It isn't the case that in those days we were unthinking and now they are very self-directed and thinking. Your life role wasn't open to question in the same way that it is now. . . .

That turning point—recognizing, defining, accepting ourselves and the kinds of possibilities that life had—came late for most of us; some of us, twenty-five years later, were still floundering. A few, like Evy, had reached an understanding of themselves early, in the commonplace but bearable conflict with parents that teaches you your identity: for her, in the Scandinavian ex-logger father who decided that education was turning her into a Communist; in the mother convinced that this daughter, who was to be a minister's wife, had lost her faith. Bearable conflict: it made it possible to accept one's own children's struggles with equanimity—with sympathy, admiration.

And what was it, finally, that this reasonable, orderly Evanston had made of us? The care that the town and our parents had lavished on our upbringing was still evident in the remarkable physical health of the class as it entered middle age: the women most often slim and energetic in this era of the diet, the men rather athletic, still bringing home golf and tennis trophies from the local clubs, hiking, climbing, skiing, sailing; remarkably few had died, and nearly all of these by accident or war. And the inner qualities? It seems to me that they are aspects of one essential character which we all shared to some degree: the dutifulness, the dislike of conflicts, the concern for what is personal and private, the rather abstract sense of propriety; the eagerness to master techniques that has made us useful public servants but not political leaders. Evanston, twenty-five years ago, was already what the nation at large only aspired to be, but its success made it a middle kind of place, a place without extremes—of wealth or poverty, love or hatred, intellect, ambition. The route was clearly laid out for us and we followed it, perhaps too readily, to such rewards as it could offer.

Much that was beginning in 1946 and that has been the substance of our lives seems now, as I write, to be ending; a sense of national decline has become almost commonplace, the bitter truth of our generation's middle age. Atomic energy, the system of alliances and international legislation that would put reasoned agreement in place of war and oppression, the civil rights movement—all these and what they have made of our lives are matters for other chapters. But the meaning of these events and perhaps their causes were there all along, if we had noticed: they were inherent in what the middle generation was capable of knowing and responding to and what it was not. Sooner or later, simply to survive so much history, we had to discover that meaning, and for some of us, the discovery came early and easily. Evanston, several people had concluded, had been sheltered, protected; life, as we would have to live it, was harder than that.

Frank Carlborg's experience has a symbolic clarity that is expressive for all of us. He was good enough as a mathematician so that after several years of teaching, and with a wife and children, he received a fellowship that enabled him to take the several years necessary to earn a doctorate at the University of Chicago. There, he was electrified by the exposure to first-rate minds in his field—and felt that he was already too old for it. The feeling was one of simultaneous discovery and loss, of having been *cheated*. Great work in mathematics is generally done early in life or not at all. It is a matter not only of talent but of the luck of having the right kind of challenge at the right moment.

The discovery had begun earlier and became, in time, a rejection of a part of the past, which is oneself. Frank had finished college and gone through the Army as a mathematician assigned to the Redstone Arsenal in the heady early days of rocket building. He was married and teaching at a small college in northern Illinois, and he and his wife had their first small child. Then they bought fifteen acres with a decaying log cabin far out in the country, surrounded by hundreds of acres of woodland.

—I spent three years rebuilding the log cabin, Frank said. Full log, chinked with mortar—oakum was behind the mortar. Oakum and then a wire mesh and then the plaster would go into this wire mesh. We had a long road—about three-quarters of a mile—that I had to maintain, grade, and I bought a jeep. I plowed it and graded . . . sowed a garden patch with my corn. I loved it—. . . .

—Everything was hard—we'd get snowed in and have to stay there for two days in the winter. . . .

I would have liked that, I thought.

—I've thought about this a lot. In Evanston, our lives were really quite organized. There was the Y to take care of you—it was a safe place to go—and there were church groups. I got the idea that everything was going to be all right—that if you just went along, you didn't have to do very much, just be a nice boy and don't do anything bad, and all these good things would come to you. The world was suffering out there, in the Depression, I really didn't understand. . . .

And then, in the woods?

—It carried on with me really until I went into the woods and bought this log cabin. And all of a sudden nobody was flowing things into me, I was left all alone out there. . . . It was at that point that I realized that if anything was going to happen I'd have to do it myself. The system, the organization, that carried me along so nicely, arranged friends for me, kept me out of trouble, got me into college, graduated me—really wasn't going to take care of me anymore. It was all up to me. . . .

That, which perhaps never could have been taught, was the thing back in 1946 that lay ahead of us to learn. They were hard years in which to do it.

5

Your Town, My Town

It was a morning in late summer in an apartment in New York. Over mugs of coffee Spencer Beach was remembering, not without irony, the place where we had both grown up.

—My earliest impressions of Evanston were curious. My grandfather was old Evanston—I believe he knew John Evans. We lived in that old part of town. . . . This childhood atmosphere that I had was that Evanston was a very small town that went north as far as Northwestern, south as far as Main Street, and west about to Ridge Avenue. Everything else was sort of foreign country. . . .

It had been a shock to discover that this was not so, as you did at the age of eleven or twelve when the transition to junior high school exposed you to people from other parts of the town that you had not known existed.

There was more to the impression than the limited horizon of childhood. Evanston really was a collection of villages which accidents of geography and history had united in a city, and the local feelings persisted. On its reduced scale, Evanston's history is an alternative version of the national history: particularly in the quarter-century since World War II, it represents how life might have been for the country at large, a little less imperfect, a little less uncivilized. The same conflicts have been at work, but in Evanston the turmoil and the violence have found outlets in new social forms, new institutions. If the conflicts of these twenty-five years have not been resolved, they have at least taken forms that enrich city life rather than destroy it. It is worth trying to understand how this could have happened.

In Evanston, just as in the Midwest generally, a university was bound up with the social and political life from the beginning. And as in those states, settled by New Englanders, where the founding of a state university was one of the first legislative acts, it was a university dedicated to practical and utilitarian goals rather than the abstract pursuit of knowledge. Indeed, it was Northwestern that founded the town of Evanston rather than the other way around. In the decade before the Civil War, a group of Methodist laymen headed by a Chicago doctor, John Evans, bought the several hundred acres along Lake Michigan, with a grove of old trees, that were to be the university campus. A couple of years later, the university business manager drew up the original street plan of the town that was to adjoin. The qualities that those men planted are still there: the Methodist earnestness and hatred of gambling and alcohol (the original town charter specified that no drink was to be sold or consumed within four miles of the university); the Lincoln Republicanism sympathetic to Abolition (free Negroes and, later, black Civil War veterans were among Evanston's early settlers).

Besides their appreciation for practical learning, the New England settlers brought with them the idea of the township as the smallest subdivision of government, conferred on the inhabitants by the state. A township, like the larger county, represented the central government, for which both collected taxes. A village or town, on the other hand, was created locally by a group of settlers who applied to the state for incorporation. It might grow up wholly within a township, or it might spread across township and county lines with a resultant dilution of local authority under several jurisdictions. The town of Evanston had the good fortune to become, through the gradual stages of its growth, coterminous with the township of the same name.

When the state legislature laid out the Illinois prairie in the rational squares and rectangles of counties and townships, it failed to take account of the sweeping curve of Lake Michigan on which Evanston was placed. Half the township, in effect, was in the lake. Being half the size of its neighbors, however, was to prove a fortunate accident of Evanston history. It was possible for the town of Evanston, over the next century, to expand, absorbing other villages and scattered settlements, until its borders coincided with the borders of the township. Confined by the lake on the east and by Chicago and two other townships on the other sides, Evanston remained compact in population and physical size.

The neatly rectangular street plan platted by the university business manager, complete with space for parks, was incorporated a decade later, in the midst of the Civil War, as the Town of Evanston. This was the "very small town" Spence remembered from his boyhood, geographically near the center of the township and central in most other ways as well. A decade later, the rest of the university property along the lake to the north was added and with the vagaries of state law the town became legally a village. About the same time, in the early 1870s, the separate villages of South Evanston and North Evanston were incorporated as the distinct entities that to some degree they have remained throughout Evanston's history. Meanwhile, another permanent fact of the city's life was growing on the west side of the township: a distinct black community which by the mid-70s was populous enough to support a Baptist church and, by the 80s, its own newspaper, the *Afro-American Budget*. In 1892, as Evanston continued to expand north, west, and south within its township, the village assumed the rights and taxing powers of a city. Four years later, it absorbed the black community reaching to the western part of the township—and with it the central fifty-acre site where the city's high school has remained ever since. The process continued into the 1930s, when the last fragments of unincorporated township land were annexed and physically the City of Evanston was complete.

Throughout this history, the relationship between the university and its town has been interestingly balanced. Neither has dominated the other. The points of controversy that exist today between the two have been present from the beginning: the untaxed university land; the payment by the university for services not covered by taxes; the expedients of mutual encroachment which occur and re-occur to politicians and university bureaucrats. Throughout, Northwestern has intervened at critical points with practical benevolence to ensure the planned development of the environment it had provided for itself: in 1855, to grant a railroad right of way to the west of the town, away from the lake front—and the campus; in the 1870s, with land for what would be the first water works built on the shore of Lake Michigan; later, with land for parks, schools, and other buildings, and a picturesque lighthouse during Evanston's period as a lake port (silting closed the piers in the 90s). The university's foresight assumed a contemporary tone in the 1960s when resentment over its westward expansion into the still-present black community produced a promise to go no further; the solution was a landfill of several hundred acres, pushing the campus out into the lake.

Evanston's growth from a city of sixteen thousand in 1892 to a city of eighty thousand in 1970 parallels the national growth. It can be traced in the town's real estate records. A house built in 1900 for ten thousand dollars might sell for fifty thousand dollars or sixty thousand dollars in 1927—and a third or a quarter that ten years later, if it could be sold at all; it was nearly 1970 before the same house would again reach the heady level of the 20s. It is significant that it would still be the same house—the rise and fall of the real estate market has worked for preservation; and the explosive growth that followed the two world wars took place within the framework of the state's first zoning law, passed in 1921 and, much amended, still operating today. In matters that affected its growth, the town has had the knack of being able to decide what kind of place it wanted to be and of anticipating the events that would contribute to that character.

In the course of the 1920s, while the City of Evanston was reaching its geographical limits, the population nearly doubled and began to come in sight of the figure of ninety thousand that had been laid down as an ideal maximum. By 1930, the town's black population, following the national movement from rural South to urban North, reached nearly 8 percent of the total. In geography and population, the town was now almost complete. What was possible thereafter was refinement and preservation rather than growth. In that sense, the town was anticipating by nearly forty years concerns that have only recently become prominent in the nation at large. The contemporary anxiety over what we now call pollution, for example, can be dated in Evanston from 1927, when the town's first smoke abatement ordinance was passed.

In Evanston, the concern for preservation against the forces of expansion produced a kind of working balance between various extremes—homes and factories, private houses and apartment buildings, wealth and poverty, voluntary agencies and departments of city government. What the people of my generation, growing up there, sensed as an absense of extremes, of profound challenges, was also that happy mediocrity which Benjamin Franklin, that most practical of Americans, identified as the chief blessing of democracy: in the absence of extremes—of instantaneous perceptions of absolute evils and absolute means of righting them—it is possible to move pragmatically toward distant goals, keeping open the option for other solutions along the way. It is probably characteristic both of Evanston's limitations and of its pragmatic virtue that the town's one national figure (after John Evans, the founder) should have been a man always known locally as General Dawes. A Chicago banker who served on Pershing's staff in World War I, Charles Dawes achieved the eminence, in the 20s, of serving as Vice President to that figure of American political fun, Calvin Coolidge. He lived to an immense age in a turreted Victorian mansion with a cool and airy outlook on a town park and, beyond it, Lake Michigan. There, in his retirement, he composed sentimental popular songs which were performed with respect by Evanston's musicians, and there it was customary for younger men to consult him about the baffling Republican politics of the 30s and 40s. The town, which even today remains a bastion of Republicanism, would find nothing ironic in the connection of its chief political figure with the silent respectability of Calvin Coolidge.

The Evanston of the 1930s was thus peculiarly suited to forming the consciousness of the middle generation. Like any childhood place, it seemed immutable—and it very nearly was in fact. The succession of schools I went to— the elementary school, the more distant junior high school, the high school a mile and a half away—were unchanged from the time when my older brothers attended them ten years earlier: the red brick, the indestructible brown battle-ship linoleum in the halls and classrooms, the high ceilings and spacious windows, even the teachers themselves. The other structures that gave the town its child's-eye shape seemed equally permanent. The worn city hall, with its shingled tower echoing a French Renaissance château con-tracted to the dimensions of a city lot, dated from 1892; the library, standing nearby in cool, gray-limestone dignity, had been built in 1906. Both, like Fountain Square itself, with its department stores, the dime stores where one could buy things that really cost no more than a nickel or a dime, were fifteen minutes away from any part of the town by any of the several bus routes one rode for three cents (later, when I was twelve, the fare rose to seven cents).

The range of services that the town accepted as normal seems astonishing in the light of city life elsewhere and since then—that was part of what my classmates meant when, looking back, they said that their lives had been "protected." The public library itself had been founded in the 1870s, one of the first free libraries in the state. Trash collection and disposal were as normal a government ser-vice as the mail that popped through the front door slot in the morning and afternoon. Every spring, men from the city appeared with tank trucks to spray the city's trees— there were about twenty-five thousand of them, mostly elms, planted on the ten-foot strip of grass between the cement sidewalks and the street—and at other times to prune dead branches.

The mosquito problem was solved by a different kind of agency and just as efficiently. Until the early 30s you were driven indoors at dusk, raging at the number and ferocity of the Evanston mosquitoes and scratching—much of the town had once been lakeside swamp, the breeding grounds were everywhere, and nothing, it seemed, could be done about that. Then men began coming around with tanks of spray on motorcycles, covering every patch of standing water, every puddle—and the mosquitoes vanished. Illinois state law encourages such local initiative by limiting municipal borrowing and taxing powers. To get around that limitation, local commissions (such as the North Shore Mosquito Abatement District) have multiplied, their policies made and their revenues collected by volunteer trustees; the actual work is carried out by a small paid staff with no need for another self-perpetuating department of the municipal bureaucracy. It seems, no doubt, a small benefit to remember gratefully after so many years, but civilization is the sum of such beneficent trivia.

A surprising range of health services filtered down through the school system. One was constantly being tested—vision tests, teeth tests, blood tests, posturegraph tests, foot-flatness tests, speech tests—and then for those found wanting remedial exercises were prescribed. I remember in the late 30s having my teeth examined as part of a control group when the town was considering the merits of fluoridating its water; with characteristic caution, the town waited till 1947 before making fluoridation official for the whole water supply. (A decade after that, however, in many other American towns fluoridation was still a frantically controversial issue.)

If I have dwelt on the not very interesting services that

Evanston's citizens provided for themselves and their children, it is to suggest the kinds of tiresome minutiae that civilized life requires; and to suggest also the kind of old-fashioned, optimistic, Victorian activism, still persuaded of the perfectibility of human society, that took pains over such matters. Today when every demagogue will promise miracles of spiritual regeneration but has only the most rudimentary notions of how to make the buses run or the garbage get picked up, it seems worth remembering that it is on precisely such elements that civil life depends.

The energy and earnestness of that older Evanston were enshrined in an early-Victorian white-frame house half-way between Northwestern and Fountain Square, the home of Miss Frances Willard and since her death the international headquarters of an institution that seems peculiarly of the place, the Woman's Christian Temperance Union. There, white-haired ladies in long skirts and pince-nez, like idealized grandmothers, conducted troops of Evanston schoolchildren past exhibits—such as the tiny brass opium pipes grateful Orientals had surrendered to Miss Willard during a campaign in the Far East—that seemed as remote from our lives as the moon. With the repeal of Prohibition only a few years past, the WCTU's persistent concern with keeping people from alcohol seemed, of course, absurd, even to a child. But even then the organization was campaigning against drugs that today have become far more immediate and threatening than whiskey or opium. And one cannot but be awed by the sheer personal force with which Miss Willard and Midwestern women like her set about altering the national history. Ten years after the incorporation of Evanston as a town, at a time when educating women was not something most Americans of either sex perceived as a necessity, Miss Willard was the first president of the Evanston College for Ladies (she remained as its dean when, a little later, it became the Northwestern Female College and made the university coeducational). In the same spirit, she became one of the earliest campaigners for temperance and woman suffrage, that dual movement, moral and political, which in time compelled a masculine nation to accept both votes for women and Prohibition.

That spirit, with its unyielding pursuit of whatever goals seemed to promise practical human benefit, was still very much a force in the Evanston of our youth, even though its great accomplishments were in the past. It was the spirit, which at the time I despised, of the old ladies only a generation removed from Miss Willard with their peace petitions circulated in the face of the German armies subverting Spain and overthrowing France. It was the spirit of the woman in a tiny Evanston shop who disappointed me after I had ridden my bicycle miles in the hope of buying lead soldiers by telling me that she did not, as a matter of principle, sell such things. And it was the spirit, finally, of another old woman on the streets of Evanston the day after Pearl Harbor. Schoolboys were already singing the songs that had sprung up, quite literally, overnight—"We're going to get the dirty Jap"—and one such woman was there to rebuke us: for the hatred, the delight in killing, the contempt of Japanese for being Japanese.

Although it seems quaint, archaic, in its view of life and in the practical, limited means by which it sought to realize that view, the WCTU was simply a rather specialized expression of the moral seriousness that is at the heart of Evanston and the Midwest still. That purposeful optimism was likewise the motive force behind the program for health and education and all the other services that Evanston's children took for granted. Together, they instilled a sense of what one's role would be as a person—and as a man or woman—so strong, so clear, that it rarely had to be expressed directly. We had few uncertainties about the kinds of behavior that were possible for us.

At the reunion itself and in the course of the summer, I had noticed after the lapse of twenty-five years a certain constraint in talking to the women that I did not feel with the men, even when I thought I had known both equally well. There was a difference, apparently. Those distinctive modes of behavior that you learn in earliest childhood had always seemed like means of self-expression, but they turned out also to be barriers. At school around the age of nine or ten, when the boys were learning to wrestle and play marbles and organize wars on the dusty playground and the girls would be somewhere engaged in hopscotch and skipping rope, we were learning distinct languages as well. It was then, quite suddenly, that the boys acquired a large vocabulary of swear words and obscenities to be used freely among ourselves but never around adults—or girls. It was a secret, a language the girls would not use and apparently did not know. (I could still be shocked, long afterward, when I heard a girl ask a boy on my son's school track team if he'd "fallen on his ass" in the high jump—it was not supposed to be something a girl could say.)

At each stage of growth, the town provided a remarkable variety of situations in which its children could practice their roles. For both boys and girls there were organized sports to go out for and formal meetings to conduct, in school and independently in Y clubs. From the age of eleven or twelve on, there were also evening dancing classes, some quite informal, others held at the Woman's Club of Evanston, by invitation, and requiring dark suits or dresses, white gloves. All were carefully supervised and taught not simply dancing but appropriate forms of conduct. Later, as we progressed through increasingly formal dances and dates, there were other kinds of occasions that we arranged for ourselves—"casual" was the approving word we used for them. Pat Lopez, contrasting her own immensely satisfying children, her adult life on the North Shore, remembered—

—I went to the beach with my friends and we sat there all day long and then the boys came and sat all around—and we just sat—and talked. . . .

It came back. There were girls lying out all day in the sun while the last ice was still breaking up along the rim of the beach, and by April or May they were burned mahogany color. And then the summer with the groups of girls lying on towels, the boys in their groups moving around them restless as sandpipers: there would be a portable radio, a deck of cards, the experiments with cigarettes, the earnest, only apparently aimless, talk as we tried out our impressions of ourselves.

Formed, like the rest of us, by that past, Julie Chasin could only be appalled at the idea of the coed dorms her daughter, who had just finished high school, might be living in the next year at Northwestern. Julie had gone there herself, had delighted in the flourishing sorority life of that time, with its dates, dances, football games. It was not its disappearance that bothered her or the new scope for casual promiscuity Rather, it was the loss of a part of life that had been distinctively feminine, a part of one's sense of being a woman. Why on earth did the young reject it and why did the colleges acquiesce?

—It's great to put kids on their own to a certain extent but . . . as much as I liked dating . . . who wants to live across the hall from—a bunch of boys? You have more fun with girls—at that point in your life, this is the time to have fun with your friends and—what are you going to achieve by it? To me—there were so many things I enjoyed doing in college that were . . . girl-oriented. Like sports—we had a great bunch. This to me was so satisfying . . . singing. . . . I think kids miss so much if they don't get this in school, because after you're out—. . . .

For the women of our generation at a place like North-western, the sororities and all that went with them had seemed overly important. I remember tales of the week when the pledges were made, the mothers anxiously soliciting recommendations from alumnae, the daughters crushed by rejection. Too much could be lost—it was not something one would be sorry to see disappear. But the alternatives? Bobbie Collins, who had gone back to Northwestern for a graduate degree in middle age, had been president of her own sorority, had enjoyed it, but felt no need to preserve it if it was no longer needed. Yet her feelings about what was taking its place were much like Julie's. Communes, for instance, one of the novel institutions that have been springing up in Evanston as elsewhere: she had gone to parties at one with a fellow graduate student.

—This girl lived in a commune and I found it very depressing. It's an old house. . . . A group of boys live on the first floor, a group of girls live on the second floor and—very ratty surroundings. A couple of mattresses stacked up where they sleep. It isn't just that I'm older, I think I never would have been comfortable living that way. . . . You're more forced into interaction than you are in a more impersonal living situation. Supposedly they've moved in with friends—but by golly!

That feeling for privacy is part of the answer to the question that puzzled me earlier: why, if the system was so well designed—first to define one's role as man or woman, adult, then to connect the two in the shared role of marriage—did it fail as often as it did in the middle generation? There were not only the disastrous or merely empty marriages. There were also those who as adolescents had never had a date, never gone to a dance, and who as adults had remained solitary; there were others whose life in high school had been the reverse and who had ended the same way. In both cases, home, family, were at the center of outward-reaching circles, increasingly remote and impersonal, and for most of us that private view of the world was a strength. But for others it was not a vehicle for communication but a confinement within the barriers of self, sex, age.

This sense of privacy, of careful cultivation of one's self within accepted limits, was one of the reasons local loyalties within Evanston were so strong. Discovering one's identity meant finding out what was valuable about one's neighborhood, what made others inferior to it. There were, of course, real differences: south Evanston was a mixture of apartment buildings and big older houses from before World War I or earlier, relatively transient; north Evanston had been mostly built in the great growth period of the 20s. And there were several other distinct communities within the city's narrow compass, most notably the one that was nearly all black. And yet the actual differences were not great enough to account for our feelings, which were stronger than the unifying force of the school system, for instance, could overcome. Nancy remembered clearly her sense of south Evanston, where she had grown up, and the contrast with north Evanston.

—I think south Evanston was a very different place from north Evanston. It was more old Evanston families on the one hand and on the other hand commuters who had very little identification with the town of Evanston. We were always told that the people in north Evanston were *nouveaux riches*.

For the boys growing up there, this sense of difference naturally took aggressive forms. In high school there would occasionally be carloads of north Evanston boys heading for south Evanston to "clean the plows" of their rivals. One man remembered being part of a mob of boys armed with clubs and gathered on the lakefront for a battle with a crowd from New Trier, Evanston's competitor to the north. (Police came and there was some shoving and shouting but nothing much happened.)

This aggressive sense of membership in a distinct group extended outward until it became a quite strong feeling of being not so much a person from Evanston as a Chicagoan, a Midwesterner. It was a feeling, for instance, of being set apart from the East that among the men, at least, persisted into middle age: the complacent verdict across the whole political spectrum from liberal to conservative that whatever Richard Daley's faults as a mayor might be he was at least competent, he ran the city a whole lot more effectively than New York was run, and it remained a bearable place to live and work; he was one of our own.

Chuck Phalen, one of the few men in the Class of 1946 who had gone into advertising, had run head-on into the New York competition.

—In Chicago in my business when we all started, we knew that to make it you hadda go to New York. Fifty percent of us wanted to take a shot. The money. The glamor.

Chuck had gone to New York as a television producer, then had worked for a while in Los Angeles, and when I saw him again was putting together independent packages in Pittsburgh. But in New York, now, it was we, the Midwesterners, who had won, even if he had not—

The Chicago guys who hung around Howard Street* and Cooley's Cupboard and what not—no Ivy League background, they still talk like we talk when we get drunk—you know, that Evanston nasal twang that comes out. And they are running the show! . . . Toughies, street fighters. . . .

From the perspective of the 1970s, it seems improbable that one's sense of identity should have been formed on

*The border with Chicago. On the Chicago side of the street there were bars and liquor stores.

sectional rather than racial lines, but that was the case. In spite of the existence of a sizable black community, those mobs of teenage boys gathered on the lakefront for a fight were all white; there might be an occasional fistfight between a white boy and a black one, but at the time that particular form of group solidarity rarely took on a larger meaning. The hostilities were there, all right, but, at least among the whites, so deep they were almost unconscious. Instead, there were elaborate and contradictory feelings about other groups of whites: Jews, for instance.

When I was ten or eleven, a new boy joined our class at school, an event unusual enough in itself to set him apart: a boy with curly hair, a prominent nose, and a voice that I remember as whiney. An incident has stayed in my mind like a hallucination: a crowd of boys on the playground in an impenetrable circle, shouting, jeering, and myself struggling to get through, to find out what was happening, and seeing finally this one boy at the center—the indelible feelings of rage, helplessness, pity, injustice. And someone told me: he was something called a Jew and his father had done a terrible thing, had bought a house in the school district under his adopted name, which was not instantly identifiable as Jewish. It was the first family I was aware of as Jewish.

The incident stayed in my mind not only because it was violent and cruel but because it was rare. Whatever the feelings of prejudice planted in us, they were abstract and unspecific. When, during the Depression, the Jewish population of the other North Shore towns increased, people gave their decorous Anglo-Saxon names what they considered a humorously Jewish twist. Winnetka was Winnetski, Glencoe, Glencohen, Highland Park, Kikeland Park; of the latter there evolved an almost Joycean pun—"It should be called Flower Town because there's a Rosenbloom on every corner." Yet Evanston itself was apparently not much desired—there was not even a synagogue there till long after the War, and individual Jews were so scarce that we were less able to identify them than the more numerous Swedes, Germans, and Poles.

Similar exclusions applied to Catholics and Orientals, both almost as rare as Jews in our experience. The Catholics went to elementary schools with unpronounceable names like St. Athanasius'—but then later joined us, there being no Catholic high school in Evanston, and became less distinct. I was aware of one Catholic family in our neighborhood, and it was surely no coincidence that when they moved away their place was taken by another. One woman remembered being asked for a date by the one Chinese boy in the class—and then feeling uncomfortable about it and making a transparent excuse; she had been afraid, she said, of what other people would think. Halfway through the War, six or seven Japanese suddenly appeared in the high school and became, in name at least, members of the Class of 1946—it was a consequence of the relocation program. The same woman who had been afraid to go out with the Chinese boy got to know one of the Japanese girls well. She tried to get the girl a job at Cooley's Cupboard, the restaurant where she was working herself.

—I guess that was maybe my first experience with overt prejudice. The manager before he saw her—something came up about the fact that this girl was Japanese, and that was it! I don't think it was the War or anything. Cooley's just simply didn't—. . . .

All this, of course, is a part of the past that has been swept away without regret. It was one of the changes that was already beginning in the world beyond Evanston, but the same kind of change was at work, though not very consciously, in the Class of 1946. The sense of difference that was part of one's identity was balanced by a kind of courtesy, a sensitivity to others' feelings that made us extremely reluctant to refer to the things that made them different. Nancy remembered the feeling—there had been an incident that fixed it for her early—

—You were very cautious about mentioning to these people that they were Jewish because they naturally would be embarrassed about it and wouldn't want it brought up. There was a boy in fifth grade with a "Jewish" name and I remember asking him what he got for Christmas—and everybody in the class gasped! You *didn't ask*. This is another one of those things that had no meaning for me at this time, and why did it stick in my mind? Maybe because I didn't understand it.

The prejudice nearly every white remembered in his parents—against Jews, Catholics, and so on, not to mention Negroes—was not always open, but where it was, it was something to be argued about, already setting the middle generation apart from the one that preceded. We disliked the feeling because it was unreasonable, because it caused pain to others. And because it was enshrined in custom rather than in law, when the time came the whole edifice of discrimination collapsed without much resistance. Even in 1946, the first sit-ins had been tried and had succeeded in Evanston's restaurants, notably Cooley's. It was the beginning of many such changes.

Several people in the class married Catholics, others Jews. Although in one or two cases this caused a painful breach with parents, in general the event hardly called for comment. (One man married an Indian, another, settled in Tokyo, a Japanese.) Today, Evanston's Jewish population is substantial, and there are four synagogues where twenty-five years ago there were none. A Jew, even a religious one, is more likely to refuse membership in an Evanston club than to be refused. The extent of the change became real for me one Saturday night at my hotel, a deteriorating symbol of the old Evanston. There seemed to be a party going on in what had been the main dining room at the back of the hotel: a small band, people dancing to bouncy tunes that only someone who had grown up in the 40s would recognize—"Tampico, Tampico, On the Gulf of Mexico"—and in the lobby there were boys with flushed, excited faces, and middle-aged men in skullcaps. It was, I realized, a bar mitzvah. Later I was told that the North Shore Hotel was the one preferred for such festivities. The old feelings seemed largely to have disappeared.

To me, a native returning, the Evanston of the present seemed starkly different from the one I remembered, as unimaginable in 1946 as a bar mitzvah at the North Shore Hotel. Yet 1946 had been the beginning: it was in that year that a revived chapter of the NAACP and a new, militant organization, the Congress of Racial Equality (founded four years earlier in Chicago), had led those first sit-ins at Evanston's restaurants and lunch counters. Twenty-five years later, the town had become a theater for every tactic in the Pandora's box of civil protest. There were strikes of city employees, student strikes at Northwestern and in the high school, sit-ins and torchlit parades supporting such causes as open housing and school integration. The changes this turmoil had produced, which to me seemed so striking, were effectual and apparently permanent; the difference from bigger cities and other parts of the country was the absence of destructiveness, in part because in Evanston the issues were matters of custom rather than law. But as in the national history of these twenty-five years, the original catalyst for much of this social and political change was Evanston's black community. Even in 1946, that community was symbolically at the heart of the town, as it had been geographically almost from the beginning, but we had somehow failed to notice.

Although the contrast between the Evanston of 1971 and that of 1946 seemed to me so remarkable, the transformation had, of course, been gradual, event by small event. In the 1940s and early 50s, however, the town was already bringing together the conditions for what was to follow. Sheer dullness was the quality of the local politics that every member of the Class of 1946 remembered—it was one of the reasons why, for most of them, political activity of any kind seemed both futile and distasteful. There seemed to be no issues. The town's political forms functioned as if designed to avoid rather than resolve conflict. In its national politics, the Republican unanimity was unbroken. Spence, who remembered his boyhood Evanston as such an old-style small town, told me about the first Presidential campaign he could remember. There had been a mock election in his class at school.

—There was only one person in our class who was for Roosevelt, and so we were utterly astonished when Roosevelt won.

It was a portent of the future that the one person was also the one black.

Although the city had expanded to the limits of the township, vestiges of the now redundant township government survived with important budgetary and taxing powers. Such matters were decided by a majority of those attending the annual town meeting, a relic, like the township government itself, of the New England heritage. With an average attendance of forty or fifty people, the town meeting was a very private if not actually secret affair.

The city government itself was in the hands of a mayor —a succession of faceless men—and a board of part-time aldermen. It was a remarkably quiet, rather informal government. I talked about this with a slightly older Evanston man, a doctor who has been active in local politics.

—To my thinking, he told me, the town has come from

an oligarchy in which there were a few big families—
they'd call up the mayor and they'd tell him what they
wanted and that's what the city did—to where we have
something of democratic processes. . . .

He remembered, with incredulity and outrage, just how
quiet the city government had been:

—The City Council meetings were secret! . . . That's just
a bunch of crap. When I was in high school or even later
when I was in Northwestern, I was not aware of many of
these violations of just basic—it's a real tyranny! . . .

Warren Spencer is black. Where that feeling of outrage
led him was to the leadership of the NAACP—and much
else.

The old, dutiful Evanston, believing and doing what it
was told, reached a climax of sorts in 1951, when an elaborate civil defense program went into effect. Twenty years
later, the black-and-yellow signs identifying the shelters
were still dotted around the center of the town; a member
of the class, a fireman in a nearby town who had studied
such matters, told me with approval that there were
enough basements to house more than half the population,
and they were still regularly stocked with water and con-
centrated food. (A few days after I heard that, the City
Council, in the casual new style of the time, voted to abolish the program—and then changed its mind the following
day when someone reminded the aldermen that the program was supported by federal money.)

In that same year 1951, the town's leading citizen, General
Dawes, finally died. He had been born two years after the
town's original incorporation, and his life spanned nearly
all that it had been. But already the town, half city, half
suburban village, was changing physically in ways that
heralded the social and political changes of the next two
decades. In 1946, the year of the sit-ins, the town removed
the symbolic circle of trees, greenery, and antique fountain

at Fountain Square as more suitable to the carriages of the past than the cars, trucks and buses of the present; the city government moved from (but did not tear down) the old town hall in favor of the commodious clubhouse of the Evanston Country Club, only a few blocks away, whose golf courses and greens had long since surrendered to houses. Two years later, the town acquired its first parking lot, and in 1952, in the face of a continuing siege of cars and growing competition from new suburbs and shopping centers surrounding the North Shore, it floated the first parking bond issue in the state. In 1948 also, the old covenants in some Evanston deeds restricting ownership to Caucasians were invalidated. The suburb-city was becoming a city on a contemporary model.

In 1952, by referendum, the town adopted a city-manager form of government, retaining its mayor as a ceremonial figure presiding at the weekly—and now extremely public—meetings of the eighteen aldermen who make up the City Council. The city manager serves without contract, at the pleasure of the council. The heads of the city government's departments are appointed (by the city manager, with the approval of the council), but other city employees are protected against even such indirect political pressure: they have been under a civil service system since 1895, and now in addition, a majority—policemen, firemen, teachers, garbage collectors—are unionized. The demand for an ever more elaborate range of public services has been met not by expanding the city government as such but by multiplying the semigovernmental agencies and commissions that provide specific services on a disinterested—but not always apolitical or noncontroversial—basis. The titles of the new commissions are a mirror of shifting American social concerns since the early 50s: the Evanston Recreation Board (1953), the Human Relations Commission, with broad investigative powers (1961), the Citizens' Advisory Commission on Integration and the Evanston Youth Commission (both 1965), Neighbors at Work (1968), a black organization which has done everything from opening a black bookstore to sponsoring day-care centers to campaigning for an ombudsman for the high school (NAW, the acronym by which it is known locally, suggests its spirit); 1969 spawned the Mental Health Board and a City Council Housing Committee concerned both with implementing the city's new open-housing ordinance and with investigating the still newer question of public housing.

The kinds of services the town now felt called to provide reflected some interesting changes in the character of its population. The total increased only slightly, by about 10 percent since the War, to around eighty thousand. The number of Jews, on the other hand, had grown from nearly invisible to substantial (in 1971 at the high school there were now several prizes for proficiency in Hebrew, sponsored by local synagogues). And where the percentage of blacks had been less than 8 percent at the end of the growth period of the 20s and around 10 percent at the end of the War, by 1970 it had reached 18 percent. As in the rest of urban America, moreover, the blacks were increasing faster than the whites: in the school population, under the careful balancing of Evanston's integration program, they now numbered 21 percent; and as in bigger American cities in the 60s, the total population remained about the same, for the increase in blacks balanced the decline in whites, who were beginning to move to other towns still free of Evanston's big-city problems and high taxes.

In the same postwar period, the population was growing at both ends of the spectrum of age rather than in the middle, so that a population graph now swells at the ends like a barbell and is pinched in between. The elderly, the retired, seem to be staying in Evanston, moving from houses to apartments or retirement homes. All but one of

the hotels have become retirement homes in fact—and in
some cases in name as well. By now, fully a quarter of the
population is over fifty-five, as large a segment as the children or perhaps a bit larger. Hence, in many of the stores
around Fountain Square, what would have been kids' jobs
when I lived there are now filled by elderly retired people:
in a period of affluence and inflation, it has not been easy
for them to hang on. The checker in the supermarket or the
dime store, the clerk behind the cigar counter at the hotel,
is likely to be a commanding, white-haired lady in her
sixties, with the middle-class dignity of one's mother; the
man folding out a store awning on the street, washing the
windows, will be not a boy, not a Negro, but a well-dressed
gentleman with the bearing of a retired businessman.

Since the War, the traditional Evanston Republican
majority of 80 or 90 percent has shifted to the point where
it is at least possible for a Democratic Presidential candidate to carry the city, as Johnson did in fact in 1964. At the
local level, however, *official* politics remains as dull as ever,
if not more so. The mayor and aldermen are nominated by
petition and appear on the ballot without party identification, often unopposed. In contrast to a national election,
which generally brings out close to 80 percent of the voters,
the biennial City Council election in an off-year is decided
by not more than half the voters and usually far fewer. It
is as if Evanston's citizens have decided that it doesn't matter *who* is on the City Council, and in a sense they are right.
The real business of the town is carried on regardless, by
civil service specialists and the various commissions. The
policy questions that come before the City Council are so
general that any citizen can understand them, and in the
public and fully reported council meetings an interested
group in the audience is often decisive. The real politics in
Evanston has thus become *unofficial*. A neighborhood or
interest group sufficiently organized to make itself heard

can, in effect, become a participant in policy-making for the town as a whole.

In 1946, there were two neighborhood organizations in Evanston: one, of very long standing, devoted to providing the Fourth of July parade and fireworks display; the other, a traditional immigrants' social-political club whose membership was in the Polish district of southwest Evanston. Today, there are sixteen such groups permanently organized and representing every neighborhood, in several cases with rival groups in the same area. Together they represent somewhat more than 10 percent of the city's households and are about equally divided between those whose aims are defensive (to preserve the town as it has been, keep it residential, keep out public housing, keep taxes from going higher) and those which consciously promote change. (A department of the city government obligingly keeps track of the organizations, their officers, meeting places and times for the benefit of anyone who wants to join.) These groups constitute the active minority which appears week after week at the meetings of the town council and whose testimony has repeatedly provided the pressure that decides key issues. In a real sense the neighborhood organizations *are* the city government in its day-by-day decision-making, and similar groups spring up and die out again as the issues warrant. It has become a quite direct if unofficial kind of democracy, made all the livelier by the fact that the opposing groups are evenly matched, though they differ in their tactics.

Evanston, then, seems to be responding energetically to a question that elsewhere has hardly been asked: the question, simply, of what becomes of an American city when it is fully developed and can no longer expand, when its population has become more or less stable. Is there an alternative to physical and social disintegration? If there is, can the city's people achieve it for themselves, from their own resources, or must they, in order to survive, surrender the authority over their lives to ever larger and more remote organs of a central government?

Evanston's current answers to these questions are particular and have evolved, in a series of experiments, since World War II, but their history is longer than that, in a sense, perhaps, as old as the town itself. Its present policies for the schools, housing, industry, and race relations reflect studies that go back to the late 30s and the War years. A comprehensive antipollution program instituted in 1963 is a lineal descendant of the original smoke-abatement ordinance of 1927. Many general goals of town policy were first expressed in an influential *Plan of Evanston* published in 1916. Indeed, the Evanston Public Library houses a voluminous accumulation of studies, reports, and long-range plans dating at least from the opening of the old building in 1906, and they come out now faster than they can be acquired and catalogued. (A recent reorganization of the city government responded to Evanston's penchant for self-study by creating a planning department to attempt to coordinate the ceaseless plan-making of all the other departments and agencies.) It is possible, therefore, that other cities faced with similar problems cannot emulate Evanston's solutions without having lived its history as well. Yet the example of Evanston is instructive nonetheless, if only because it argues that there *are* solutions.

And what is it like to live there today? In the spring and summer of 1971, implementing a government reorganization of the previous year, the new city manager appointed new heads of various departments, at salaries ranging from about $15,000 to about $30,000 (his own is $35,000). Three of these men were in their twenties, two in their early thirties, two in their early forties—their average age was thirty-two;

the city manager himself was twenty-seven. The contrast with the past is remarkable, but it is not only that the people running the government are young in a city where so many are not. Constant and often abrasive communication has become the distinctive feature of Evanston's civic life: these are men who must be able to face everything from the subtle hostility of a single reporter to the shouting anger of the new-style City Council and committee meetings. It is not a job for a soft-spoken or reflective person.

The new quality of Evanston life is reflected in its weekly newspaper, *The Evanston Review*, which was acquired a few years ago by Time Inc., and since 1969 has faced competition of a sort from a lively Negro tabloid, *The North Shore Examiner*. The *Review*'s format is unchanged since its founding in 1925; the pages of real estate and supermarket and automobile advertising are as numerous and lucrative as ever (black-run real estate firms and car dealers identify themselves with photographs of their managers). But the news columns, once about as lively as a telephone book, are now filled with sharply detailed reporting of the City Council meetings and other political activity, and the editorials are acerbic; a weekly feature is an investigative team's report on the local significance of a broad issue like environmental quality (what chemicals go into the city's water supply and why). Readers' letters in this increasingly communicative and vociferous town may run to several pages. The difference is not chiefly new ownership or competition. What is different is that the life of the city is being carried on in public, in the committee rooms and in the streets. And it is being reported. The decorous quiet of the past has vanished.

Evanston, in its way, within the framework of its established institutions, is responding to the present. The form the response has taken can be seen in its health services and in its police.

There are three hospitals in Evanston, as there were twenty-five years ago: a Catholic one, a small black hospital within the black community (founded at a time, forty years ago, when there was no hospital between Chicago and the Wisconsin state line to which a Negro would be admitted) —and Evanston Hospital, affiliated with Northwestern's medical school, which is the real focus of Evanston health care. The same collection of substantial, rather dull red-brick buildings is still there as in 1946: they have been preserved, restored—but around them Evanston Hospital has expanded with new construction to the limits of the available land. As you enter the hospital, you are met by a security guard (a plastic label on his lapel identifies him by name and office) who happens to be husky and black. A casual visitor finds himself directed first to the public relations department, then to one of a platoon of assistant directors of the hospital who will show him around, finally, perhaps, to the director himself; each of these functionaries, like the officials of the city government, is a master of the art of avoiding embarrassment to the hospital and of detecting and soothing the irritations of its public. And like Evanston itself, the hospital is both quite open and politely but firmly secure.

Black patients and staff are now in evidence at the hospital, as they were not twenty-five years ago (remedial teaching and a day-care center are part of the effort to recruit blacks). The hospital is still short of black professionals. Indeed, the town's few black physicians consider that the hospital is run like a private club; it is a situation they intend to change. Yet the hospital reaches out into its community as it did not when I knew it. It provides free testing for the afflictions of old age, such as glaucoma. It has recently established a pediatric outpatient department, complete with staff doctors, nurses, and researchers, that offers the kind of child care that in the past was limited to the white middle class. It is an imaginative step toward solving the national dilemma of delivering essential health care to the entire population at a bearable cost, and it seems likely to expand into other areas. And just as mental health has become an official concern of the town, the hospital now gives an entire floor of one building to its psychiatric department, treating both outpatients and those who are hospitalized.

Even though Evanston remains a relatively peaceful, self-contained place to live, over the past decade every category of major crime has increased steadily, particularly those—murder, assault, rape—that involve personal violence; in that period the number of major crimes has grown one and a half times while the population, though changing, has remained stable. The value of goods stolen each year in the town now amounts to almost three-quarters of a million dollars, or about ten dollars per person, more than half of it automobiles (usually recovered); burglary is the other big category of theft (the goods are generally *not* recovered). On three occasions in recent years, the rage of the black community has been stirred by the death of black prisoners in dubious circumstances. Each time, the case was voluminously examined and reported on—by the Human Relations Commission, the City Council itself—and the suspicions were allayed, though the anger remained.

The city's response to these facts of contemporary life has been an overhaul of the police department with the appointment of a new chief, an enlargement of the force and improvement of its equipment, and a therapeutic reaching out into the community. Today, the force numbers about 135 men of whom 15 are black, but the total is still relatively small (the ratio of police to population in a major city like Chicago, for instance, is three times as great). The police reorganization provides for work with the young that begins in the elementary schools. Several "liaison officers," as they're called, are assigned in plain clothes to the four junior high schools. A staff of social workers ("outreach workers") concerns itself with the young of all ages, the victims as well as the offenders, and aims to identify and if possible reform potential delinquents. Despite the presence of Northwestern's famous criminology department and police-oriented courses at other colleges in the area, most of Evanston's officers, including the new chief, are still high school rather than college graduates. The department offers a pay raise to those who complete the equivalent of three years of college; about a fifth of them have done so.

One evening during the summer of my return to Evanston, I wandered over to the new police headquarters to see for myself—the officer manning the complaint desk that night, as it happened, had been a year behind us at the high school. I remembered a rotund smooth-faced serious boy who had been a shot-putter; he had grown into a man of massive girth with an immense, Edwardian moustache. He was one of the town's fifteen black policemen. A few days earlier, the most visible of Evanston's three black aldermen, a fiery law student in his twenties, had had another run-in with the police and had responded first by threatening to resign, then by introducing an elaborate proposal for a civilian police review board. We talked for an hour or more while he soothed telephoners complaining about stray dogs, and other cops, coming and going, kidded him about his appetite and brought him hamburgers and milkshakes. What did he think of the alderman? How was it that Evanston's police seemed not to get along with him—or vice versa? What did he think of the idea of having a review board looking over his shoulder? I was curious to see if he would express an opinion on any of these matters, but what I heard was yet another version of Evanston's meticulous public relations sense—"on the one hand, but then on the other hand." He had been well chosen for the job.

In the spring of 1970, a few months after his promotion from captain, Evanston's new police chief was confronted with a frightening situation. National Guardsmen had shot the students at Kent State. Northwestern's students, like so many others, went on strike and, among other things, occupied the lovely, leafy section of Sheridan Road in front of the campus, the shortest link between Chicago and the rest of the North Shore farther up the lake. The message went out to students elsewhere—there was to be a rally filling the university's football stadium. At other places in these years—Columbia, Berkeley, Washington, Chicago—students' defiance of the local government ended in clouds of tear gas, enraged head crackings, mass arrests—or, as at Kent State, in panicky gunfire and death. Evanston had managed to avoid violence. How?

I talked to the police chief about this (his wife is a woman of the Class of 1946): a tall, black-haired, husky man, identifiable in any crowd as a cop, with an air of furious energy barely contained. A year after the event, his feelings were still intense, but he had held them in, held back the police, day by day, from doing the obvious thing and using whatever force was needed to remove the hirsute undergraduates from the road. Instead, their approach had been custodial. Barriers blocked off the section of road, traffic was rerouted, and a few officers were assigned to protect students and townspeople from one another. As the day for the protest in the stadium approached, a National Guard unit was called in—and then kept discreetly out of sight. After a week or so, the undergraduates got tired of sitting on the road—no one would arrest them—and gave up. The twenty thousand students poured into the stadium, held their rally, and departed peacefully—word of the National Guard in its hiding place got around and it was enough.

The episode had tried the policemen's nerves, but the expected violence had been prevented.

Two years earlier, in 1969, one of the characteristic issues of the 60s had produced a characteristic response, arrived at by familiar tactics. The City Council had passed an open housing ordinance (Evanston-fashion, it is called *fair* housing) establishing a review board with impressive powers of subpoena and injunction. It was the climax of several years of agitation—parades, demonstrations, sit-ins, angry testimony before the City Council—and it had pitted an uneasy alliance of blacks, students, and conscious liberals against the town's middle-of-the-road home owners and taxpayers, mostly, of course, white. (The demonstrations, I was told, generally took place on Saturday mornings, when student labor was available, and for some of the students, at least, were a source of pocket money.) Symbolically, the campaign placed two members of the Class of 1946 on opposite sides, with a close-up view of what was happening.

The town's oldest and most active real estate firm is also the only one actually on Fountain Square and therefore a natural target for a sit-in. Bill Jennings, now the company's executive vice president, thus found himself in the improbable position of confronting a crowd of noisy demonstrators intent on making him have them arrested. His response was an interesting one. Here were people who were concerned about housing. What could he do for them? He went around the office talking to the people one by one, trying to find out what their needs were, what he might in fact be able to offer them—and discovered a problem which he, as a real estate broker, could not solve.

—None of these individuals really were in the housing market—so what was the parade all about? They were demonstrating on behalf of third parties with whom they weren't personally acquainted, seeking a solution to housing problems they thought they perceived.

At that point, finally, Bill called in the police and the demonstrators were led off to court.

One focus of the campaign had been Evanston's traditionally liberal Unitarian church, now with a substantial and well-organized black membership—it was near enough the center of town, for example, to be a rallying point for marches. Ken Mills, the scriptwriter, was a member, living in what is known locally as a bi-racial neighborhood. What results had the fair-housing ordinance produced? One of the town's two black realtors had joined the Evanston Real Estate Board but both continued to do their business chiefly with blacks moving into the black community. Houses and apartments to rent were still expensive and scarce and the brokers and owners made their decisions not so much on the grounds of race as on the pragmatic question of credit and reliability. And as blacks moved into border areas like the one Ken lived in, the white families continued to move elsewhere—he could tell me the racial composition of every block adjacent to his—

—All of Florence Street right behind us is black. The next block over on Ashland is mixed. The next block may be all white. The block after that is mixed. The last white family moved out behind us about two years ago. . . .

Recently, the issue has shifted. The question today, as in so many other towns across the country, is whether or in what form Evanston will accept a federally subsidized housing development. Those who fear it (yet another Evanston taxpayers association sprang up in opposition) have visions of high-rise buildings on the disastrous New York and Chicago model, flooded with imported incompetents who will overwhelm the town's police and relief budgets. Those who favor the project have more reasonable goals, to provide inexpensive, small-scale housing for the town's own poor—black, white, elderly. The issue is complicated by the fact that there is virtually no remaining undeveloped land. Several proposals were made to slice off pieces of the city's scarce and scattered parks.

One small indicator of what the town might decide came late in 1971, when the City Council quite casually put an end to the seemingly changeless local prohibition against liquor. The Methodist university had built the principle into the first town charter and it had been repeatedly affirmed; now, with a simple vote by the aldermen, it was gone. Yet the move was made with customary caution: liquor licenses were to be issued to one hotel, one restaurant, one private club. The WCTU announced immediately that it had no intention of leaving town—it felt, indeed, all the more needed.

There is another issue underlying all these local questions of contemporary urban America—deeper than questions of housing, schooling, police, deeper, even, than the matter of race, though that has been a powerful motive. It is the question simply of what kind of town Evanston is to be: whether it can continue its controlled and rationally limited self-improvement or must become something very different, denser and more fragmented, a city like any other city. It is at a point that has been forecast for other cities but mostly not reached. I have described the town's past because it is the past of us, the middle generation, but in another sense, for the country at large, it is the future: a mature society beyond further growth, committed not to limitless expansion but to the cultivation, preservation, refinement of what already exists. What kind of future is going to be permitted by the forces within and outside this small society? It will be a place without great extremes, where humane services multiply and passionate conflicts are talked out through increasingly local and informal government—not acted out in deeds of real violence. The arts will be much prized, as they are in Evanston with its exhibits of local painters, its twenty-five-year-old symphony orchestra, but they will not, probably, reach the heights that come from extremes of passion, rage, violence, poverty, wealth. Altogether, an equable life. Will Evanston achieve it?

That question, it seems to me, is one that Evanston's whites and blacks are going to have to answer together. Looking at the middle generation, one is not so hopeful about what their answer will be. The hostilities are open enough now so that they are compelled to talk about them, talk to each other, but it is a self-conscious dialogue marred by incomprehension and suspicion.

Hence, in June, a few days before graduation, I asked the high school to introduce me to some students, and it produced two members of the Class of 1971 whom I'll call Frank and Barbra. They were part of the first class to go all the way through the radical new system introduced in 1967— as the Class of 1946 had been the first of the postwar classes. Frank, athletic and good-looking, reminded me of a friend who had joined the Marines after two years of school and had made a career of it, but Frank in the fall would be going to one of the Ivy League colleges and had dreams of being a lawyer. Barbra, in the current fashion, was in blue jeans and wore her hair long but was at the same time soft-spoken, feminine; it was not hard to associate her with those vanished girls of twenty-five years ago. She would be going to a Midwestern university and already had rather specific ideas about a career (physical therapy)—thanks, presumably, to the school's elaborate testing program which in 1946 was in its first year.

We talked easily while I explained what I was up to: past and present, change, comparison, contrast. Since Frank had played basketball, I tried to get them to imagine a time twenty-five years ago when their school's team was all white. They could not imagine it.

—When we came in first place three years ago, Barbra

said incredulously, they were all blacks and one white!

What of the racial animosities I had been hearing about from white adults, parents—fights in the cafeterias, the washrooms, on the streets? Was it possible these days for blacks and whites at the school to be friends?

—Well—*we* used to be pretty close friends, Barbra said, and they both laughed—because, of course, Frank was black and she was white. *He* can talk very well about the whole thing, she went on, still kidding him. He has white girl friends. He goes either way—

—And white *boy* friends, Frank said. He wanted that clear.

We talked a little longer, but I had an answer, not so much in their words as in their easy, unselfconscious friendship, reaching across but not ignoring the differences of race and sex.

It was time for them to get back to class, for me to go. How did they feel about the school now that they were ready to leave it? Had they *liked* it? Were people still proud of it? Frank answered for both, in words almost identical with those another man, also black but twenty-five years older, was to use a few days later—

—I think everyone does feel proud of the school. "I come from Evanston"—that sort of speaks for itself. . . .

6

In Black and White

—It was *all* bad, Bennett said. All black kids had a bad time at Evanston High School.

We were sitting over gin and tonics in a room off the bar of a black social club in Evanston, an Evanston still officially and, it seemed, immutably dry. Until that summer, the way my particular life had gone, there had been one previous occasion when I had sat down over a drink with a black man. That was normal enough for a white man of the middle generation—it was not so much that one avoided Negroes as that work and social life did not bring them into one's way and one did not seek them out.

I had asked Bennett, as I did everyone I talked to in the

Class of 1946, what his general impressions of the school had been, and that had been his answer. Surely, I suggested, that was too sweeping; I remembered black boys in the class that I had known fairly well who must have felt differently.

—Well, he admitted, I couldn't say everybody, but ninety-eight percent of them. And the two percent that didn't had psychological problems—serious behavioral or . . . personality problems. Evanston High School as we left it sort of represented the last of the segregation kind of thing . . . social isolation. . . . I would say that our class represents the last of the antebellum thinking for a lot of reasons.

I tried again. Hadn't there been some *good* things about the school for blacks?

—The only good day that we had in all the four years was when Robeson came to school. That was one day where black kids felt that something happened at the school that they could relate to. . . .

It came back. It must have been 1945 or 1946 when Paul Robeson, the black American bass, had sung for an assembly of the school. It was about the same time I was taken to see him in a production of *Othello* that had come to Chicago, with (ironically, it now seems) the Princeton-educated Puerto Rican José Ferrer as Iago, white devil to his Moor: Robeson was not a great actor, I suppose, but an overwhelming physical presence with a velvety deep voice that filled the theater like none other I have heard.

Other Negroes in the class told me similar things, with more or less vehemence, depending on their temperaments. I had asked Roy King, the carpenter, for example, if he had any recollections of racial hostility at the high school—

—I don't feel that there was hostility, he told me. There was indifference, which is worse. We were nonexistent.

You can almost fight hostility, but indifference—it's the worst thing in the world. . . .

What is astonishing about our black contemporaries' perception of the situation is that we, the whites, were totally unaware of it at the time (and in most cases remained so); and that we were able to live with the same set of facts and find in them the opposite meaning. A number of the whites remembered specific instances of discrimination against Negroes—incidents that had made us aware of race, that had stayed in our memory as injustice, as a needless and arbitrary cause of pain to another person. But none of us, I think, either at the time or later, were able to see such isolated incidents in relation to each other, as parts of a system of exclusion. What was missing was emotional conviction, imagination. Then as now, we accepted the idea of equality, opposed arbitrary exclusions based on race—at least in theory. But we failed to see these principles as having any special application in Evanston. If we thought about it, we would have said that the same opportunities were open to Evanston's blacks as to its whites. And in a sense, that was so.

Bennett had spoken of the real destructiveness of the experience for the blacks, and there seemed in fact to have been losses. When the Class of 1946 entered high school in 1942, about 10 percent of us were Negroes—about seventy people. There were forty by the time we graduated, 6 percent; the rest had left to join the service or had simply vanished for whatever reasons. And of those who did graduate, nearly half could not be located when it came time to plan the reunion. (In contrast, all but about 20 percent of the whites were found, and of the missing, three quarters were women, difficult to locate, presumably, because of their married names.)

But at the same time, there were quite a number of blacks for whom the opportunities had not been closed. One man had become an electrical engineer, the first black member of the national Society of Electrical Engineers. Another was a musicologist, the head of the music department at a black Southern college. Still another, a teacher in a town in central Illinois, had been its first black alderman and was president of the teachers union. And there was Bennett himself, an official of the Department of Commerce with responsibility for implementing programs to encourage minority businessmen. Unlike the whites, nearly all the black men had been impelled into political activity of some kind, into leadership.

That drive toward leadership began in the feeling of white indifference, of painful deprivation in a white system, but what the whites remembered, looking back from the racial violence of the present, was an absence of hostility. Relations, as Jack Stauffer put it, had been "good but aloof." A scientist described it in scientific terms: the "blacks were exposed to similar stimuli and responded in a similar way" and he was surprised when I suggested they might have felt differently—

—I guess I was just unaware that they were being denied any rights. . . .

Dan Magen summed up the general impression as well as anyone:

—There were some Negroes I felt I knew pretty well. They weren't any best friends, they didn't go over to your house and you didn't go over to their house. . . . It was just kind of the way the situation was in those days. . . .

The situation.

—That's an unusual situation that we were in, Roy had said a few days earlier, with ironic understatement, it was as if he were answering Dan or all of us—and of course in a sense he was. We were conditioned very, very smoothly, Roy concluded—to stay in our place.

"Our place" was a part of Evanston known universally

among whites as Colored Town. (In the past, it was as often Niggertown, but by our time *nigger* was a word you more or less consciously did not use.) Here again I discovered a curious difference in perception. When I realized that there *was* a difference, I began asking the people I talked to what they had called that part of town where most of the blacks lived. For the whites, it was always Colored Town, but for the blacks the question itself was—what? embarrassing, insulting, another instance of white perfidy? Only one person, a woman, came close to an answer. Had she called it Colored Town as the whites did? I asked.

—Oh, you did? I didn't know that. "The west side of Evanston"—I never called it anything.

What was wrong with the question, the idea? If the white areas had such a clear sense of neighborhood, signified by names—north Evanston, south Evanston, Lincolnwood, Ridgeville—why hadn't the same thing been true in the black community?

Late in that summer, still puzzling over such questions, I was driving through the outskirts of Annapolis on the way to visit a friend, threading my way uncertainly through the narrow, confusing streets of a place I'd never been. It was the mostly black community ringing the historic core, with the vivid life of the streets—the color, movement, small shops, restaurants, laundromats, liquor stores—of a black Southern town, and it seemed for a while as if the whole city must be black. It came to me: suppose I were arriving there to live, a solitary white among so many who were different—where *could* I live and what kind of work could I do, what would be allowed? There would be fear, rejection, the fear of rejection, and always the sense of being arbitrarily set apart, not an individual with one's particular set of responsibilities, qualities, limitations, but a type, an abstraction: *the white man.* Probably you would not do very well in such a situation, and no

matter how you struggled to separate yourself from the
abstract type, to be yourself rather than a mere racial label,
you would never be certain that your failures were merely
imposed from the outside and not due to your innate inade-
quacy, inferiority. And so you would seek, probably without much choice, refuge with others superficially like yourself—other whites—in a part of the town where for some
of each day you could get away from all that, be yourself.
No doubt it would be called White Town.

That made it a little easier to see what had been wrong
about our idea of Colored Town. One had more or less
known all this for a long time, but knowledge is abstract
and there is an immense distance between knowledge and
conviction. It does one no credit to have lived into middle
age with such knowledge before transmuting it into conviction, but as I mentioned earlier, we of the middle gerera-
tion were slow learners in a lot of ways.

A few of us reached that point a good deal sooner. For
Evy, for example, living and working with her minister
husband on the West Side of Chicago, it had come through
actual rather than imagined experience. After seven or
eight years, their children were the only whites in the local
schools—and it then seemed necessary to send them elsewhere, to a private school where they would not be
alone—

—I guess we want our kids to know who they are and
schooling is part of finding out who they are. And this kind
of insight, when we use it in reverse for blacks and Puerto
Ricans—it works in *so many* ways. . . .

But at any rate, the part of Evanston that was called
Colored Town was a fact of the time and place as it has been
a fact of America. Perhaps it seemed more distinct and
separate than it actually was because, in our minds, we had
to assign the Negroes a physical place corresponding to
their social place. And Colored Town was the one thing

that set Evanston apart from the blissful rest of the North
Shore, the thing that a little later, with the sophistication
of college education, some of us realized was Evanston's
"colored problem." (With the War still fresh in our minds
and the Nazi solution to "the Jewish problem," such a
phrase, one would think, might have sent a tremor of horror through one's whole being, but it did not.) One man
told me that at the time there were posters on buses in the
South advertising "Come to Evanston, Haven of the Negro." Whether that was so or not, Evanston—Colored
Town—was indeed a haven: the only place on the North
Shore where a Negro could or did live. That was not accidental. The founders were Abolitionists as well as teetotal-
ing Methodist Republicans. One of the two junior high
schools we attended was called Haven.

Evanston's Colored Town was a rough triangle west of
the center of town, bounded on the east by the high embankment of the Chicago & North Western Rail Road
tracks, on the west by the drainage canal of the Sanitary
District of Chicago, merging on the south into the Polish
neighborhood of southwest Evanston. And at the center
was the high school, which it was impossible to approach
without passing through some part of Colored Town—that
was part of one's education, one's consciousness. I sensed
it as a place with a vibrant, teeming life of its own, small
grocery stores and funeral parlors and churches, hospital
and school and YMCA, lodges and clubs, illicit liquor and
whorehouses and Saturday night slashings behind the
shades of the neat, small houses. It was a complete community, parallel to the white one. And of course it *was* parallel
precisely because every area of Evanston life from which
blacks were excluded had to be duplicated or it didn't exist.

All this, however, was more a matter of custom and
individual discretion than of law or public policy. Even in
the matter of housing and despite the existence of cove

nants in some deeds restricting land to Caucasians, the boundaries were not quite as clearly drawn as they seemed. There were in fact and had always been Negroes living beyond the boundaries of the railroad tracks and the canal, as there were some whites living within them.

The number and subtlety of these customary exclusions seems amazing in retrospect. Because we, the whites of the middle generation, recognized them only in fragments rather than as the shameful whole they were, it is useful to enumerate them. Besides the question of where one lived, there was the complicated matter of schools. One's impression that with one exception the elementary schools were all white was not quite correct. In fact, seven of the thirteen schools of the time were white and there was one in the center of Colored Town that was virtually all black (one or two dark-complexioned Italian families living nearby had an occasional child in it)—there, however, except for a gym teacher, all the teachers were white. There were blacks from fringe areas at the other schools, in one or two cases a noticeable number—in doubtful cases the principal or even the board of education would decide who went where.

Some of the Negroes went from elementary school to seventh and eighth grade at the two junior high schools— that was the point at which we began to come together (but not all: the black elementary school included the next two grades as well). At that point a few of us formed the friend-ships that in some cases were to be the only ones we ever had with a Negro. Yet they were limited—it was under-stood that we met only in the context of school, never afterward, in our homes—and when we all went on to high school, a strange thing happened: we drew apart again. This was partly a matter of a difference in the academic program. In the junior high school, each class with its leaven of blacks followed the same program (literally—we went from class to class in a body, in silent single file); in high school, however, the whites typically were taking courses that prepared them for college while the blacks typically were not. The exceptions experienced difficulties. Ada Garrett, for example, a black girl of extraordinary intelligence and grace who sailed through the high school in three years and into one of the most renowned of the Ivy League women's colleges, remembered a curious incident in an algebra class—

—I did what the teacher told me to do. And—I think the first marking period before the exam—I got a four,* *just like all the other Negroes.* And when I did the exam, I did it all right, so then after that I got ones. . . . I think I figured this out for myself, I didn't ask my mother or the teacher about it: I never really felt the need to demonstrate my abilities. . . .

There was a difference in expectation, on both sides: Negroes, like other untalented students, were expected to take not algebra but something less rigorous with a title like "general math," and it is possible the teacher was surprised and bored to find a Negro in her class—assuming another unteachable failure, a mistake. One woman in the Class of 1946 who particularly admired Ada remembered a later and different incident in an English class taught by a formidable but kindly white-haired woman who had the reputation of being the best in the school. Ada had announced that she was going east to college. That would be a mistake, the teacher told her—the Negro situation, the isolation, it would be too hard—

—And the last I remember her, she was saying, "I am going to go to the best school I can get into and I don't *care* about the *Negro situation!"*. . .

This was still the spring of 1945.

It was not only in the classrooms that we were pulled

*The marking system was on a scale from 1 to 6 (failure). A 4 was somewhere below the dead level of mediocrity but not failing.

apart. In sports, the contrast with the present was also remarkable. In the junior high school, the sports program in football and basketball had been elaborate and apparently made no distinctions between whites and Negroes (the home room I was in performed the unprecedented feat of winning the school football championship both years, in good measure because of a wonderfully athletic black boy, Paul Stephens). On the high school teams, on the other hand, there were virtually no black players. There were one or two who fluctuated between the varsity and junior varsity teams in football and basketball, but by our last year there were none on either of those varsity teams, nor in swimming or baseball (nor for that matter on any of the other suburban high school teams in our league). Admittedly by then some of the best of the black athletes, such as Paul Stephens, were already in the service, but those who remained didn't make the teams either. In the case of the swimming team, the school had no pool, unlike the other big schools with which it competed, and the team practiced at the local YMCA, which was all white. That was the reason there was no pool, we were told: so that whites and blacks would not swim together. Considering the tightly pared budgets of the 30s and 40s, that may or may not have been the reason, but it was what we believed.

Why was it that, except for track, there were so few blacks in the sports program? One black man told me he looked down on the coaching—the coaches were too old-fashioned to learn much from (white athletes agreed). And as in so many other things, Colored Town had its own parallel program in football and basketball—he thought the black basketball team was *better* than the white team at the high school (the black team played against pretty much the same players on a Y team—always at the white Y). In the pattern of black-white relations in other areas of Evanston's life, there was, it seems, a sort of mutual repulsion, like the positive poles of two magnets, rather than a formal school policy. If a black boy might feel that he did not *want* to go out for one of those sports, he also knew that he probably would not make the team if he did, and there would be no challenge to the coach's discretion.

Did it matter? Today, when in most schools the importance of sports has mercifully diminished, it is not so easy to reconstruct the feelings of a boy of sixteen or seventeen twenty-five years ago, with all the adolescent boy's anxieties—fearing and half-expecting failure, asserting and at the same time doubting himself, trying to find out—focused on a game. But, yes, it mattered. It had mattered a lot, for instance, to Bennett—

—I played semipro ball as a twelve-year-old kid. I played center and I played guard. And I played with guys who were adult—I had a *reputation*. . . .

Bennett was stuck on the JV team, a team, he told me, that was scored on only twice in our last two years while the varsity was losing more than half its games. When he went to college, he chose a small black school in the South —one like those that in recent years have become a major source of black professional football players.

—They let me play on the football team and I sort of had a regeneration. I no longer felt that—because of the fact that I was sort of excluded, I had serious doubts about my ability. . . . I made all-conference as a freshman—all-conference both years and first team both years. . . .

The same kind of unacknowledged separation existed in the school's extracurricular and social organizations. There were, for example, social and athletic organizations for boys and girls whose function was to sponsor worthy projects and dances. Everyone in the school was theoretically a member—their officers were elected by a school-wide vote—but none of us seemed to notice that the officers and the small group of people active in other ways, as well as

those who went to the dances, were always white. It was
simply the pattern of social life in Evanston. If Negroes had
insisted on participating, no one, probably, with the awkward Midwestern courtesy of Evanston, would have prevented them, but they didn't insist, they would have felt
uncomfortable, unwanted.

—We didn't push to go to the Y, Roy King commented,
or to become members of Trireme or Pentangle or Quadrangle [the girls' and boys' organizations] or anything. We
were just beautifully excluded, we were not part of that, we
knew that that was *taboo*, we were *not to go over there*. And
no one ever told us that. . . .

The school's officer-training unit was ambiguous. At a
time when the armed forces for which it was preparing
were still officially segregated, it was a local organization
without national connection, an MTC (for Military Training Corps) rather that an ROTC. It was not clear whether
that was a device for keeping Negroes out or letting them
in, but the effect was the same—there were none. I asked
Walker Davies about that—I had remembered a boy with
a smooth, tan complexion, the slow, hooded smile that a
few years later was called *cool* (our word at the time was
casual). Maybe, I suggested, not joining the MTC had had
something to do with money, the cost of those snappy gray
cadet uniforms?

—We were all aware of the fact that all the organizations
were white—not a matter of cost but of people being discouraged: basically, discouraging people. I think that if any
parent, black or white, felt that a kid really *wanted* to get
into anything—you're going to find the money from somewhere, even if you've got to pay two dollars a week to keep
it. . . .

By the end of high school, in 1946, the separation was
nearly complete. A sensitive white like Frank Carlborg
noticed that something had happened—and wondered—

—My observation is that they disappeared. I was in the college-bound group and wound up in the advanced courses in math and physics because I happened to be good in that. . . . And by the time I got to the senior level, Bobby Ball was about the only black boy that was still around. . . .

Bobby, who became an electrical engineer, was the one Negro almost every white I talked to remembered, usually with particular affection. And what Frank said had a literal truth in the sense that, for one reason or another, nearly half the Negroes who had started with us had left school by the time we graduated. But there was something deeper and stranger than that. For most of us, there has been no blacks our own age in the first seven years of our schooling, and then in seventh and eighth grade—whether deliberately or not and whether we recognized it or not—we were exposed to a notable and attractive minority, boys and girls who were athletic, intelligent, friendly and unselfconscious. And then between the junior high school and high school, we began mysteriously to change, to draw apart. The whites mostly were not aware of what was happening, but if you were black and sensitive, you noticed immediately and remembered with rage and pain.

—I had a very hostile—a hatred for whites, Bennett told me. It started from freshman in high school. Kids that you knew—a lot of the kids that were in my class at Haven: the problem was that all of a sudden, over one summer—in high school, eighty percent of the kids don't even know you anymore, they don't even say hello to you in the hall. . . . It wasn't a unique experience with me, it happened to all the black kids that were at Haven, with very few exceptions—the guys like Paul who were football heroes, it was a little bit different, but the average guy went through this sort of Coventry thing. This was a pattern: it was almost conspiratorial.

The whites of the middle generation, reading this, will be surprised and disbelieving, but it was so, I think, and to me it remains mysterious. Although I have no sufficient explanation for whatever it was that happened, the experience in school was indeed preparing us for the life we would enter when we left; and because that was about to change, it was in that sense, as I said earlier, that we were prepared for the past, not the future.

The past was an Evanston where a tiny black hospital had been founded because Negroes were not admitted to Evanston Hospital; not only not admitted but not, I think, employed in any capacity. It was an Evanston that indirectly set aside the least attractive of its beaches—"the free beach"—for Negroes. In the central Fountain Square area where half a dozen good and moderately priced restaurants were always full, there was not even a lunch counter where a black person, shopping in the stores, could pause for a hot dog or a hamburger. The local movies were no longer segregated, but they had been. Even the town's bus drivers were all white until some time after the War, when the revived NAACP noticed and objected.

That systematic separatism established a pattern that very few of us, black or white, were able to outgrow. Among the white men I talked to, perhaps as many as half had known at least one Negro in something approaching friendship while they were in school. A smaller number, going into the newly integrated Army and Navy during the Korean War, had formed the kind of bonds the service seems to instill in young men—Jack Stauffer, for example, found that he and a Negro from New York were almost the only Northern enlisted men on the ship, and they went on passes together, kept in touch afterward. Even in the impersonal situations of contemporary business and civic affairs, fewer than half the men had had any real contact with blacks, and I could find only a handful who as adults knew any blacks in a social way. For the women, at all of these stages of our lives, the proportions were even smaller.

The roots of that separateness were in earliest childhood. One of the counting rhymes you learned was "Catch a nigger by the toe" (I was indignant some years later when it was suggested that it should be "Catch a *bunny* by the toe"—it was like censoring *Huckleberry Finn*). Surprisingly in the reduced circumstances of the 30s, for some of us the only contact with a black person was as a servant—at the low point, a live-in maid who cooked and did housework and laundry six days a week (Thursday was the day off) could be hired for seven or eight dollars a week, and it was a service a good-sized family could still permit itself. It was not that you looked down on someone, black or white, for being a servant; indeed, it was often the only opportunity you had to know a black person well. The real point, however, was that with rare exceptions we never saw our parents in any but an unequal relationship with a Negro.

Hence, when the time came and in school you began to meet blacks your own age, there was discomfort on both sides; it was a relationship with strict limits. Ginny, whose father was a milkman, lived within a block of Negro families, but until junior high school those children went to another, more distant school while Ginny's was all white. Then, when she started the seventh grade—

—One of the girls was my age and we used to walk to school together. And we got to be pretty good friends, although there was a kind of hesitancy on her part. I think her mother and my mother tried to discourage this friendship.

The same odd thing happened to Ginny as to so many other whites when she went to the high school: socially, the black girl disappeared.

—I never thought about her being black or white until we got to high school. And then in high school we hardly even spoke. . . . And I remember that it sort of bothered me, and yet I made no effort to renew the friendship because I knew it was just not socially acceptable. . . .

Bobby Ball figured in several stories like that one. His father was a chauffeur for a Jewish family, one of the few of any kind in Evanston that was seriously rich, and apparently Bobby lived there with his family. As a result, all through elementary school, he was always the only Negro. I knew him first in junior high school, a good-looking, intelligent boy telling us enthusiastically about the marvelous car his father drove, it had an unheard-of luxury, electric windows—you pressed a button and they went up or down; later he was more reserved. He was a boy with an air of tactful good breeding—of wealth—that made one feel almost gauche by comparison. And it was Bobby who became the electrical engineer. With help from his father's boss, he was already well started on a career that could have taken him, it seems to me, to any level whatever, when, inexplicably, he died, still in his twenties, as if his death had been something contrived in a mediocre novel. (When I went back to Evanston, one of the first things I noticed was a painted sign, already wearing dim, on a building next to one of the black churches—The Robert J. Ball Memorial Youth Hall—and I remembered.)

It was through Bobby that Allen Kerr discovered the puzzling fact of race. They lived nearby, Allen and his family—after the stock market debacle and the loss of his father's business—in his grandparents' house, which was also served by a black couple. Allen had asked him over and—

—Bobby Ball came to my house to play. I can remember. . . . being disturbed by the fact that he was black, so I got very uncomfortable when I brought him home. It was a feeling that I became conscious of and I was surprised because it was something that was there and I didn't know about.

The feeling, I suppose, had to do with fear of displeasing one's parents, of causing pain to a guest by bringing him into an awkward situation. Hence, one avoided such situations and one's parents' views were felt rather than expressed—they did not have to be. A little later, however, Spence had willfully insisted on inviting his entire class to his birthday party. Since the class included Bobby, his mother had to explain why that was not possible: "We don't go into their houses, dear," she told Spence, as he remembered the words, "and they don't go into ours unless they work here. It's not that we're any better than they are, it's just that we're different.... " They arrived at a civilized compromise: the party became a picnic at a forest preserve near Evanston—and Bobby came.

Several people remembered a curious incident that occurred in about the sixth grade. They were in a speech class, a meeting conducted by a student chairman according to parliamentary procedure, and Bobby held an office of some kind. The teacher interrupted and moved that he should be voted out of office, but the children spontaneously voted against the motion and in the awkward pause that followed Bobby started to cry. Finally someone suggested that he could resign, and he did. Later, however, on their own, they elected him to something else; whatever the teacher had meant, they assumed it was because he was— colored was the word we used.

The other side of the isolation, the simultaneous bringing together and separating of black and white children, was fear: you fear what you do not know. The white girls' impressions of Negroes, naturally, were formed by black girls, and if they were unlucky in whom they met the effect was an ugly mixture of condescension, fear, hostility. The black girls they remembered as *tough*; they used strong language to which white girls had not been exposed; by junior high school they were seen smoking in the washrooms and on the way home from school. Pat Baldwin, for example, so fulfilled in the life of her family, really liberal in the reflection of her lawyer husband and her attractive children, remembered the transition to Evanston's other junior high school in south Evanston.

—At Nichols School there were a lot of—blacks. And generally not very attractive people—some were quite a bit older. One girl who was friends—and actually I think it was kind of a false friendship, I think I thought I was being very democratic by being friends with her because I actually didn't feel very much this way—stole my purse and that disillusioned me. . . .

The step from elementary to junior high school was a serious one, with the nervously exciting prospect of a different and more demanding curriculum, homework for the first time; Negroes were part of the difference. John Colwell, a big athletic doctor with an air of confidence, a man I could never imagine fearing anyone, had been afraid to go to junior high school "because the blacks were there." Why?

—It must have been feedback from my older brother and sister and older kids. . . .

Bill Jennings, nearly the opposite of John in everything but intelligence, had more specific memories of the source of that fear, which he had faced with elaborate prudence.

—The physical development of the blacks at an early age has always been intimidating to me. I don't know what to do with a twelve-year-old that obviously can throw me through a plate glass window if he chooses to do so—so it's a problem . . . because I'm not much for throwing people. . . .

It was an irony of which, with a dry chuckle, Bill was conscious that he, of all the people in the class, had had to confront that possibility in fact, as an adult: first there was the open-housing sit-in at his real estate office on Fountain Square, and then—

—On two occasions I've been gotten out of bed at two o'clock in the morning and brought down to the office and ... somebody has thrown somebody else through the plate glass window in a brawl. . . .

People drank elsewhere and then congregated at an all-night restaurant nearby. Each time, the fights had been blacks and whites, but he had not been able to find out whether a black had thrown a white through the window or vice versa.

Even in the 40s when we went on to high school, the mutual fear and hostility occasionally broke out in a fight, but on the whole, because the relations were distant, that was unusual. Chuck Head, who had played football, remembered these fights as the athletes on both sides asserting themselves—

—They'd be the ones that would do the fighting, the big strong ones. . . . It was more talk than anything, and if it ever came down to anything, it'd be on an individual basis ... in the locker room, where you're all sweaty and worked up anyway. . . .

Another man remembered that an outstanding black athlete—a football hero a year or two older than we were—had asked his sister for a date. She refused, but among her brother's friends there was much talk of violent reprisal. Later, in a car full of boys driving past Northwestern, he had seen a black boy walking with a white girl—and they stopped the car, got out, and beat the boy up.

By 1946, all this was on the point of drastic change, was, indeed, already beginning to change. And when it came, this transformation grew out of the same kinds of experiences we all had had. For a few of us, the whites, the grain of perception which in time became the pearl of justice was buried deep in childhood: some incident, trivial in itself, in which a black person our own age was arbitrarily set apart and at the time we were powerless to do anything about it or to understand. What we were discovering was, in the polite term of the day, discrimination.

Ken Mills told me of something that had happened his first year in junior high school. It was just before a vacation and the white YMCA was having one of its periodic learn-to-swim campaigns: boys recruited by the gym teacher were encouraged to go for a series of lessons at a nominal fee and—

—The gym teacher having to tell the black kids that no, you can't do what the rest of the kids are doing. It was probably the first time that I could see how he was hurting and how the kids were hurting. That strikes the bell for me —the first time I was aware of it. . . .

About the same time in the other junior high school, there was a brief attempt, in the gym classes, to teach us square dancing. It was one of the rare occasions that brought the boys and girls together in that setting. Spence remembered, while we were dancing, looking up at the spectators' balcony raised several feet above one end of the gym and—

—Suddenly seeing Bennett sitting in the balcony of the gym. He was asked not to participate in the dancing. . . . Another colored guy . . . and Bennett. . . .

For most of us, any large sense of the meaning of that incident and all the others like it was still years off. For Bennett, however—sitting in the balcony watching us square-dance so that no one could carry home tales of black boys dancing with white girls—the awareness was already almost as old as consciousness. When he was eight or nine, his family had moved away from the all-black school to an area where they were between two schools and within reach of both: one all white, the other, an older one called Noyes, with a few Negroes. His father tried to get the children into the white school, but—

—They wouldn't let us in, so we had to walk over to

Noyes. Every morning when we went to Noyes we would pass by [a white girl of the Class of 1946] and a couple of her cronies going the other way. That was a daily ritual.

The girl, apparently, lived closer to the school Bennett was attending than to the white school at which he had been refused. Hadn't he felt terrible about that, hadn't it seemed very wrong?

—My first reaction was to become hostile. The next one was to wish I was white.... About the same time, I realized that it was a good thing to be black, I began to develop self-pride, and that what I should do would be to spend some of my life doing at least one thing: to make things better for the blacks.... That's what I've been doing ever since—that one thing a thousand different times....

Bennett's life, it seems, had been a paradigm of the Negro experience in our time: from awareness to hostility to organization and leadership in a multiplicity of forms. The nervous white observer needs to remind himself that these three stages, in Evanston as elsewhere, seem to be necessary for us to pass through before we can reach the ideal that, not long ago, we were calling integration—a time when two men will be able to talk together, act together (or for that matter, in opposition) as individuals rather than as unwilling representatives of their respective races. This process in Evanston differs only in that it is a little farther along.

Bennett had made his life an experiment in the means of carrying out that process. After the early sit-ins that in 1946 opened the doors of Evanston's restaurants, he had chosen to go to that small black college in Georgia, then to Roosevelt, the new city college in Chicago, finally to UCLA. At each place he had involved himself in the student and local politics, finding out what each faction—black activists and Muslims, white liberals and leftists—was capable of. The same impulse had led him into a black studies group in the

50s, at a time when only a few specialists knew that there was such a subject; and into a Midwestern black political organization ready to support whichever side had most to offer. In Chicago, he taught for a while in one of the city's transitional high schools and lived in the Cabrini housing project which recently has been known as the place where two policeman-peacemakers were shot at random (at the time it was, he thought, already sliding toward the social disaster built into all such projects). At the same time, he was organizing an almost successful aldermanic campaign against the Daley machine. Finally, a series of government jobs had placed him in a position where he had a hand on aid to black business and, in 1970, had made him the obvious black opposition candidate in the first contested school board election ever held in Evanston.

His life need not have turned out that way. The crucial question—for a man, a town, a nation—was whether the hostility could be organized, could be converted to purposeful action toward possible goals; or whether it would remain mere hostility, expressed in the random violence that had become a commonplace of American city life. For Bennett, the turning point had come after he returned to Chicago from his first two years of college in the South. I remembered him clearly from high school: self-assured and intelligent, I would have said, but not unfriendly, not filled with generalized hatred for whites—my ignorance was another measure of the barriers in the way of our knowing one another. But he had come back seething with rage—at being sent up to the balcony in a movie, having a gun pulled on him when he tried to get off a bus by the front door, watching a black soldier being beaten up by a group of policemen—and then in Chicago in 1948 something had happened.

—I was on the subway, and you know these side seats that really seat three people—well, there was a white fellow and two black women, and he had moved so far away from the woman next to him that he left about six inches. . . . So what I did, I just sort of moved in between . . . and then I threw a hip and he went falling out on the floor. And it was so ludicrous. . . . I said, "Well, this is kind of ridiculous, this guy hasn't done anything to me, he has a problem about hating blacks, but I'm sort of getting out of hand with this. . . . "

After that, at Roosevelt College, he had made an effort to get over the hatred, get to know whites, work on the student council. In 1971 he was still making the effort when he and his sister were the only two black members of the Class of 1946 who came to the reunion.

—Not, he concluded with a smile, that I developed any what you might call trust, but I began to understand. . . . It was helpful.

If you were black, you necessarily began to understand much sooner than if you were white, but even in 1946 at Evanston High School there had been a portent of the kind of changes that were to come. That spring, it somehow came about that a boy named Bill Hodge was nominated for president of the boys' sports organization, Quadrangle, for the following year. A ripple of amazement went through the school, we stopped one another in the hall to exclaim over it ("Did you see who got *nominated?*"): Bill was a black boy a year behind us, short, very dark, with the heavy muscles of a sprinter in his legs and all over his body. In the fall, he was regularly breaking 10 seconds for the hundred, a fabulous performance for a schoolboy when the college-level world record was still 9.6. Because of his speed, he bounced back and forth between the JV football team and the varsity, a sort of secret weapon. Bill's running for president of an organization that hardly any Negro had ever participated in produced an amused and rather defiant reaction—why not?—and he was overwhelmingly elected.

Several men in the class remembered the incident and asked me what I thought it had meant. For some, it had been a liberal gesture which they recalled with pride. Others looked on it simply as a joke, an adolescent thumbing of the nose at the authorities, and we had the satisfaction of hearing that the lofty and remote superintendent of the high school, a man always referred to with a hush as *Doctor* Bacon, was deeply displeased. For me also it had been a joke, but a cruel one: one of the duties of the president of Quadrangle was to represent the school at meetings of similar school organizations elsewhere on the North Shore, and since these took place in white homes, he would not be received. In truth, the election meant all of these things, and even the liberal idea of it was not as fatuous as it sounds. A couple of years later, a fraternity at Amherst achieved notoriety by being the first to pledge a Negro; the national fraternity ordered them to remove the boy; the Amherst group refused and instead disaffiliated itself from the parent body. As it happened, seven boys from the Class of 1946 had chosen to go there (it was the biggest group at any college other than Northwestern or the University of Illinois); and the controversial Negro pledge was a boy from Evanston a year or two younger.

The incident had another meaning that none of us perceived and that it took me twenty-five years to piece together. It was simply that Bill had been nominated in the first place because he had *wanted* to be; long before federal laws had led solitary boys and girls past lines of hostile white adults to schools in Alabama and Arkansas and Georgia, Bill had, apparently, set out to open as many of the supposedly restricted doors as he could reach at Evanston High School. He had been, a black classmate told me, the first to join the officer training unit, the MTC (not being a member, I hadn't noticed). He had also entered the school drama club—and been cast, in a one-act melodrama about the Civil War, as the plantation's black butler, with the necessity of counterfeiting a suitable accent and demeanor. Going back to the school twenty-five years later, I wandered into the palatial theater that was near the heart of the reconstructed school and sat down in the darkness to watch a student musical in rehearsal. Half the students on stage were black; I could not see that there was any distinction of race in the parts. It was one of the things that Bill in particular—but others like him—had started. And running for office in the school and being elected had, in turn, been the culmination of a series of acts of extraordinary determination. But it was also a beginning.

There were other beginnings. Eunice's father, for example, had come to one of Evanston's churches after the years as a missionary in China and—

—Having Negroes in the church went without saying, because already—that was something we did. People generally *conceded* that that was something we did—*of course* the church was open.

I was surprised. For me, it was another discovery.

—But at social gatherings—we had an interracial conference. . . . Our youth group would have conferences with other churches . . . lots of back and forth with Chicago churches. . . . The social evening where we had interracial dancing was very hard for some of the people in the church to accept. . . .

The result? The church had split and her father, she told me without rancor, had left the pastorate. But it was a beginning.

If what Eunice Luccock and Bill Hodge were quietly doing in 1946 represented two factors in the equation of change—awareness and purposeful action—another factor, hostility, was also beginning to be in evidence. About the same time a curious new institution appeared in Evanston: it was called Bump Day. On that day, which was Thursday,

the matrons shopping at the department stores around
Fountain Square and the girls walking in slow groups from
the high school to Cooley's Cupboard had a disconcerting
experience. They were jostled on the sidewalks by gangs of
small black boys. It was not violent, no one was ever
knocked down or hurt, but it was awkward, embarrassing.
What followed has been the familiar history of the past
twenty-five years, in Evanston as elsewhere. Beginning
with the sit-ins in 1946, the restaurants were admitting any
Negroes who wanted to go, but by 1971 three of the five
places in downtown Evanston where I used to go with my
parents had vanished and the prices in the remaining restaurants were no longer such as to encourage families. A
Negro could now live anywhere he could afford—the more
distant and previously all-white suburbs, one man in the
class told me wryly, had made a great show of attracting
black airline pilots and budding corporation vice presidents—but too many of Evanston's Negroes still faced the
inexorable facts of credit; any more complicated complaint
would be ancient history before the Fair Housing Review
Board had completed its deliberations.

Evanston no longer had a beach set aside for blacks, and
there was even a city agency that would pay the nominal
cost of a season membership for those who could not afford
it. The YMCA had closed down its subsidized branch in
Colored Town and made up the difference in membership
fees for those who wanted to transfer—but still it found
black members hard to attract. At Evanston Hospital, black
patients were no longer barred (they now had a way of
asking, though, one woman told me, if you'd *mind* sharing
a room with a Negro, and one's doctor might well object
on medical grounds); black employees were now much in
evidence though not on the professional staffs. Above all,
the elementary school populations and their teachers had
been smoothly and intelligently balanced; but three years

after that began, the superintendent was fired, and part of the issue—or what people, at any rate, *thought* was part of the issue—had been the way he was carrying out the integration program.

At the high school several years before I went back, one of the last vestiges of the old system had fallen away. It was a time when the kids still went to the school dances and black couples were now going too. Then the question of mixed couples came up—white girls were dating black football players and insisted on going to the dances—and the school felt that was going too far. The man who was president of the local NAACP at the time had gone to the high school to discuss the problem—

—So we went over to protest this particular thing, and they were coming up with the deal, well, if the white girl's mother would write a letter saying she was aware of the thing—well, hell, who writes the damn letter? So anyhow the advisers were coming up with the thing that high school is a preparation for life and these kids are going to experience discrimination in life, so we want to discriminate against them here so they won't feel too bad. I said, "Oh brother, I'll never forget that reasoning. . . ."

The dances, before they began to die out, were indeed integrated, and the girls went in whatever company they chose. By the time I was visiting the school again, the whole issue was so far in the past that to students like Frank Weston and Barbra Oberholz it sounded as antediluvian as the era when Evanston's basketball team went into its games without a black player.

Frank and Barbra's experience was possible *because* ours had been almost the reverse. Apart from Eunice, in the group I interviewed there were only one or two whose parents had any sort of social relationship with adult Negroes. We remembered, as Marge Shearer did, being told over dinner what was wrong with the high school, the

organized hostility of Negroes against whites—and argu-
ing about it: "Hey, wait, I *go there*, I haven't seen that.
. . ." Janet Warren's parents were "courteously racist"—
both courteous *and* racist, unwilling to give pain but with
no doubts as to the natural inferiority of Negroes or the
propriety of segregation—and she had set out from there
toward her career as a labor lawyer whose concern was as
much racial as it was legal or economic. Nancy Lloyd had
been sent to a liberal Midwestern college (a station on the
Underground Railroad, among the first to admit Negroes),
but what stayed in her mind was a Christmas vacation
meeting at Marshall Field's in Chicago with a black girl she
knew there: after the rush of greeting, both girls were
awkward, embarrassed, because their mothers were with
them.

You construct your adult self out of resistance to your
parents, and the hopeful rhetoric of the War gave our resistance its particular content: it was all such constraints, on
both sides, that, at its best, its most conscious, the middle
generation set out to cure. Had we succeeded? A good
many doors had been opened in the town, the schools, but
was that all we had wanted? Was it possible now for a black
person and a white to talk together, decide on common
goals and work for them?

I sat far into one evening with Roy King in a corner of
the living room of the house he had built. Like others in the
class he had wondered how to take someone coming to
interview him, particularly a white man: should he dress
up, take a shower? He had decided I'd better see him as he
was, in his work clothes, with his shoes off. He talked about
his reluctance.

—Kids can see my black skin, your white skin, and in a
few minutes it's all over. They see you as somebody they
like or dislike. But here as adults, we are skeptical—
I'm wondering if it isn't a bit of fear that we have of

one another or insecurity in some respect.

While we talked, his family was elsewhere in the house. From time to time one of the four boys looked in, was introduced, shook hands, customers telephoned and left messages, neighbors came in, said hello, and went out again: the murmurous warmth of a black community on a summer evening, a very different feeling from the Evanston I knew. Hadn't there, I asked, been changes in the twenty-five years—the high school where his sons were going, all the other things?

—A lot of people do a lot of big talking, but how many people really mean anything? I see very little actual progress—people-to-people progress. . . .

So a few doors had been opened in Evanston, but Colored Town was still there, though the name was not much used anymore, a distinct, living entity near the center of the town. The last open land between the high school and the canal, which I remembered as the cornfields I walked through to school, had been built up with new houses. The black community hospital had expanded. There were a couple of new schools, a new park, more sidewalks and paved streets. And that was where, if they were still in the Chicago area, the black members of the Class of 1946 were most likely to live. It was no easier, apparently, for a black person of the middle generation to go out through whatever doors were open than for a white to go in. Ken Mills had chosen to live in a "bi-racial" neighborhood on the edge of the black community and was counting his white neighbors as they moved away. Frank Carlborg, by then, had already seen a similar hopeful experiment through to its conclusion. In the early 60s, after several years of teaching, he had gone to the University of Chicago to work on his doctorate in mathematics and had lived in an area near the university which at the time was a beacon of integration in the liberal weeklies—

—They said if integration can't work there, it'll never work. And that's just about right—it's failed. Even the people who were most wrapped up in it and made investments, totally committed—we know some people who bought land in the face of this coming black wave—they're now giving up and moving out, going to the suburbs. . . .

By the time he had the degree and could take his family away, it was no longer a place where a white person—where anyone—could live.

—We were sitting once in our dining room window, looking out—and a little old lady was knocked over and her purse taken and a black boy ran off. We watched it! Ran out. But it was too late. . . .

In Evanston too, if there was not the familiar violence of the South Side or of any big city, there had been a defensive drawing in of the black community, a new hostility; or, perhaps, simply a coming to the surface of old hostilities, always there but not recognized. Not very long ago, Chuck Head had returned to Evanston from his farm and had gone to the Negro community (as he now called it) to take flowers to a woman who had worked for his family and was sick. His wife and mother were with him and—

—This group of Negroes cornered us in an alley and they came in from both ends . . . in cars. They never got out of their cars or anything, but they had us cornered. . . . I was the only man. . . .

They waited for a while in the car until a black minister appeared, explained, and they were able to leave. Whatever might or might not have happened next, it would not be possible to see in the incident merely a painful stage of growth that must somehow be lived through. What Chuck had seen was—

—These young toughs going around patrolling the Negro section of the town, watching for whites coming into their area. . . . And it was rather frightening. . . .

Then what do you do? Barbara, for one, had been led by way of her local PTA into the midst of the bitter Evanston school board election of 1970—with all the diffidence and discomfort of any member of the middle generation thrust reluctantly into politics. The campaign went on for months. It set her against her own parents, who were bitterly on the other side. And after all the torchlight parades and protest marches, the bemused Chicago television and newspaper coverage, the ferocious invective of school board meetings and public hearings—the opposition board had been defeated and the dismissal of the controversial superintendent had been sustained. But the era of the uncontested school board election, arranged by a select caucus of leading citizens, was over. The issue, she thought, had been not integration itself, not the superintendent: "It was to elect a quality school board." In defeat there was still the satisfaction of having had the privilege of seeing "intimately black and white people working together"—but in the aftermath the good will had diminished, the people had drifted apart again.

Bennett, in the Class of 1946, was one of the opposition candidates Barbara had been working for. Had the election, which looked so divisive to an outsider, really brought people together and had that relationship fallen away again since then? His judgment was summary—

—The error that was made was that the liberal whites that were running the campaign never came out and got the black votes. . . .

The election had been not only a contest between blacks and whites or between the middle generation and its elders. It had also been *within* our generation, and there any thought of communication across the barrier of race had been an illusion: however decent our intentions, that, for us, seemed not to be possible, for us it was too late. And our children? We had struggled to expunge the stereotypes of race from our speech and from our thoughts, we had, like Lou Joyce, asked our parents not to talk of such things in front of our children. I had been impressed by the unselfconscious ease that two of the students I talked to at the high school had with each other, Frank and Barbra, black and white. Frank was feeling the same kinds of pressures the blacks of the middle generation had lived with—but in reverse. The night before I met him at Evanston High School, there had been a demonstration by an organization of black athletes during the school's athletic awards ceremony. (Officially, I was told, there were no racially defined organizations at the school, but this was one that no white would happen to join.) Situations like that seemed to make him uncomfortable. He had no doubts that the things they were protesting were real, but—

—When there is something like a walkout, sometimes I don't know where to stand, because I feel like an *individual* —I just try not to look at color. . . .

It was with all of these people on my mind—Evanston blacks and whites, young and middle-aged, my own children and my friends' children—that I sat down with Bennett at his club to talk. We went on into the early morning, with people coming in to see him, join the discussion, leave again. I began to get tired, as if I were listening to a language I only partly understood: when he was talking to me, I could follow; otherwise, I seemed to lose the thread. We were talking, finally, about the murder of Martin Luther King and the outburst of black destruction that followed.

—His death only sort of highlighted the fact that nonviolence wasn't a way of life in the black community—the country went up in smoke.

How did *he* feel about nonviolence? Did he dare reject it?

—It's not a matter of *feeling*, it's a matter of the efficacy of a *tool*. You live in a society where you must, as a black person, institute change, otherwise you are saying that the inequity that exists will continue. . . . Doing something about that means that you have a whole range of options, from sticks and stones to words, and you pick up those instruments that you feel you can handle best.

But why the violence? Why destroy the society we both wanted to change for the better?

—That process is going to create a lot of confrontation, is going to create guerrilla warfare in the cities, is going to create literally veritable armies of blacks fighting against the police and national guards in these cities and maybe even line up some of the damned students with the blacks —I don't think the students are ever going to advance that far, though. But the black kids are. . . .

Again I challenged him, this time with the kids I had been talking to in the last few days: our experience had been one thing, theirs was going to be something different, better, more rational.

—The relationship between *people* is one thing and the relationship between the power brokers and their representatives and the people is another thing altogether. The power brokers in *this* city say that blacks and whites, never the twain shall meet, and they're afraid of blacks. And so the police here are fucked up. When you have a situation where they have killed people in a town this small—that means they're doing it at the sufferance of the power brokers. . . . The police by definition—his whole process of dealing with the public, his whole racial attitude—makes him hostile toward blacks. . . . I don't give a damn where the police are because the police are pawns in this whole goddamned game—the police are just as much pawns as those kids they shoot down and the kids that are going to shoot them down. Lynching is no longer a matter of an organized group, it's a matter of police shooting down some goddamned kid who allegedly stole or is in flight—it's all a lot of *bullshit*. They *kill* these kids. It's just an *insanity* that exists in this country and is going to continue to exist.

He was thumping his fist on the table for emphasis and I was caught up in the rhetoric. That was an *intolerable* situation he was describing. How could he contemplate it? Bennett lowered his voice a little and continued.

—You're going to have two hostile armies: the army of occupation—the police—and the kids who are just uptight about all the shit they're taking. And because of the increasing economic deprivation you're going to have large ghettoes peopled with folks who are uptight. And these same kids that are over there slaughtering people in Vietnam are the same ones that are going to come back and walk the streets unemployed in two or three years. And they're not going to take all that shit. They're going to organize and go out there and kill cops. . . . The only thing that'll stop that trend—because whites, unfortunately, the power brokers, just don't believe that the natives are restless until they burn the motherfucking place down like they did in sixty-eight—now when that happens, then everybody says, *"Well*—we better *do* something. . . ."

That year had been punctuated by the random murders of policemen—it is still happening as I write this—as the previous year had been the year of pointless bombings of office buildings, banks, and university computers and the year before of the burning and looting of cities. Did we not all have the same interest in preventing that, in preserving whatever was humanly useful or valuable?

—I don't really have a vested interest in this society. I just live here at the sufferance of a few people—I don't own a goddamned thing in this society: I was born here and I'm living here. . . .

The change I thought I had been seeing, in Evanston and

elsewhere, was in the sensitivity of people to one another as people: with such knowledge, you cannot think of a person as a *thing*—cop, nigger, honky, boss—to be heedlessly smashed. That seemed to me the hope we had amid the subhuman twitch and shuffle of violence. Did he not see it?

—I don't think there's going to be any qualitative change in the race situation for twenty-five to fifty years. Reason being that the sins of our fathers and the sins that have been created over the last twenty years of racial residential and school segregation are only going to increase over another decade. If you're creating reservations and ghettoes and school systems that destroy people and don't educate people, it means that these kids are going to come out and repeat the problems. . . . So it means that that whole process has to be reversed. I'm optimistic because I'm saying that that deterioration process may not destroy the country. . . .

If that was his hope, it seemed to me as chilling as despair. I decided later that what I heard was probably a speech, parts of several speeches, that he had made more than once: other people in the Class of 1946 had mentioned how well Bennett had spoken during the school board campaign. It was a spoken equivalent of that violence that as a nation we are going to have to live through—and that we *will* live through if we can learn not simply to listen but to understand. And to be middle-aged is to have learned patience.

My conversations with Bennett took place against the backdrop of the class reunion, a twenty-fifth reunion whose buoyant success had been marred only by the disquieting fact that, except for Bennett himself and his sister, the Negroes in the class had stayed away. It had not started out that way. What had happened?

Many months earlier, at the first formal meeting of the reunion committee, Roy King had been present and had agreed to participate. The meeting took place at the home of a committee member in one of the new suburbs duplicating, a little farther west, the towns of the North Shore. It had been a good meeting, warm with the pleasure of old friends seeing each other again after years, an auspicious beginning.

Roy had not attended the second meeting. Instead, he had written a letter explaining why he would not serve, and the letter was read out. A lengthy discussion followed. People were upset, annoyed—they had offered what they thought was friendship and had been refused. Pat Baldwin had sympathized with him—she thought the letter "very strong, articulate . . . touching and honest"—and felt estranged from the others when she tried to say so—

—There's a real—terrible snobby-sounding thing to say —blue-collar kind of attitude about minorities still—and I was very surprised to hear it. . . . And this group—not all, but many of them—thought it was terrible. They said, "Why, I *shook his hand* and stood and talked to him at the door." . . . And I thought, it's *still* way back when. I'm sure he sensed this, this patronizing kind of—this talk started going on and on, and I said, "Well, I would suggest dropping it, I think that he has a good point"—and of course this did not make me too popular. . . .

The feelings that Roy's letter generated were magnified, human-fashion, over the months of planning for the reunion. He was an "activist"—a Black Panther someone suggested—he was organizing a boycott by the other black members of the class. (I asked an Evanston police official if it was possible the town now had a Panther unit. He said much the same thing as the town's black leaders: some groups were a bit more vocal than others, but all, he thought, were on the quiet and conservative side, in the Evanston style of doing things.) I was repeatedly warned not to try to contact some of the blacks because they might be "militants" and therefore somehow dangerous. I began to wonder if all this emotion might end in a visible gesture of some kind that would threaten the reunion itself—who knows, a demonstration, an antireunion, a walkout, a bomb —since in our time there has been no fantasy so bizarre that it cannot, sometime, turn into destructive reality. All this, of course, was before I had talked with any of the people who, at a distance, seemed so threatening. The committee members themselves, I thought, would have felt and acted as Roy had—if only they could have put themselves in his place. But they would not have been the middle generation if they had been able to do that.

Another man, an easy-going realist, remembered the situation less emotionally, but even for him it rankled. It was ancient history. What could *he* do about it?

—We sat around and talked about it. There's no sense in making a federal out of it, just a bunch of people that went to high school together, and if they don't want to come there's nothing we can do about it. We're not going to start having racial meetings to say we're sorry or we treated you right or wrong. . . .

The letter vanished, so I never saw it, but people quoted parts of it to me, including Roy himself. The evening I saw him, I had had lunch with Bill Jennings who, running his booming Evanston real estate firm, would, one supposes, be the sort of person Bennett would include in that abstraction, "the white power structure." Yet only ignorance or the compulsion of violence could place him within any such monolithic bloc, any more than Roy—or Bennett himself: a man with a disciplined but individual and inquisitive mind, still teaching himself the social and human side of his business, with the courage to overcome his conscious fears

of demonstrators, hippies, window-smashers. He had
missed the committee meeting at which the letter was read
but had heard about it. It discouraged him—

—If you assume that communication isn't worthwhile,
you have no problem. But if you assume that communication *is* worthwhile, how the hell do you ever start?

That was intended as a message for Roy, which at the
time I did not deliver. The truth turned out to be much
simpler than that or than all the fears and warnings had led
me to suppose. The reunion was only a few days past when
I talked to Roy and he asked me about it. What had it been
like? Had I enjoyed it? He had wanted to go, and then—

—I went to the committee meeting for this reunion. I
was really looking forward to this. I wondered why we
hadn't had a reunion. . . . I set there and there was something wrong and I couldn't put my finger on it. . . .

Had anyone been rude to him—or patronizing? No—

—The people were very courteous, all the things that—.
But there was something wrong. The next morning I knew
what it was and I called some more black classmates. They
laughed because none of *them* would go to the committee
meeting. . . . They all agreed: "Well look, man, we were
never a part of any class at high school." And we weren't.
We might be in English class together, we might sit in
biology together, we might sing in the choir together.
When that class broke up, we went our separate ways, that
was the end of it.

The letter, then, had been simply an honest summary of
what he had felt at the time and since, speaking not for the
black members of the Class of 1946 or anyone else but "just
for Roy King."

—I wrote a letter to the committee. Because this is something I had to say. I was not ashamed of what I had to say
. . . but I couldn't go, under the conditions. And as I said,
"To be a *re*union, there must have had to have been a

union." And we were never together. . . .

But that was not quite all. He had written not only about himself but about his children, and some of the phrases had remained in Pat's memory.

—"We kind of melted into the walls when we were at Evanston High School," she quoted, "and this is how we would feel at this reunion." And he said: "I have two boys at Evanston High School now, and hopefully things are different. When it comes time for their reunion, they will go and feel part of things."

The twenty-five years, improbably, had made parents of us, and like all parents we now put our hope not in ourselves but in our children.

7

Growing Through It

On the afternoon of the reunion, fifty or so members of the Class of 1946, with wives, husbands and a handful of children, gathered at Evanston Township High School for a conducted tour. It was part of the reunion program. Clearly, we were going to need a guide. From the outside, the core of the building was as we remembered it, a red-brick mass topped with stone-trimmed Gothic towers, but it was embedded in new structures extending in all directions. In the twenty-five years since we left it, the school enrollment had doubled, yet what now existed, I had heard, was not one huge high school but four smaller ones, self-contained but connected. As the tour began, our guide was explaining what had happened and why.

—Teachers get to become acquainted with a student body of say thirteen hundred. The year before last, the total enrollment was fifty-two hundred, it's about fifty-four hundred at the present time, and it seems that the school population is going to level off at about six thousand in another four or five years. And that will mean we'll have four semi-independent schools of fifteen hundred each.

The man explaining the reorganization of the high school was one we all recognized as Mr. Cameron. Twenty-five years earlier, he had been in charge of one of Evanston High School's eleven home rooms, each, with 250 or so students, large enough to function with some of the autonomy of a small school. We were assembled in what had been the school's main office, still with the same function and mercifully in the same place, unchanged except that it is now chillingly air-conditioned; near it, also unchanged, is the high school superintendent's office, still set off by a partition of small-paned leaded glass and approached across a vaguely medieval tiled pavement that interrupts the harsh linoleum of the hallway. The area is still, as in 1946, the administrative heart of the school. Around it have grown up, like the leaves of a quatrefoil, the four distinct schools that came into being in 1967, each with its own principal, teaching and administrative staff, classrooms and laboratories built around a courtyard, each named for one of the four superintendents the high school has had in its seventy-five-year history: Boltwood, Beardsley, Bacon (who ruled the school in our time), Michael (his successor, who planned the rebuilding and the new organization and now has been succeeded in his turn). A freshman entering Evanston High School is enrolled in one of the four schools and spends his four years there, taking most of his academic courses within his own school.

—I'm not going to try to show you everything, Mr. Cam-

eron is saying. There are a million square feet of floor space
in this building and over three miles of corridors. . . .

Except that the luxuriant wavy black hair is now white
and the teacher's sober blue business suit has been ex-
changed for summerweight slacks and a sport shirt, Mr.
Cameron seems to have stepped back into our lives without
a break: a big man with a straightforward ease in talking
on his feet and a command of the statistics in which the
school abounds. He has been well chosen to lead us, a
reassurance that not everything we remember has been
swept away, that someone remains who can tell us about
our school in the language we learned there. He retired
four years ago and now often guides visitors around the
school: twenty-five hundred a year, he tells us, come to
study the nation's first educational park, the computerized
modular scheduling, the innumerable other innovations.
We set off after him, a straggling line of middle-aged ex-
students.

The building turns out to be mostly not air-conditioned,
and on this late June afternoon it is hot. We sweat. Mr.
Cameron seems to be avoiding stairs—in deference, surely,
to *our* age, not his. Somewhere ahead of us he is clearly and
steadily explaining what we are seeing, but by now we are
thoroughly confused by the sheer abundance and variety of
facilities, no longer able to distinguish the core we remember from all that has been added in and around it. Each of
the four schools is similar in plan but varies in detail. Each
includes a resource center (books, offices and conference
rooms for faculty available for consultation, student carrels, dial access to audio- and videotape in the central media
system); classrooms and laboratories; a vivarium (each
school maintains a distinct artificial climate, from desert to
tropical); a student cafeteria and a student lounge; an open
courtyard; a study hall (one of the huge former home
rooms).

Between and around the four schools are grouped facilities shared by all: the old central library, to which carrels have been added; the computer center (mostly for teaching —the school's computer services are contracted outside); a television studio with television classrooms attached; in one of the courtyards, the school's special pride, a small planetarium (astronomy is among the courses offered); the industrial arts shops and home economics rooms (the latter including a laboratory nursery school run by students, boys as well as girls); studios and practice rooms for music, art, dance; eleven gymnasiums; two large swimming pools; and a theater-auditorium that looks as big as Radio City Music Hall (and must be, nearly, to seat the number of students in the school). It is a bewildering array to take in on a warm afternoon.

We are led finally to rest in the half-darkened auditorium, another haven of air conditioning, and gratefully we sit down. Mr. Cameron is still affably discoursing, unruffled, an old hand at this. Do we have any questions? Is there anything else we'd like to know about? A few people make the effort, but by now we are tired; my own questions seem almost too complicated to formulate. We say our thanks, shake hands again, and start to leave.

My questions, if that had been the time and place and I had had the energy to ask them, would have had to do with education: its nature, value, effects. What difference does it make? Evanston Township High School—and with it the separate but coextensive elementary and junior high school system—is among the very best in the country by whatever measure. Most of us on the tour that afternoon had seen or heard of the article in a national magazine a few years earlier* in which a panel of experts ranked the high school

Ladies' Home Journal, May 1968.

the best in the nation. When we were going through the school system in the 30s and 40s, similar methods of rating it produced similar results. Were the schools really as good as their reputation—did they accomplish more fully and effectively than others whatever we mean by education? Or was it the town itself that made the difference?

There were, it seemed to me, quite a number of qualities that the members of the Class of 1946 had in common. Most of these we shared with others of our time, our place, our generation; they were the marks of men and women who grew up in Evanston, in the Midwest, in those years. But in the course of the summer, driving around the country to talk to the people of the Class of 1946, I discovered something else. The quality that set them apart as a group, that ran all through, black and white, auto mechanic to professor, housewife to lawyer, was something I have found no better name for than intelligence. Not the quality measured by IQ tests but rather a kind of disciplined reasonableness: a practical self-awareness, an ability to perceive and interpret events and to express one's perceptions in distinct and personal terms. It is not a quality that in Evanston was ever raised to extremes of eloquence, passion, or intellectual accomplishment, but it is a very serviceable quality for getting one through life. It seemed to be the one thing that all of us had taken from our Evanston schooling, however it had been varied by the particular set of abilities we brought to it or by life since then.

This was the quality Frank Carlborg was talking about when he remarked that, on balance, going to Evanston High School had been "a tremendous advantage."

—You go there—I don't know that the schools were that great, but the courses were there and they were competently taught—but you come out of it with a background that turns out to be valuable. You're reasonably well spoken, you're reasonably well acquainted with the successful things that are done in the world, so you're not dazzled by somebody that can use the language a little bit . . . that has known the president of a company. . . .

The class, on the whole, agreed. It was not just complacency about one's past but a sense of distinct value received. Walker Davies, despite the social exclusions he had known as a Negro, remembered the experience, in his diffident way, with gratitude—

—ETHS was just like saying—you know, in high school terms—you gotta be from Harvard. That may be a little way out, but that's the way people—people even nowadays . . . I've found this to be true—

And in spite of all the changes, Frank Weston, a black student of twenty-five years later, was able to look back on his own very different experience in almost the same words.

Those in the class who still lived in Evanston, who had children of their own in the schools, felt much the same way—that the schools were as good as they had been or better. The exceptions were people who somehow resisted, or failed to recognize, the kind of education that was offered. Several of these were women I remembered as popular in all the social ways, who had gone on to college and there had experienced a kind of startled intellectual awakening that reflected badly on what had gone before. In the style of that time and place, intellect, apparently, was not a social asset in a girl. If it happened that in other ways she was equipped for popularity and liked the feeling of it—if she was sought after for dates, parties, dances, clubs—unconsciously she might keep her intelligence to herself. Later, she would realize what she had done and resent it.

It is easier to describe a school system's services and programs than to assess the education they are meant to sustain, especially if the education is one's own. The services in the Evanston schools were remarkable for their

range and variety, and many that were normal there in the
30s are still novelties elsewhere today (elementary school
libraries, for instance, with trained librarians). But education is not chiefly a matter of services or systems or theories
of instruction, although they contribute; it has to do with
the attitudes to life and to one's own mind that a teacher
instills, not so much by what he teaches as by the qualities
of life and mind reflected in his teaching. For us, what was
special about Evanston's schools was our teachers.

It was a notably stable group. Of the eighteen or twenty
teachers I had in elementary and junior high school, there
was *one* teaching for the first time—the others had all had
from several to many years' experience and a few had
taught my much-older brothers. (By way of contrast in
time as well as place, there has never been a year in which
that could be said of the teachers my own children have had
as they have gone through, collectively, nearly fifty years
of schooling in reputable systems in the East.) Part of the
reason, of course, was simply the Depression itself, the
scarcity of other jobs, but longevity in itself is no more a
virtue in teaching than in any other field. They stayed,
really, because to teach in the Evanston system was a final
goal (it still is, in spite of starting salaries that are substantially higher, for instance, in Chicago). That feeling was
present in their style of teaching: both kindly and severe,
with an assurance and firmness in matters of discipline that
spurred you to strive for mastery of whatever was being
taught. The fact that until we reached seventh grade all of
these teachers were women, and unmarried women at that,
seemed to make no difference. They were sharply defined
as *teachers*, their role undiluted by marriage or motherhood.
They had the presence to teach us baseball or soccer with
as much sureness as history, arithmetic or painting—and to
administer to the boys an occasional sharp lesson in the
proper deportment toward a lady or a girl our own age.

That strong sense of discipline, of eagerness to please, was accompanied by an equally strong sense of one's place in the hierarchy of school and authority. As a child, you noticed gratefully that you stood in the same relationship to your teachers as your teachers did to the school principal or the principal to the superintendent—and so on up to whatever was the ultimate: on the rare visits from the principal or the even rarer tour of inspection by the superintendent, your teachers suffered the same quicksilver anxiety you did yourself under too close scrutiny. That feeling for authority suited the formal Midwestern courtesies of the time. And paradoxically, because the authority, the discipline, were so clear-cut that they hardly needed to be asserted—because we all, principal, teachers, children, know the rules—we were left, at each level, with considerable freedom to decide things for ourselves. For the children, that meant that from first grade on an important part of our learning was done independently or in small groups; weeks of such work culminated in a written report—laboriously scratched out in ink with much nervousness about blots and erasures—that was also presented orally to the rest of the class. At longer intervals, the class found itself responsible for an assembly program, presenting its work formally to the entire school. Working individually, each child worked at something like his capacity.

In the elementary and junior high schools (seventh and eighth grades), the gradually changing curriculum—each year with a little more responsibility, a little more homework in increasingly demanding subjects—gave you a feeling of purposeful progress through the hierarchy of the grades. For Roy King, junior high school had been the two upper grades of the nearly all black elementary school in the heart of the Negro community (those on the fringe of that area were able to go to one of the two mainly white junior high schools where everyone else went). Hence, for him and for the others in that school, the transition to the high school was a big step. He remembered with gratitude the white teachers readying them for the change—

—When we got to seventh and eighth grade, they were preparing us to compete against the students from Nichols and Haven [the two junior high schools] in high school. "You will have to know this in high school, you will have to know that in high school." . . . It was a good experience.

All the teachers at Foster, the black school, were whites except the gym teacher, and that circumstance was to persist for another twenty years. It had not yet occurred to anyone that there might be something unsuitable in a black school staffed by white teachers. On the contrary—

—They were, when I look back, Roy thought, unusual in that we were not—these were professionals . . . dedicated to teaching, and I don't think they made any difference in the color of skin.

At the same time, the rest of us in the two junior high schools were nervously looking forward to the immense high school, with its three thousand students, where the teachers would give us homework every night in things like Latin and algebra and the seniors had the stature and the self-assured bearing of grown men and women. It was not so much what our teachers told us to expect as what we worked out among ourselves: that the time had somehow come for putting childhood behind us. (When I was at last a freshman at the high school, I resigned from my Y club under the impression I had outgrown such things and then for the same reason got my first job, delivering telegrams after school.) And as it turned out, that first year in high school was as bewildering as anything we could have imagined. We had progressed in a body through the elementary and junior high school grades, with thirty others that we knew, in school and out, almost as intimately as we knew ourselves. After such seclusion, in high school you found yourself, with a shock, in a home room with two hundred and fifty others you'd mostly not laid eyes on before, who lived in parts of Evanston where you'd never even been— and the unfamiliar names and faces changed with each class. That was the quality that had impressed the few people in the Class of 1946 who disliked the school: they remembered it as huge, impersonal, remote.

Compared with the present, the curriculum we encountered when we entered high school at the beginning of World War II was stripped to essentials but nevertheless extensive. It included the basic sciences, mathematics, English, history. At a time when thousands of American high schools offered *no* language courses, at Evanston there was a choice among four years of Latin, three each of French, Spanish, or German. Class assignments were still at random as they had been in the lower schools, so that the required English and history courses brought together a range of abilities. In other areas, there was a separation more on lines of social class than intelligence: those who were expected to go to college (at the time, 60 to 65 percent, compared with about 10 percent of the middle generation at large) naturally filled their programs with science, mathematics, one or two languages; those without such expectations spent most of their time in business courses, home economics, industrial arts. In the sciences and one or two math courses, there was a beginnning of the homogeneous grouping—"tracking" in later educational jargon—that, with the boom in testing since the War, has become an obsession of American schools. At Evanston in 1946, however, one still made the choice oneself between the hard or easy version of, say, the physics or chemistry course. (By the time homogeneous grouping was finally abandoned in the late 60s, Evanston High School was operating as many as eight "tracks" in subjects like English: eight distinct levels of ability in each of the four years, to which students were assigned on the basis of intelligence and achievement tests.)

What the high school offered, then, was a particularly effective form of the kind of "education without frills" that restive taxpayers today keep saying is what they *really* want. At the time, it was all we knew, but we began to appreciate its worth when, in 1946, we faced the problem of getting into college or finding a job in competition with all the others.

—It wasn't till I was applying for college, Ralph Mann remembered, that I realized how valuable graduating in the upper third of Evanston High School is vis-à-vis any other public high school. It was a recommendation in itself. . . . I think we had probably one of the best educations that was available at the time.

Roy King, whose real learning of carpentry had come when he went to work for his father, had gone through the vocational program and appreciated it in the same kind of way.

—I took wood shop along with everything else. It was beautiful as far as I knew, it had top of everything. . . . I thought I was *good*—until I got out on the job. . . .

Julie Chasin, who had taught for several years herself and remained involved in education, could still feel what the school had accomplished in forming her life in middle age—

—The people that I have kept in contact with, most all of them that I know are very active people, interested people, and involved people. . . . Our interests developed at that time, and for all of us, it kind of formed our life pattern. . . .

From the perspective of the present, it seems astonishing how much subtle discipline was built into the high school, how much direction most of us were prepared to accept without question. The several school publications, for instance, were characterized by controlled but enthusiastic assent. The eight-page weekly newspaper was produced by junior and senior students from the English journalism course (the teacher was the faculty adviser). It was, in fact, quite professionally made up, carefully edited, not badly written, and year after year its standing among the best in the country (like the school itself) was certified by organizations like the Columbia Scholastic Press Association. It was also, I think we recognized, rather predictable. The kind of scandalous controversy that distinguished student newspapers of the 60s would have been inconceivable. It was not chiefly that the paper was produced under the scrutiny of the faculty adviser but that the student editors and writers, aspiring to the ideals of responsible and objective journalism, practiced a strict self-censorship.

When it came time to produce the senior year book (like the newspaper known as *The Evanstonian*), the faculty adviser gave us her ideas for organizing it and we gratefully accepted, having no other experience in book-making. She also intimated that Dr. Bacon, the school superintendent, regarded the year book as a vehicle for presenting the school to the public and that there were subjects he would be pleased for us to cover (some rather Pre-Raphaelite frescoes that no one knew were in an anteroom of the library; the school's new testing and guidance program). Again, it would not have occurred to us not to comply.

Ultimately, it was Dr. Bacon who set the tone for the school, a remote figure with an aura of scholarship and icy dignity whom one saw occasionally at a distance, on the platform at a school assembly in the gymnasium, a man with the bearing of a patrician J. Edgar Hoover in mint condition. Our teachers seemed to look to him with the same kind of awe that the elementary school teachers felt for the principal. Without irony, they taught us the required four plays of Shakespeare from Dr. Bacon's one book, a slightly expurgated textbook edition. Roy King told me about the one time he had actually seen the great man.

—Who ever knew anything about Francis Bacon? He was the big lion that no one ever saw. I saw that man *once* and I was wrong then. . . .

Roy had gone out from his wood shop class to buy ice cream at Monticello's, a student hangout across the street from the school. He was coming back with several packages of ice cream under his arms when he passed Dr. Bacon in a courtyard. The superintendent nodded gravely and spoke to him; here, no doubt, was a student on some official errand.

A few, like Jim Crandall, had automatically resisted any form of authority they could discover—and twenty-five years later looked back with regret. Jim as a freshman had been an outstanding student. And then—

—I was a bad kid and I ran with a bad crowd.

The school, evidently, had made some effort about him —he had had some of its notable teachers—but it had not worked.

—I think sometimes they overdid the rules business— you couldn't leave the school during lunch hour. Now the minute they told me that, the first thing I had to do was leave the school during lunch hour. You couldn't take your car off the lot during school hours—well, I immediately found ways to do that. There were so many restrictions. . . .

Even in 1946 there were a few signs of the changes that were coming to the school as to the town and the nation. In that year, after cannily making them official organizations complete with faculty advisers, the school quietly abolished the several fraternities and sororities that some of us turned to for relief from the impersonal bigness of the place. In the spring, an educational planning committee came into being, with equal representation, though not equal weight, for teachers and students (the appointed students were a carefully chosen cross-section of classes and accomplishments, including several Negroes). And it was also the beginning of an elaborate aptitude testing program which its director encouraged us to go through without charge.

A couple of years later, Dr. Bacon at last retired. Through the 50s and 60s, the school grew to double its 1946 enrollment and experienced the national revolution in curriculum and educational technology, though in its own way and still largely within the old framework. In 1967, all these changes came to a head in the drastic reorganization reflected in the rebuilt school that Mr. Cameron led us through on the class tour.

In Evanston today, when you look up the high school in the telephone book, you find a listing for each of its four component schools: Beardsley, Boltwood, Bacon, Michael. Under each school, there are numbers for its principal, its health service, its guidance counselors—and its social worker. There is also a listing for the office of the superintendent, the man who presides over the entire complex as Dr. Bacon did in our time. When I dialed the number, a man's voice answered "Scott Thomson." I said I wanted to talk to the superintendent and the man said he *was* the superintendent. I explained my business and made an appointment.

As one of the high school's twenty-five hundred annual visitors, you receive a self-adhesive lapel badge that enables you to wander unchallenged through the halls; it is printed in what are still the school colors, orange and blue ("Hi! I'm visiting E.T.H.S.") and has a line where you can write your name. An assistant superintendent leads you into a small conference room and shows an elegant and appealing slide/tape presentation of the school produced by students a couple of years back. She remarks that the administration had thought the script too favorable to be persuasive, but that was how the kids wanted it—to show how good they think their school is. Proms are coming back, she says hopefully a little later (one was held this year and forty couples went; in 1946, the yearbook devoted a two-page spread to the year's six big dances).

The visitor also receives a folder of materials describing the school. An attractive leaflet headlined "We're Number One" lists the school's facilities, faculty and student attainments. A statistical summary, another handsomely gotten up leaflet, graphs enrollments for the past ten years and emphasizes the number of courses in each department, costs per department and per student, tax rates in comparison with those of other high schools in the area (by this measure, five of the ten school districts listed are more heavily taxed). There are reprints of magazine articles about the school and copies of the architect's plans for the rebuilt school as an aid to finding one's way through the maze of halls, stairs, courtyards. Several offset-printed handouts describe, in fairly technical terms, particular features of the school that educators come here to study: the media center; an impressive list of current innovations in teaching ("mediated self-instruction"), equipment (teaching machines, the vivaria), organization (team teaching, paraprofessional teacher aides); the resource centers; and modular scheduling. For those who wish to inquire more deeply, there are the *Course Planning Handbook* used by the students, a 64-page description of courses that rivals many a college catalogue, and the current *Annual Report*, a 160-page paperback book assessing achievements, problems, and long-term goals in each academic department and in the high school as a whole. Clearly the school is conscious of having a story to tell and a receptive audience. After the chaste silences of twenty-five years ago, the new spirit is striking.

Looking through the various handouts, you find that a student now chooses among close to three hundred courses, compared with perhaps seventy in 1946; the total includes the basic academic courses like English or the sciences—taught by separate faculties within each of the four schools—as well as those (such as auto mechanics or film-making) that require special facilities and draw their students from the entire school. There are half a dozen work-study programs. Each department offers at least a few courses in the form of seminars or independent projects. There are also advanced placement courses and in the sciences two college-level courses (biology, chemistry-physics). There is a separate department of combined studies with its own series of interdisciplinary courses in literature and social studies. Although fundamental subjects are provided for at several levels of difficulty, there is also a good deal of the kind of exotica that a very large, well-equipped and well-staffed school can afford: print-making, film-making (and several television courses); Greek (returned to the curriculum after a thirty-year absence), Japanese (but not Chinese), Hebrew. Students find their way through this plethora of possibilities by way of distribution requirements (to graduate, they need four years of English, two each of social studies and physical education, one each of math, science, art), leaving room for seven purely elective one-year courses.

As a goal, this great range of student choice determined both the physical and the philosophical structure of the rebuilt school. It was expressed in three notable innovations: modular scheduling; a number of new facilities, particularly the resource centers; and an idea of the student as in large measure actively self-educating, through independent study, rather than passively taught. Modular scheduling means simply that the school day is divided into twenty-one fifteen-minute modules ("mods"), with a five-minute passing period between each; courses are organized in a weekly, rather than a daily, cycle of such units. A course may thus be scheduled for anything from six mods a week (creative writing) to sixteen (chemistry-physics); a typical course runs to nine mods meeting three times a week, three mods at a time (fifty-five minutes, including two passing periods). Although it sounds simple enough, when the range of possibilities is distributed among three hundred courses and fifty-five hundred students, it becomes a problem that only a fairly capacious computer can handle, with abundant human assistance.

A freshman at the high school may have a dozen mods a week scheduled for a study hall, much as in the old days. As he rises in the school, an increasing amount of his time is unscheduled, in blocks that may run to six or seven mods (a couple of hours)—a third or more of his time. He is expected to be working independently in whatever environment he thinks appropriate, which may be anything from a school cafeteria or student lounge to an open laboratory, his school's resource center, or the central library.

As you roam the halls of the new ETHS, you are, indeed, struck by the constant physical movement—students on their way from one center to another—and the amount of social talk—students leaning at windows in conversation, sitting on floors, legs outstretched—that goes on in cafeterias, conference rooms, student lounges. With your memories of the tense silences of twenty-five years ago, breached at forty-minute intervals by the shuffle of feet moving from one class to the next, it is not easy to know what to make of it. The school authorities, of course, have long since raised their own questions and concluded that the millennium has not yet arrived. In the preface to a recent annual report (suggestively headed "Beyond Modular Scheduling"), the superintendent announced the discovery that when students are free to study virtually anything, they are also free—as they always were, of course—to study nothing. There are students who, when presented with the time and facilities to investigate a subject they have chosen, would rather go to the cafeteria, drink coffee and talk; those who did badly in the old, tightly structured system, it turns out, do even worse in the new, less organized one. The school's response to this almost existential insight has been characteristically strenuous. There have been surveys of students and teachers as to how much unscheduled time is good for students at each level. Scheduling for freshmen has been tightened so that most of their nonclass time is assigned to study halls or counseling. The reading program has been expanded. A core of "retrogressed learners" ("hall wanderers" in the school's vernacular) has been identified and a new laboratory school within the school has been designed to rescue them. And a number of old-fashioned forms of discipline have reappeared, along with some new ones.

If the image of the old school was architectural or mechanical—an orderly structure created once and for all by ingenious men, a Midwestern brick Parthenon—the new one is more like a living organism constantly responding to its environment. What is it like to be part of this organic process? When I went for my appointment with the superintendent, Scott Thomson, I had to wait in an outer office while a couple of black students and a coach went in to see him. When they left twenty minutes later, he came out to get me and we sat down at one end of a long conference table. The delay had been merely one of those small crises that have become almost routine for American school and college administrators, a newly perceived and seemingly unresolvable grievance. In this instance, the black athletes felt that their coaches were not directing them toward college; their word for this was exploitation.

The superintendent is a man in his late thirties who has come to his present job by way of a doctorate at Stanford, further study in Oregon and Malaya, and a superintendent's post in California. While we talk, he sits attentive but relaxed, a man with an air of being able to convert every thought instantly to speech controlled and edited for public consumption: clearly not one to be ruffled by the day's conflict, whatever that may be.

Had he, I asked, had to face the kinds of mass confrontation that have been such a feature of other American schools? Evanston, it seems, has been fairly quiet. A year earlier, five hundred students had walked out to join the Northwestern protest of the Kent State shootings. In his first year, in the aftermath of a black walkout to celebrate Martin Luther King's birthday, he had faced a sit-in that began in confrontation and ended in elaborate negotiation of issues too complicated to summarize; it had been settled with a compromise.

What about the new racial hostilities that one has heard about elsewhere, especially in the big cities?

—The black community is very aware today and has been for three or four years. There's a black consciousness, and as a result . . . there's been a drawing away from contact. . . . I've spent a lot of time trying to get the black and white coaches to work together.

Was that the reason there were no black organizations within the school? (I had heard of one such group called the Evanston Athletic Association, which was to lead a black athletes' walkout a few days later.)

—There's not officially a black student organization. No organization can have a racial clause in it. There was a black student union a couple of years ago, but it can't have a charter here. This year there's an organization called Organization Black—maybe all the students in it are black but the charter is open to students of all races.

What about bomb threats, vandalism in general? I had already been told about the large sums being spent in some nearby schools to replace smashed plumbing (not just a few broken windows or light bulbs). It was only a few months since an epidemic of school bomb threats had flashed through the country, to the point that in some areas any kid capable of dialing a telephone could close his school for the day—and it happened day after day. But in Evanston?

—In a comparative sense with other schools, our vandalism isn't bad—it's not *good*, he hastened to add.

And bombs, bomb threats?

—I have yet to spend a year in a school system without having a least one bomb threat. . . . We have a search procedure, we check out ash cans, stairwells, any unlocked doors. They got a routine thing.

There had been no school closings, no actual bombs. The procedures, which he described in detail, were typical of the Evanston way of doing things: thoroughly thought out by a man with strong nerves, then carried out by a discreet security force.

That left drugs among the problems disrupting American schools, and again the comment was forthright, balanced, predictable—and probably accurate.

—We're in pretty good shape in the drug situation. It's partly the result of the nature of the community, partly the result of the programs we've had. . . . You're not as anonymous in Evanston as you might be in one of the newer suburbs. There's a lot better community control here—in the positive sense of the word.

A little earlier, we had been talking about the teacher contract negotiations, just concluded. In an era when teacher strikes had become almost commonplace, Evanston had never had one. Why not? Was it something about the teachers the school attracted?

—There's a real pride in the school, a very infectious pride. There's something built into the school that makes you want to extend yourself, and most of these people are truly extending themselves. It's a wonderful thing. If you knew how to buy it, you'd go out and buy it . . . a tremendous internal standard.

As I got up to go, I asked him what he thought of the periodic efforts to compare the country's eighteen or twenty thousand high schools. Where did Evanston rank now? "Number One!" Dr. Thomson replied, but with a laugh. Schools, of course, cannot be ranked like entries in a ledger. Nevertheless, if you were part of this one, you had no doubts.

It was several days after meeting Dr. Thomson that I asked him to introduce me to a couple of students, partly to see how the school's public relations sense would respond. The result was an hour with Frank and Barbra, whom I've mentioned earlier. They were, I suppose, as consciously representing their school as their superintendent had been, and yet the warmth of their feelings for the place was as real as his. We talked about courses, what it was like to be part of the small school within the much larger one. For them, graduating with the first class to go all the way through the new system, it seemed to have worked very much as intended.

—I base myself mostly on my own school, Barbra said, I never venture out just for social reasons, to go to another school. I used to, but now most of my friends are here and I just stay in that one school. . . .You have the small school and you can see your teachers. . . .

But the courses sounded so demanding. Didn't it seem tough, a grind?

—I guess you don't really think about the work, Frank said. You have your goal, and I've always had my goal in mind. I guess I thought of work as just a means to attain a goal. I get a kick out of walking into class with something under my belt. . . .

Both were clear about what they were going to do after high school. That of course was another of the things the school had intended: to make it possible for people like Frank and Barbra to find out what their goals were and to provide means for realizing them. They seemed like lineal descendants of the Class of 1946, and except for Barbra's hip-hugging bell-bottomed trousers, either of them, it seemed to me, could have traveled twenty-five years back through time to our own youth without serious discomfort. There were, however, other ideas about how well the school was accomplishing its objectives.

For the last couple of years, systematic opposition to the kind of acceptance Frank and Barbra represent—and to the superintendent's disciplinary reforms—has been expressed in an underground newspaper put out by a shifting "collective" of students. While the award-winning official school paper carried on much as in the past, as a vehicle of the school journalism course, the opposition paper turned up several times a year under a variety of titles (*Gadfly, Revelation Now, Toehold*) and in various colorful formats. To get around a high school regulation, it was given away rather than sold, and when funds ran short there were appeals for donations and a money-making film show (W. C. Fields, the Marx Brothers) to recoup. The school does, however, scrutinize the paper and one or two issues have been confiscated; in the delicate balance prevailing between the school and the collective, the word *shit*, which appeared ritually somewhere in each issue, was apparently O.K., but a number of similar words were not.

Some of the material is standard fare lifted from big brothers in the underground press: denunciations of the war in Indochina, furious polemics on both sides of the Arab-Israeli conflict, a critique of welfare with the unstated assumption that every American family has an inherent right to an annual income of $5500. In one issue there was a cautiously oblique criticism of the shenanigans at the Chicago conspiracy trial, suggesting that Abbie Hoffman and his colleagues may actually be agents of the CIA or the State Department (along with the editors of the leading Chicago newspapers). There is also a Menckenesque regular feature listing current American inanities under the heading "Congratulations": ". . . to Leo Hershkowitz, a noted archeoligist [sic], who has confirmed that New York City Hall was built over an 18th century madhouse. . . ."

Much of the agitating, however, was local and specific. When the Evanston Bus Company raised the fare on the high school buses, there was an editorial calling for a boycott until it was reduced (proposed solution: state subsidy). When the school decided to discipline students moving around the school without a pass ("hall wanderers") by stationing teachers in the halls to check passes and issue corridor warning notices like traffic tickets, the paper reprinted the relevant directive to the faculty with a diagram of the school showing where the teachers would be found (proposed solution, sympathetically addressed to Dr. Thomson: abolish hall passes and let students go where and when they want as long as they're orderly). Under the heading "The Politics of Grades" there was a proposal for replacing report cards with self-evaluation (the high school still places much emphasis on grades, grade-averages, and class standing, and even some conservative parents I talked to thought it excessive). An end-of-school issue included a detailed constitution and bill of student rights for the school. In several recent issues there were sympathetic reports of a "free school" being organized by ex-students seeking an end to oppression in the basement of the local Unitarian church.

Late one Sunday afternoon near the end of the school

year, I went to visit one of the young men involved in producing the paper (I'll call him Stuart Fisher), at his home across Sheridan Road from Lake Michigan. There were half a dozen boys and girls, juniors and seniors, there when I arrived, all members of the collective. They had been having a picnic, one of the happy alternatives, Stuart noted later, to the middle generation's institution of dating.

I explained myself. What was it like to be part of our school in the present? What had struck me about the school now was the immense range of choice for the students, the free movement from one ingenious facility to the next, but what rankled with Stuart was the apparatus of control, the restrictions by which the school attempted to direct its students within the large framework.

—Legally, you are not allowed to be in the other school, other than your own, but this is violated constantly. The school's gone to great extremes to prevent it. Everyone's required to carry an ID card at all times, with your school and your picture on it. . . . They started requiring you to show your ID card if you wanted to get something to eat. . . .

The ID cards were another innovation, but not one the school officials talked about, any more than the hall passes or the corridor warning notices that went with them. Actually, like the students in the school-sponsored survey, Stuart could see a need for some forms of discipline, but—

—I lay the blame on the junior highs, where you come from a very restrictive, very tight schedule—when you come from an environment like the junior high school suddenly into the high school, it takes a lot of will power to adjust, to discipline yourself to go to your classes and make good use of your unscheduled time. . . .

There was more—for example, the effort to control who went in and out of the school, for whatever reason—

—The school has hired four full-time security guards

and there's another guy that patrols the outside of the
school in a Cushman cruiser and they're equipped with
walkie-talkies. They're responsible for any disturb-
ances. . . .

The school's annual report actually lists a security staff
of eleven, including a chief (compared with sixty-seven in
the janitorial and maintenance unit). Presumably the
school's program for the bomb threats and the occasional
fire planted in a trash basket or locker also included keeping quiet about its security force.

—They tore down Monte's last year, just to keep kids
from going there because they used to sneak out and then
come back. . . .

Monte's was Monticello's, an ostensible drugstore across
the street from the school, which had served the same function in our time and, in addition, had been a hangout for
black students comparable to Harry's Pool Hall, at Fountain Square, for whites. The school had bought the land,
torn down the building, and surrounded it with a chain-
link fence ten feet high. Monticello's would have been a
natural headquarters for whatever drug business there was
to be done. Were there dealers in the school as one heard
there were elsewhere—boys with outside contacts and a
regular supply of drugs for sale?

—There seems to be a general decline in psychedelics,
acid, and there is unfortunately a gruesome use of really
strong depressants like heroin. . . . They found some drugs
earlier this year. Most of the dealing that goes on in school
is some kid whose brother brought back a pound when he
was in LA last summer, from Mexico. There isn't any
organized group coming in with stuff and selling it in the
school . . .

Stuart's view agreed with the superintendent's, but I
wondered. I had noticed ostentatious convertibles parked
on streets around the school campus, sometimes with

gaudily dressed men lounging in them. One man who lived a couple of blocks away was convinced he had seen a drug transfer one morning from such a car to a boy on foot.

And socially what was the school like now? Were the town's racial tensions in evidence? You could diagram the cafeteria tables that were all black, by custom, Stuart thought, and there had been fights, but the real division was between jocks and freaks.

—Everyone here today is freaks because they're left of center and—you know, the attitudes. And jocks I guess I break down as people who're completely apolitical . . . totally socially oriented. . . .

But wasn't *freak* a drug term?

—You can't orient it towards drugs anymore at all, because now quite recently there's been a very distinct trend with—a lot of jocks are smoking marijuana now and a lot of freaks are drinking alcohol, it started with wine but a lot of them are on hard alcohol. . . .

With problems like these, what about the elaborate system of guidance counselors and social workers, both unknown twenty-five years ago? What effect did they have on one's school experience?

—I've gone through about the worst of it. I've been in high school three years and I've had three counselors—great chance to get to know your personal identity! No one goes in just to talk to them. . . . I had a friend accused of possession of marijuana in school. Instead of taking legal action against him, they referred him to a social worker. Another girl friend of mine tried to commit suicide and they referred her to the school social worker. I don't know the function they're supposed to serve. . . .

In that year when part-time jobs of any kind for students had mysteriously dried up, Stuart was sufficiently a son of the middle generation to have one, with a local printer, but his feelings about it were radically different—

—Shit work—sweeping, cleaning, mopping—ugghh. . . . I'm doing slop work now for a dollar sixty-five an hour after school. . . . The intellectual stimulation is kind of lacking. It's a menial, low-class kind of mongoloid-idiot labor. I just get fed up with sitting there, folding, collating. . . .

Although he was holding a job he didn't like, getting out *Toehold*, and engaging in complicated legal maneuvers against the school (to be allowed to distribute the paper, the kids had taken their case to the board of education), Stuart had accumulated enough course credits in three years so that by the end of summer school he could graduate. And his plans then? The answer was a surprise. He hadn't found a college yet that attracted him. There were still some courses he wanted to take, he was going to stay on for another semester; besides, he got along well with his family. In its muted and devious form, his feeling seemed to me an echo after all of the pride and affection Frank and Barbra felt.

As it happened, Evanston High School, rebuilt and subdivided into its four smaller schools, with its new and much revised curriculum, had reopened in the fall of 1967 just as a complex plan was going into effect to end what was now called de facto segregation in the town's elementary schools. It was more than a coincidence. Although the high school and the elementary schools served the same community, they had their own boards, their own administrations and policies, their separate histories. The high school had always been integrated—in the sense that that was where all the students from the town, black or white, actually went—but the rebuilding had to do with making the existing integration a little more real. Between 1946 and 1967, while the high school enrollment doubled and the proportion of black students increased substantially, Evanston might have done what many similar towns did: build one or two new high schools in other parts of the town. The new schools would have been largely white while the old one would have become increasingly black; the racial antagonisms already present would have deepened, perhaps beyond the possibility of healing. The imaginative reorganization that was in fact undertaken was simply a happy consequence of the local geography: there was no more suitable land on which to build a new high school. But the effect was to make of the school a theater in which something like real integration could begin to occur.

The two events—the rebuilding of the high school, the desegregation of the elementary schools—had a deeper connection. From the age of seven or eight there comes back to me an image of a black woman arriving at our school, leading by the hand a small, unwilling colored boy. It was a warm, bright day, almost hot, that must have been early fall: the woman had an air of having come on foot a long distance in the heat, from somewhere on the fringe of the school's attendance area. A couple of years earlier I had been through it myself when my own mother led me off to the school for the first time. They had come, we somehow knew, to ask that the child be allowed to attend the school, and they vanished into the principal's office. Not much later, they were leaving again, pushing out through the heavy glass doors of the school, across the playground again, and away, and we knew they would not be back. It was a case, apparently, within the discretion of the principal. Others grew up with similar memories waiting to be understood and in time became protagonists in Evanston's integration drama. It was that earliest experience, part of the education the town had given us, that gave the program its particular shape—and that made it seem not only necessary but possible.

In the elementary schools, although segregation seems not to have been a formal policy, one school near the center of the black community had been largely black from the beginning and by the late 50s was entirely so; another was clearly going in that direction. The process by which Evanston moved from that condition to integration—and the kinds of conflicts that the process generated—is instructive; it is worth looking at in some detail. Because the integration program brought into the open the deepest kind of conflict and because at the same time it was made to work, it revealed more about Evanston and its history in the past twenty-five years than any other event.

Until 1950, when they were merged, Evanston's schools were divided between two school districts quite different in character: north Evanston, with most of the black population and the town's one all-black school, 21 percent of its children black, the school attendance districts fixed on neighborhood lines; south Evanston, with a black school enrollment of only 3 percent and a policy of open enrollment. In the middle 40s there had been detailed studies of the racial mixture in the two districts, long-term projections. Even earlier, in both districts, there had been an occasional pairing of all-white schools with ones that had a substantial number of Negroes—for example, for combined assembly programs.

In 1958, the all-black school, Foster, burned. Its children were temporarily transferred to other schools and a debate swelled over rebuilding it elsewhere so as to change the ratio of blacks and whites. In the end, the school, like other Evanston schools since the War, was rebuilt on the same site; there was no other place to put it. Nevertheless, the question had been formulated, and in 1961 the board of the combined school district went on record as favoring integration. The immediate result was a series of workshops for teachers concerning what, in the language of education, was called "human relations." Two years later, the school board encouraged black children to transfer to white schools from Foster and another that by then was two-thirds black; and it established a citizens' committee—on "intercultural relations"—to study what to do next. The following year, 1964, partly in response to crowding in the elementary schools, the board took another step toward integration: the sixth grades were transferred from the elementary schools to the junior highs, henceforth known as "middle schools." Since the junior high schools had always drawn from both the black and white communities, the effect was to bring the two groups together a year earlier. The same year, under continuing pressure from civil rights groups and black aldermen, the board took the crucial step: a resolution deploring the "psychological and sociological disadvantages" of de facto segregation and promising to develop a plan to eliminate it. A year later, to implement this policy, the Intercultural Relations Committee evolved into the overtly named Citizens Advisory Commission on Integration.

The new commission collected a large body of testimony from neighborhood and other community groups and within a year produced a plan to desegregate the schools with minimum displacement of the white majority. The heart of what was soon known as "the integration plan" was a decision to abolish the all-black Foster School and transform it into an abundantly staffed and equipped laboratory school, which children from throughout the town would attend voluntarily. The attendance lines for the remaining schools would be redrawn so as to include some of the black children in adjacent formerly white schools within walking distance. The remaining blacks—those in the center of the black community and hence farthest from any white school—were to be broken down in neighborhood groups and transported by bus to the re·

maining schools. The plan was approved in 1966 and that
fall the first stage went into effect: a laboratory kindergarten at Foster School with an enrollment limited to 150 children, about 20 percent of whom were black (165 actually
applied). The school board conducted a block-by-block cen-
sus of the town, and, as at the high school, computers were
used for the complex task of redrawing the school attendance zones and distributing the black children to the nearest white schools so that the proportion in each would be
about 20 percent without actually overcrowding any
school. In September 1967, the new laboratory school, after
its year of experiment at the kindergarten level, was in full
operation with all six grades, the busing program had
begun, and, as a later report put it, the schools were "fully
integrated." Or so a majority of Evanston's citizens supposed. What remained to be done?

At this point, a new factor entered the already emotional
equation. The superintendent elected to retire, and a
successor, Gregory C. Coffin, was called from the posh
Connecticut suburb of Darien and charged with carrying
out the plan already decided on. Four years later, Dr. Coffin
was to make himself the focus of the most bitterly contested
election of any kind ever held in Evanston. The election
was one for the school board held in the spring of 1970,
which as far back as anyone could remember had always
been for a single slate of carefully chosen candidates, so
sedately uncontroversial that the vote often ran as low as
five hundred out of an electorate of around forty thousand.
If he accomplished nothing else during his four years in
office, the new superintendent succeeded in bringing into
the open most of the fears that the town's blacks and whites
had about integration and about each other.

The integration plan was the latest stage of a historical
process that in a sense had been going on as long as there
had been a town of Evanston; in another sense, however,

it was merely the first of many practical steps that followed naturally from the basic decision to integrate the schools. Under Dr. Coffin's administration, it was discovered that a number of unforeseen practical measures were needed to make the program work.

In the summer of 1967, for example, a few weeks before the busing plan went into effect, the school district organized a voluntary institute on integration attended by nearly half its teachers. Later institutes supported by federal grants developed teacher and student resource materials on such subjects as the Negro in American history (black cowboys as well as white). The institutes' staffs, either in person or on videotape, were eminent and varied: from militant Chicago black power advocates to Jonathan Kozol, the white author of *Death at an Early Age,* to John Hope Franklin, the eminent black chairman of the Department of History at the University of Chicago. Perhaps inevitably, however, some white teachers, particularly the older ones, were frightened by the intimate and sometimes hostile rhetoric of these meetings, and they were followed by quiet resignations, early retirements.

At the same time, there was a determined effort to increase the number of black teachers and administrators in the district. In 1963, three years before Dr. Coffin's arrival, about 7 percent of the district's teachers were black, appointed and promoted, as a report observed at the time, strictly on merit. By 1969, the professional staffs of all the schools had been integrated and there were now nearly eighty black teachers out of a total of seven hundred—about 11 percent. The proportion of Negroes in administrative positions also increased dramatically: by 1970, they held exactly a third of the posts. Here again, however, there were criticisms which in time devolved upon the superintendent. Some of the new black assistant principals were said to be casually or inadequately qualified under the long-time standards laid down by the board of education.

By such practical measures, the integration program sought to identify and respond to the anxieties of all concerned—parents, teachers, children, blacks and whites. If the program was to do what it intended and not simply drive its participants apart in new and excruciating ways, it could not be imposed by the fiat of a board of education vote or the power of some outside authority: it was essential that it should be the act of the whole community. It depended, to begin with, on a large body of painfully gathered data about all the school district's children and their parents. It continued through door-to-door surveys and explanations, a running commentary of information and persuasion in mailing pieces and reprints. The key arguments were partly moral, partly the principles accepted by the Supreme Court in its famous school desegregation decision of 1954: that segregation was harmful, psychologically and educationally, to both black and white pupils; and conversely, that integration is positively beneficial, educationally as well as psychologically. The laboratory school has gone a long way toward realizing these claims.

When the laboratory school began its first year of full operation in the fall of 1967, its budget was swelled by a federal grant of $125,000. Its six hundred pupils (out of nine hundred applicants—a measure of acceptance that prevailed in each following year) were a carefully chosen cross-section of the school population. The school featured team teaching, individualized instruction in a nongraded setting, novel programs in every subject area, an audio-visual center producing materials for the school district as a whole as well as the school—literally dozens of imaginative experiments, including several programs that brought the school into intimate relationship with the community. One member of the Class of 1946 was among the select group of teachers who staffed the school, and she conveyed its excitement.

—What happened, Evy said, I worked in the Lab School and we worked like dogs and we really did some good stuff. And the only problem was, you never had time to sit down and figure out what you were doing. You just kept jumping all the time. . . .

Jumping: it had not been the style of the Evanston schools I remembered, but it seems to have been Dr. Coffin's style, and he put his mark on the Lab School and, through it, on every school in the district. Apart from Lab School innovations that were taken up directly by the other elementary schools, the children themselves were feeding back into the conventional middle schools when they reached sixth grade and compelling the schools to adapt to their different expectations. Bob Dawkins, the school district's black Director of Pupil Services, explained what happened.

—They were used to a nongraded, team-teaching setting. The environment was totally different. Many times these youngsters were confronted, say for example in math, with math that they had had at Laboratory School because they were able to move as fast as they could possibly go. So therefore the middle schools' teachers were pulling their hair out. . . . That's when the staff, the principal, the parents, had to get together and say, "It's time to make some changes. . . ."

There were also some rather specific disappointments: the integration plan in itself was not a panacea. Many of the Evanston parents whom I talked to in the Class of 1946 had tales of a breaking down of discipline, of racial hostilities. A recurring word was *intimidation.* Sometimes this meant no more than that white children were nervous in the presence of groups of blacks; in other cases it meant fights, robbery, knives pulled out of pockets. Whether it was in fact a policy, a good many parents and children—and some teachers as well—*believed* that there were dual standards of discipline and grading. Ralph Mann told me about his son

who was now in the same junior high school—middle
school—where we both had played football together long
ago.

—Things that you and I would never have done—it's
being done today out of hand. And the kids *know* there's
going to be no discipline . . . smarting off in class to teachers, not only the black kids but the white kids as a result.
. . . When my boy was in Lincolnwood, he learned right
away that the blacks and the whites were squaring off and
when it was king of the hill it was always the blacks against
the whites—the type of thing that would never have happened when we went to school because there wasn't this
conscious integration effort. . . .

Ralph, however, was not against the integration plan,
and he was not unperceptive of the sources of the hostility—

—The blacks suddenly found themselves in a white island and banded together. . . .

Another man told me of boys and girls who wouldn't go
to the bathroom for fear of being beaten up; they went in
pairs or they didn't go. A carefully unprejudiced member
of the class found himself in the awkward position of
raising a boy who now hated blacks as a result of similar
experiences. A woman teaching at one of the integrated
schools noted—perhaps with the cautious sense of public
relations that seems ingrained in all Evanston officials—
that it had been rather difficult to get the school's black
parents to join in the various PTA activities. As for the
children—

—I feel that in some respects we have failed or the parents—the children still tend to group themselves when
they are left, for example, on the playground. . . .

It is hard to say just how much Dr. Coffin—one very
busy executive among hundreds of teachers and administrators, thousands of children and parents—contributed to

the special character that Evanston's integration program assumed. He does seem to have been a man who threw off ideas faster than his staff could take them in—and then took the thought for the deed. He tended also, in speeches and in articles in educational journals, to picture himself in heroic terms, a white knight clashing swords with black extremists and a reactionary white Establishment (his north Evanston neighbors, for instance). In thinly generalized terms he attacked the immorality of school "board members who care more about being re-elected than they do about the results they produce." (In fact, the difficulty was not one of getting members *off* the board but of luring competent citizens onto it and perhaps getting them to stand for even an uncontested reelection; for that purpose, a delicate system of persuasion had prevailed since the 1920s: the school board caucus, by which various civic organizations sought out candidates.) Two months after the busing program went into effect, Dr. Coffin told a national conference on education, "Don't think for a minute that we had a lot of extreme liberals on our board of education" and went on to denounce "the white power structure of the city . . . the mayor, the city council, the downtown service clubs"—in effect, his employers, the board of education. A year later, Dr. Coffin was describing his role in some of the by-products of the integration program: the formation of a black teachers organization, an all-black school advisory council, his participation in open-housing demonstrations (for communication with the black community, gaining *their* support, *their* trust, was of course what this was all about). Talking about such things, he remarked prophetically that "needless to say, this could result in a limited tenure in this superintendency."

The prophecy was self-fulfilling. In June of 1969, taking account of its own discomfort with the superintendent, the mutterings of parents, and a recent resolution by one of

Evanston's home-owners' associations, the board voted quietly not to renew Dr. Coffin's contract, which would expire
the following June. What happened next would have been
unusual in any community or any comparable situation; in
Evanston, it was inconceivable. The very next evening at
a mass meeting held at one of Evanston's four middle
schools, Dr. Coffin encouraged the formation of a movement dedicated to reversing the decision by firing the
board and retaining himself. The next school board election would not take place till the following April. There
were ten months in which every possible feeling could
display itself.

The Negroes and conscious liberals who favored Dr.
Coffin were persuaded—and he said nothing that might
make them think otherwise—that his dismissal meant the
undoing of the integration program: the black children
would be transported back where they came from; the exciting laboratory school would go back to being just another all-black school in the midst of a black neighborhood.
Letters appeared in *The Evanston Review* comparing the
superintendent favorably with Jesus Christ. Organizations
and counterorganizations sprang up quite literally overnight. Both sides employed lawyers and public relations
firms; a petition with eleven thousand signatures favoring
the superintendent's retention was delivered to the school
board. Through the rest of the summer and the fall of 1969,
there was a series of increasingly crowded and vociferous
school board meetings, carried to overflow crowds on
closed-circuit television. These were regular meetings concerned with mundane matters like budgets, tax rates,
plumbing, but the unprecedented public attendance of two
thousand or more made it difficult to carry out any ordinary business. Speakers ranging from aldermen to schoolchildren seized the microphone to demand that the board
resign. At one meeting a black leader filibustered for two

hours when the board attempted to adjourn, reading from the works of W. E. B. Du Bois, which he happened to have with him. Organizations like the Human Rights Commission and the president of the Evanston High School board came forward with offers of "mediation" between Dr. Coffin and the school board (the board declined). A squad of police stood by at each meeting to protect the board members and lead them away when it was over. Near the close of one meeting, a black member of the board proposed, with fiery rhetoric, that the laboratory school be renamed in honor of Martin Luther King. The board, thankful to find anything on which it could agree with its audience, approved the motion on the spot.

One demonstration by the pro-Coffin forces, starting from the Unitarian church, for some reason marched *through* several Evanston department stores in the vicinity of Fountain Square. Ken Mills gleefully remembered a torchlight parade, including women with small children in strollers, whose goal was the home of the elderly white school board president, a woman, in northwest Evanston.

—They were in a sense protected and in a sense shepherded and in a sense *looked after* by the police. They marched on the sidewalk and when they got to this residence they kept marching—it was an endless line around the block in northwest Evanston, which upset them something terrible.

Didn't the other side do anything?

—No counterdemonstrations. Evanston's way is usually to try to ignore it—that's Evanston's standard response to a situation. . . .

Officers of the Evanston PTAs inevitably provided much of the leadership and the day-to-day organizational work on both sides. As a result, the caucus system broke down. First the black caucus members resigned in a body; then the state PTA directed its own members to withdraw. If the caucus had seemed reasonably representative in the past, it clearly no longer was.

An important issue through much of the campaign was the school board's refusal to state its reasons for firing the superintendent. The board insisted (no doubt on the advice of the new lawyer hired for the campaign) that like any employer it had no wish to discredit an ex-employee. The pro-Coffin forces countered that the board could not give its reasons because it had none—other than its dislike of integration. Finally, in August, the board acceded in a sober pamphlet, "The Report of the Board of Education on the Superintendency of Dr. Gregory C. Coffin." This document argued persuasively that integration of the schools had been the board's policy long before Dr. Coffin was hired to further it, that this policy had not changed, and that integration itself was therefore not an issue. And the report cited the superintendent's administrative carelessness in handling funds and programs, dealing with personnel and with the board itself—and supported these charges with unsigned letters from disgruntled teachers who had quit or were planning to do so.

There, on the whole, the matter rested, until the following February, two months before the school board election. The board refused to resign or to reinstate Dr. Coffin; the opposition continued to view this decision as an Establishment conspiracy to abolish integration. Then early in February 1970, the pro-Coffin group produced its own thirty-nine-page booklet, which, at least by intention, was a point-by-point rebuttal of the school board's report. The limping caucus nominated three school board candidates committed to upholding the board's decision (one was a black woman who felt the superintendent had been lax about consulting the black community). Two days later, the pro-Coffin forces nominated their own three-man slate, also including one Negro, who as it happened was Bennett

Johnson of the Class of 1946. With the one pro-Coffin member who would remain on the board, they would be a majority and would, they thought, be able to overturn the board's decision and reinstate the superintendent.

When the election itself finally came in April, it was almost an anticlimax. The majority of Evanston's white citizens had remained aloof from the demonstrations, the shouting matches at the school board meetings, but they quietly organized and when the time came they *voted*—giving the anti-Coffin candidates 51 percent of the record ballot. Ken Mills dejectedly summed it up.

—This is probably one of the few white superintendents of schools in this country who had the full backing of the black community. But we lost the fight. That was the year they brought out the old people's homes. Literally. Wheeled people in to vote. . . .

Throughout the campaign both the winning candidates and the school board itself had insisted that they favored the integration program and that there would be no change in the basic policy. If change had ever been the object, moreover, the black boycotts that followed the election—first of the schools, then of local stores—made it clear that it would be a perilous step. In June, when his contract expired after the year of turmoil, Dr. Coffin quietly departed. Ironically, more than a year later when the school board was still looking for his successor, the schools were being administered by the associate superintendent, the black ex-principal of the former all-black elementary school now dedicated to Dr. Martin Luther King.

What, finally, did this curious affair signify for Evanston? Why is it instructive for the country at large, increasingly faced with the need for similar decisions? Part of the meaning can be found in an elaborate study which Dr.

Coffin initiated six months after the first black children entered their new schools. (Financed by substantial foundation grants and carried out by an independent research organization, the study was not finished till a year after the superintendent had left; it was a final stage in the program of analysis and response which characterized the integration plan from its inception.)

In general, through two hundred pages of text and more than a hundred statistical charts and tables based on voluminous testing and observation, the report confirmed many of the white parents' complaints, which critics of the school board had tended to dismiss as racism. Integration of the schools had not brought the two groups together in any deep sense. There were indeed hostilities along racial lines. Particularly in the middle schools, a majority of the teachers, black and white, thought there was a dual code of discipline, though nearly all abhorred the idea. Among the black children bused to white schools, there seemed to be some lowering of self-esteem, hence, among the boys, more troublemaking, more referrals to psychologists and social workers. The teachers as a group, again both black and white, viewed their white pupils somewhat more favorably than their black ones. Academically, the report showed, integration had apparently not harmed the black or white pupils, but neither had it raised their achievement. At each level, the white children as a group were still well above the national norms, the black children at about the norms for black children and significantly below the performance of their white counterparts; both groups continued to progress at about the same rates as in the past and in the same relation to each other. These findings are, of course, in contrast to assertions about the academic benefits of integration that have been repeated so often they are accepted as established fact.

The report also suggested a possible reason why there

was greater racial hostility in some schools than in others. The black children on the outskirts of the black community —who were able to walk to adjoining white schools when the attendance lines were redrawn—were more like their white counterparts than those who were bused: in family income, education, job status, and so on. The bused children, in contrast, came from the inner core of the black community and were transferred to more distant white schools; they went, that is, as a group, and one that was less well off in all those socio-economic ways than the whites they joined or than other blacks who went to closer schools. It was from the more distant white schools that I heard the most about violent incidents.

I have deliberately summarized these findings in the dry language of the research study because it is necessary to be cautious about generalizing from such data; and because any town adopting real integration as a goal—as many will in the next few years—must be aware of the complexity of the undertaking and the time needed to carry it through. Except in the laboratory school, for example, Evanston was unable to take any account of the social and economic differences between the two groups it brought together. The goal itself will only be more difficult to achieve if real facts and real perceptions are concealed or denied.

In the aftermath of the school board election, the most interesting thing I discovered in Evanston's middle generation was that everyone who voted against Dr. Coffin, from auto mechanics to vice presidents, remained committed to the integration plan. Ralph Mann, for example, did not think the fears and irritations generated by the integration program and vividly expressed in the election campaign were of final importance. They were simply incidents in a long process that was only beginning and would take years to complete. About integration itself he had no doubts.

—I think it had to be done because . . . geographically

there was getting to be such a concentration down in the colored section. These kids were growing up with no exposure to white children. I think it was a good plan. . . .

Like the school board, Ralph was convinced that the issue had not been integration but the superintendent's failures as an administrator, his inability to carry out policies decided by the board; integration, if not yet accomplished, was at least in the course of being achieved. Bennett Johnson, perhaps speaking in his role as unwilling but defeated black candidate (by eleven hundred out of twenty-seven thousand votes), saw it rather differently.

—The board was a very poor board. They never defined what Coffin's area of responsibility was and what their area of responsibility was—just incredible the kinds of basic, fundamental errors they made in management. One of the reasons the racial thing got out of hand was, they failed to set up the right kind of guidelines in the beginning. They say that he violated certain policy guidelines—shit, there were none!

And the people like Ralph who thought the problem was not integration but the way it was being carried out?

—There was only one real basic issue in the campaign— the threat of legitimate racial integration.

There was something oddly uncommunicative about this dialogue, and it was, I decided, the source of the friction that culminated in the bitter election fight. On the one hand, the whites were convinced that they were in favor of integration and that it was taking place; on the other hand, the blacks and their supporters were just as sure that the whites were against integration and that it was being subverted. How could there be such a gap in perception?

The difficulty was the key word: *integration*. To the whites, it meant what had already been done, lifting the black children out of their district and moving them into the white schools. But the blacks wanted something more, something subtler and less easy to define: *legitimate* integration, Bennett called it. Remembering the half-conscious separations of the nonsegregated—but hardly integrated—schools we had both gone to, I could hardly disagree.

Dr. Coffin seems to have grasped this difference early on and to have acted upon it. In one of the combative articles he spun out of his experience in running the program, he expressed the distinction explicitly.

—There is a world of difference between "desegregation" and "integration." The former describes a physical condition; the latter, a state of mind. One must precede the other, for without desegregation there can be no integration. Mere desegregation guarantees nothing, but it is a first step.

Bennett himself told me as much, in a number of different ways, but it took me a while to understand.

—When we were in school, there were just blacks and whites sitting in the classroom. When you talk about integration, you do things to make the black kid feel that he's part of the school. . . . When he came on the scene, Coffin was not an idol of the black community. He really wasn't tuned in to the black thing at all. But the thing I admired about the guy was that he was a student—he *learned*. . . . Over a period of months, he found out what he needed to do in order to integrate the schools and he did it. And this was why he became a bad guy. . . .

Could the integration program have been taken as far as it was without the superintendent's talent for stirring up hostilities? Or was that somehow a necessary motive force in the undertaking? Evy, who had worked under him in the laboratory school, raised the question herself.

—Coffin's hiring was with the understanding that integration was occurring . . . and then the question comes up whether or not there may have been conflicts because of the kind of guy he was, very strong and possibly very arrogant.

. . . In Evanston, we don't like people who are abrasive. . . .

Abrasive had become the word for the superintendent as *intimidation* had become the word for the relations between the black and white children in the newly desegregated schools. And yet, if Evanston's black adults could not reach a stage of reasonable communication with whites until they had passed through the stages of self-consciousness and then hostility, perhaps the same thing was true of their children. In any case, where elsewhere this process has produced burned school buses and bombs and murdered children, in Evanston the violence was only verbal: the town was able both to express its buried antagonisms and then somehow, in those frantic public meetings of the school board, to give them harmless outlets. As much as anything, perhaps, that result was the answer to my basic question about the uses of education: whatever their flights of rhetoric, these were, black and white, a civilized people. And perhaps too, if they had not had, at the right time, an administrator capable of viewing his employers as enemies and himself as a martyr—a man who made himself the target of the fear and hatred he had aroused—the integration program would not have worked as well as it did.

Dr. Coffin's parting gesture suggested that he underestimated his north Evanston neighbors no less than his school board: when his contract expired and he moved away, he rented his costly home to a Negro family. The gesture may or may not have been meant as spite, but the neighbors, who were pleased to have voted against him, were imperturbable and in fact went out of their way to welcome the new family ("if they can afford the house, they can't be *that* bad"). They were, Ralph Mann concluded—

—Very nice people. They kept the place up better than *he* ever did.

It was north Evanston, of course, that had the final word.

8

꘏꘏꘏

Lives: Staying Close

Late on a Saturday afternoon in August of that reunion year, a hundred miles from home, my wife and I found ourselves in a predicament. As we drove off from another classmate's house, something went wrong with the gear shift and the car coasted feebly to a stop. It was one of those new towns that in the past ten years have sprung up in the rolling Maryland countryside between Washington and Baltimore: several thousand acres of Colonial houses and town houses on curving streets surrounding a golf course, a country club, a gas-lit village green with Georgian churches and small shops. Garages and gas stations were not among the amenities the town wanted anywhere near it. I imagined myself spending the next hour on the phone trying to cajole mechanics twenty miles away to come and fix the car and being told, finally, that I would have to wait till Monday. I walked back to the house we had just left to ask where I could get help.

Before I did that, John suggested, perhaps he could have a look. We pushed the car back down the street and put up the hood. Leaning over the fender, he pointed out what had happened: the gear-shift lever was connected to the transmission by a metal sleeve and the screws that held it in place had come out; we could see one empty screw hole. There must be a couple of others underneath. I was impressed. Did he work on cars a lot? No, he explained, but as an engineer he was imagining how the connection would probably have been designed.

Now what? An auto-parts store seemed as remote as a well-equipped garage. We went down to John's basement workshop. In one corner there was a cabinet with small plastic drawers all filled with neatly indexed screws of different sizes, types, threads: wood screws, machine screws, flat-head screws, round-head screws, in steel, stainless steel, brass—hundreds of different screws! He selected a couple in stainless steel that he thought would fit, went up to the car and put them in. That would do, he thought, till we got home. I went into the house with John to say goodbye again. While they waited for us, my wife and his family had been watching television—it was an afternoon when another trio of astronauts was returning from exploring the moon. We stayed a few minutes longer to see the splashdown and then drove home without further incident, marveling at our luck.

Our good fortune on that Saturday afternoon is not the main point of the story, of course, though I am still grateful. The incident is really a kind of object lesson in the rational, problem-solving competence the middle generation aspired to: in whatever field, to find out how things work—not necessarily why—and then put that knowledge to work *doing* things. John's life had been a particularly vivid acting out of several forms of competence that Evanston in our time had meant to transmit. Where he differed was in his immoderate accomplishment.

I remembered the boy I had known in junior high school and high school: John Pritzlaff, with the smooth South German features to match his name; bright, husky, good at math, a builder of models, playing football and golf. Twenty-five years later, I turned up at his house in Crofton and found him almost unchanged, only a little heavier, a little more deliberate in speech. He had been up a ladder fixing his father-in-law's roof, wearing a baseball cap, a T-shirt, shorts. We sat down in the living room to talk, our wives at one end. John's two daughters came in, introduced themselves, and without being asked went out again to bring iced tea and cookies. They sat down on the floor to listen.

—As a group, John observed, I think we were probably rather sheltered in the Evanstonian environment, and we projected that as being what the life-style of the world should be. . . .

John had learned earlier than most of us that there was a difference. With his way paid, like that of a good many others of our generation, by the NROTC program, he studied engineering at Northwestern under a five-year work-study program; it was a time when jobs were still scarce enough that students would submit to the extra year for the sake of the added qualification. In the work part of the program, he learned to be a machinist, and beyond that—

—In going to Northwestern for a quarter and then working in industry for a quarter, you associated with the shop craftsman type and the blue-collar worker. I think with this association during the formative years, you became aware

. . . that there are other ways of living. . . .

John spent three years of active duty in the Navy after college and was sent to Korea as chief engineer on a destroyer. He did not regret the three years of service that had paid for his education, and in fact, in the years that followed, it all fitted together. Immediately, with a master's degree made possible by the revived GI Bill of Rights, he was looking for his first real job in the mid-50s. By then, in contrast to 1950 when most of us finished college, a competent engineer could look forward to a beguiling choice of jobs and salaries with glamorous perquisites. Characteristically—the goals of the middle generation were modest, "enough" money rather than a lot, technical competence rather than the top of the entrepreneurial pyramid—salary was not the deciding factor—

—The GE offer was not the highest but was the most interesting and offered probably the more rewarding career. That probably was one of the better decisions that I have made in my life. . . .

The ten years that followed in Schenectady involved him in the kinds of projects that have been symbolic of the dual role of American industry since World War II: the design of a new kind of electric toaster, an electric carving knife (hot ham was the almost insuperable problem), for the much-wooed consumer; finally, a responsibility for the engineering of the Polaris missile that meant years of indefatigable commuting back and forth to California on overnight planes and growing interest in the means of underwater exploration. Again characteristically, when, about this time, he learned scuba diving, he found that the instructor did not understand what he was teaching, mastered the technology and physiology of diving on his own—and then taught the course himself.

John's special combination of skills, interests, and energy presently came together in the job that took him to the

Westinghouse underseas laboratory in Maryland and work
—first as senior engineer, then as program manager, and
finally with the rather Byzantine title of advisory engineer
—on a machine called Deepstar 4000: a submarine-like
vehicle developed jointly with Jacques Cousteau and intended to carry men to the bottom of the deepest oceans to
explore, find and bring back whatever was there, whether
that was the crew of a drowned submarine, the contents of
a sunken ship, oil, minerals—or the food for an over-
populated future. The straight line of his life had brought
him to a point where he was doing things he deeply wanted
to do, knew how to do. At high schools in the area, he
was in demand as a vocational speaker, and this was the
theme—

—I really do something that I would have done in my
own basement if I had the facilities to do it—might have
been to dabble in building a little submarine. Here at Westinghouse I've had the multimillion-dollar resources of a
gigantic company to help. . . .

John asked me if I'd like to see his workshop, and we
went down. There were a lathe and a drill press (at the time
I did not notice the vast collection of screws); occasionally
to meet a deadline on a project he had come home and
worked most of the night making a particular part. Near
the workbench were his darkroom and several carefully
labeled file cabinets of photographs recording the progress
of various projects. An elaborate electronic system he had
designed and built channeled music from the basement
throughout the house. The powered airplane models he
still built hung from the ceiling. While we talked, a gem
polisher ground away in one corner and we looked at some
of the jewelry he had made. Most of these hobbies had
contributed at one time or another to his work and others
perhaps would as the orderly scheme of his life unfolded:
golf, skiing, sailing on the lovely tidal rivers of Maryland,

square dancing (he was president of the regional association; periodically the family went off to remote hamlets in West Virginia and western Pennsylvania for gatherings of square dancers).

There had been a good deal of talk recently about how various companies were attempting to adapt to the new breed of engineers, scientists, managers: the young men in their twenties who seem conditioned to refuse any assignment until its purposes have been abundantly explained and justified; who don't, in a word, take orders as we on the whole did, on the assumption that if a superior wants something done it must be reasonable. As we went upstairs again, I asked what Westinghouse—or he—was doing about this new generation. John, of course, had long since mastered the delicate postwar art of management by persuasion rather than force. As for the new graduates, ones like those who again that spring had occupied their universities, including even Northwestern—

—The idea that the kids shall run the university—I think they're missing the fact that in real life nature doesn't offer you that option. You get out and you're going to cut down a tree, it's going to fall the way the laws of nature say, and unless you study, analyze, and understand those laws . . . you just can't go out and wield an axe and say, I want it to fall *here*. . . .

But if the universe we lived in was such an orderly place, why were there so many who could not admit its laws? What had happened to them in our lifetime?

—Since the War, the social structure has begun to change so rapidly that the center core of society has become fractionated—the kids growing up can't identify with what is right and what is wrong. . . .

Then what did he think of this new generation, in effect our children, that would be our successors?

—People are created with equal opportunities to achieve,

but their personal capabilities are by no means equal. So many people think that equal opportunity means a guarantee of equalized end achievement. There will be those that are needed to dig the ditches—as well as the guy who designs the ditch that needs to be dug and the guy that designs the machine that does the digging. Now those guys are *not* equal. But each one in his own way can achieve social fulfillment.

It was another of the fixed laws of the orderly and impersonal world that the middle generation had found waiting for it. It seemed a harsh place in which to construct so much personal happiness, so much energy and useful achievement. Yes—

—The reality—the world—is a cold, cruel place to live. . . .

John's wife's parents had retired to that new town in Maryland and he hoped that his own parents would too. It meant that there were things he could do for them like fixing the roof that day I visited him, and it was a responsibility he was glad to accept. Most of the people in the Class of 1946 had stayed close to home in more obvious ways. It was not so much that they felt consciously dependent on Evanston, on the Midwestern homeland; it was simply the shape their lives had taken, and they accepted it, they were at ease with it.

Earlier in the summer, I had spent an evening with Charlyn and Allen Kerr, one of the seven couples who had married within the class and then, after his three years in the Navy, come back to the Chicago area to live, first in an apartment in northwest Chicago, then for the last thirteen years in a newish split-level house in Park Ridge, another close-in suburb about ten miles west of Evanston. It was one of those warm June Illinois evenings. A big fan sent a rush of air across a living room that seemed filled with children and children's friends coming and going, furniture, bags of golf clubs. While we talked, Charlyn worked at a lapful of sewing, a dress for a prom one daughter was going to; at Park Ridge, unlike Evanston, proms were still taken seriously, though with some grumbling about the expense. What was it like living there now?

—Park Ridge is a very antiseptic community, Allen said. There are no blacks in Park Ridge.

—There's one black student, his wife mildly corrected him without looking up from her work. In the high school.

—I think the kids are just seeing a very small slice of life. I think they're very insulated.

—There really isn't a poor section, Charlyn said.

They thought of it, of course, in terms of their children. It was, in fact, a town much as Evanston had been twenty-five years ago, except for the absence of the black community and the patches of relative poverty that set Evanston apart from nearly every other Chicago suburb; and perhaps because of that, Park Ridge had never had that intense self-awareness, that satisfied sense of its own identity. They had not particularly sought that area or a town like that but neither had they avoided it; it was simply that it was near the plant where Allen worked as a printing salesman. They enjoyed being within reach of brothers and sisters and the other relatives in and around Evanston, but they had been comfortable in the early years on their own (the Navy sent them to Guantanamo; Charlyn taught at the school on the base).

We talked about the events of our lives, the political trials, the assassinations, the wars and uprisings, the rhetoric of violence. But these events were merely the past now, their meaning and the emotions that went with them—the rage, fear, grief—remembered but no longer deeply felt. Allen recalled his irritation with the Communist-counting Senator McCarthy—the *other* Senator McCarthy from Wisconsin—but had not been much affected. At the time, his sister had been interviewed by an FBI agent about a college roommate who was working for the government and had replied with the caution one used in those days.

—The agent said to her about this girl, "How would you describe her?" My sister said, "Well, she's just a red-blooded American girl." The guy said, "*Red*-blooded! You mean *blue*-blooded!"

We laughed. That McCarthy was disgraced and dead. It was not easy to remember a time when careers were ruined because of him and those who disagreed were too frightened to complain.

Like everyone in the middle generation, Allen and Charlyn remembered exactly what they had been doing when the news came that a President had been shot, and yet the event itself remained abstract—its meaning, finally, the thought, "that you could have history affected by some deranged man who with one bullet could create such havoc." Charlyn that day was to play with Evanston's symphony orchestra, which had started the year we graduated from high school and had recently celebrated an anniversary; I remembered her as a small girl lugging a cello back and forth to school in its canvas case—she was one of the few who started in Evanston's extensive music program and still played seriously.

—Char was scheduled to play a centennial concert for Evanston the day Kennedy was assassinated. . . . She never gave the concert.

—We all came to the dress rehearsal, Charlyn said, and everybody was there. Everybody wanted to go on with the concert as a memorial. We felt better playing than not playing. Right at the last minute, about eight-fifteen—we didn't give the concert. . . .

From time to time conversation was blotted up in the roar of a jet at O'Hare Airport a few miles farther west, where another new runway had just been finished. Charlyn put her work aside and got up to bring more coffee. We had been talking, really, not about *what* had happened over the twenty-five years but about how life had changed; what was important was the net result, now. That meant one's children and their contemporaries, the new generation about to enter adulthood as we had done. Allen had been teaching Sunday school at their church for years, had organized programs at the high school, done local interviewing for his college. For the past year an exchange student, a blond, handsome Finnish girl, had been living with them, and they were going to miss her when she went home.

—I get really upset when I read in the paper—Allen began and interrupted himself. And yet the kids I have contact with are great kids and they've got fantastic potential. . . .

His obvious liking for his own four children, his ease with them, seemed to spread outward. If there was one thing that worried him, it was drugs, the town's high school as a marketplace for drugs.

—The drug thing really is frightening the people our age today. It's not their ball game, they were never confronted with that themselves, and so they're on very uncertain ground, they feel very unsure, and it's frightening: you know they can get anything they want over at the high school. . . .

The beginning of Allen's life had been marked by his father's loss of his business and his home. The Depression had thrust him, like so many of us, into jobs, a defensive striving for independence; like John, he had earned his college degree through the NROTC and repaid it with three years of active duty. His children's feelings were of course rather different.

—The thing that's discouraging to me, I notice in my son, not so much in my daughters, is that they don't have any motivation to get a job and make money. . . . Parents do a great disservice to their children by giving them everything. . . .

In the course of the evening, the four children and the Finnish exchange student came in one by one and introduced themselves, and finally the youngest, ready for bed: attractive, self-possessed, not, one would say, children a parent need have great anxieties about. It was the children that absorbed their energies, beyond them the school, college, the civilized civic duties, a growing commitment to their church—but not politics. It was not that Charlyn or Allen was repelled by political life, as some of us were, but it seemed remote, unreal.

—I think the feeling all along for me, Charlyn said, has been that social action is extremely important. That's the way I've operated my life. I worked in a settlement house after I got out of college. . . .

She had gone from there, Allen added, to Washington, as secretary to Chicago's intellectual Senator Paul Douglas. They had both, it seemed to me, been consistent with that beginning. It was not the kind of life that unfolds dramatically scene by scene but the steady, accepting, responsible life that many of us in the middle generation had thought we wanted. Against the noisy desperation that has flashed through our time like an electric shock, it was part of my own homecoming to be able to sit down with them for an evening at peace and talk.

—I've been back at school where you're made to feel very old, Bobbie was saying. People don't do it deliberately, but good heavens! There are things I remember. . . . Most of the students weren't born during World War Two and then you're suddenly aware that you really *are* getting on—exposing the fact that you really *are* a different generation. . . .

A clock chimed in the hallway: two in the morning a few days later in my homecoming—we had been talking for five hours. Bobbie Collins—the name suited her tireless energy —had come over after dinner from a PTA meeting; I was spending the night with friends in one of the new northwest suburbs that Evanston people have gravitated to, and they turned out to be neighbors. School, which in the Midwestern vernacular means anything from kindergarten to college, for her meant graduate school at Northwestern. In the midst of raising three children, looking after a home, and being elected to things in the organizations she belonged to, Bobbie had started working on a doctorate in archaeology, and it had turned out to be one of those liberating experiences that for a good many of us came rather late in life, as if we passed through youth too quickly and then rediscovered it in middle age. Bobbie remembered herself in high school as docile, more middle-aged and middle class than she had become. But now—

—Going back to school is quite a thing. Sitting in a PTA meeting or listening to a sermon, I become very uncomfortable, I want to ask questions, and it's a *tyrannical* situation as far as I'm concerned to have to sit and listen to something that you're not in a position to question. . . .

The War and the Depression together had left their imprint—

—I well remember when we didn't have a car. . . . I make it sound as if we were poor—we weren't *poor*, but— . . .

In the year or two of preparedness, as Roosevelt called it, before Pearl Harbor, Bobbie's father had been able to go from a dull job in Chicago to the security of the National Guard and the Army. Before she could settle down to high school at Evanston there had been a succession of Army camps in the South where you learned to ride in the right part of the bus and in one Florida town the people boasted that Negroes were not allowed in town after dark. And perhaps because of that, she was able to perceive, as few whites from Evanston had done even after twenty-five years, that—

—This integration thing—I don't think that school was really integrated in the sense that there was much interaction or socialization. . . .

As for many others, jobs during high school had been a matter of course—waiting on tables at Cooley's Cupboard near Fountain Square, working behind a counter at one of Evanston's department stores. It was not a matter so much of needing a job or of saving for long-term goals, although the money provided immediate things like clothes; it was rather that you were going to *have* a job anyway, and there were things you could do with the money you earned. She had worked on the school newspaper and an annual handbook of information about the school but remembered herself as inactive and had so little confidence in herself that she didn't try for a scholarship at college.

—But what that school did, Bobbie said, was to begin to bring out an interest in things. Once I began joining things at Northwestern, I went overboard, to the point where my grades suffered. It was something you go through, a developmental thing.

She had been president of her sorority—partly, she said, because it was one way of getting a room to herself—immensely involved in doing things. And yet, she thought—

—I'm not a leader type.

After college she had worked several years for a newspaper, trade magazines, writing, editing, doing public relations. What had that been like for a woman starting a career in 1950? How did it seem in retrospect, in the light of all the talk we were hearing that summer about the oppression of women?

—I've always *sort of* been into Women's Lib, I'm told by my husband, Bobbie said, and we laughed. Our lives are pretty well set. But if this had come along when we were launching our careers, it might very well have set me off in a different direction. Anything that increases your awareness of your own culture and your own values—once you're made aware, you can never be the same again.

What followed was marriage, the three children, the parents' gladly doing without things for the sake of the children, their home, clothes, health, summer camps, education—and then a couple of years ago the explosive reawakening of going back to graduate school, deeper than the first experience of college twenty years earlier. There had been archaeological digs at Indian sites in southern Illinois, parties, the day-by-day meetings in class with graduate students almost young enough to be one's children. One learned their language, shared their concerns, hated the war in Vietnam as they did—and then discovered that the difference in generations was not a matter of age but a difference between rhetoric and action, sympathy for an abstract group and concrete help to an individual. Bobbie had experienced, from the students' viewpoint, the strike at Northwestern that followed the shootings at Kent State, the elaborate plans for political campaigning in the fall. And then—

—This year, where was it all? I was really furious. When election time came up, where were these people that were so concerned? It's hard for me to realize that they are young and fickle. In this sense, I think that we've been taken in a little bit. The idealism is fine, but they are not following through. . . .

The same disappointment had touched her more personally about the same time. A daughter had gone through a serious operation, a hazardous event with weeks of convalescence, recovery, and anxiety before and after. Bobbie had stayed away from class to take care of her, and—

—All our neighbors and so on brought dinners over

. . . and all the kinds of things that the suburban WASP middle class that's supposed to be so awful—these were the people that would rally around.

But the fellow graduate students that she thought were friends?

—Even when I went back to school, no one ever *inquired*. And I've never quite figured it out. . . . My conclusion is, these kids are very concerned about world problems . . . but not the guy right next to them. . . .

In spite of that disappointment, she was still responding, still discovering—and in the process questioning attitudes that Evanston's middle generation had accepted as a matter of course. That ingrained dutifulness, for example, that made one avoid things whose only recommendation was enjoyment—

—We seldom go to a movie just to relax—I've never even seen any of the X movies. I think duty might be really one of the basic things in the generation gap. Most of us have worked pretty hard—the PTA, being pressed into something because you feel obliged to do it: I think I've outgrown it. . . .

What about the drug business? There were lurid stories about the affluent new high school where her oldest child went.

—I'm sure that practically every kid at that high school has tried marijuana. And I never have—I really would like to some time, just to see. I can't believe it's too much different than the kids trying liquor when we were in high school. . . . I'm not frightened of marijuana, I'm kind of frightened about the whole situation—I wonder what it is basically that kids want to turn off. . . .

The attitude was, I thought, a lesson in the art of parenthood that most of us had been trying to learn: to accept your children, you first have to be able to accept yourself, your own life. And then? The children would be grown up and gone. What would be left of all that struggle? Was that all it meant to grow twenty-five years older?

—At some point, Bobbie said, you realize that you aren't going to do all the things you thought you were. . . .

And yet Bobbie was not resigned, life was still unfolding, and there were new goals beyond: the degree she was working on, perhaps a children's book about archaeology, perhaps editing, more writing. Wherever it was going, it seemed a satisfying way to live.

The hall clock chimed again, the quarter-hour, half-hour. Work started again in the morning for all of us, and it was time to say goodnight.

When I arrived one evening at Chuck Reding's house on the west side of Wilmette, the North Shore suburb immediately north of Evanston, he apologized for the untidiness of the family room. I looked around. Except for a couple of large cartons on the floor, it seemed immaculate. They were about to move to a new house and had just been packing, Chuck said. The present house was a ranch type built of glazed brick in the severe, rather heavy style of postwar Chicago suburbia; the new one would be older, near the lake, in east Wilmette. Chuck as it happened was one of the three firemen in the Class of 1946. Superficially, his life had not been typical of the men in the group—the salesmen and businessmen, lawyers, doctors, teachers—but the difference was a matter of means rather than ends. In retrospect, it had been a life remarkable for its consistent goals, purposefully pursued. One could hardly have predicted, in 1946, that it would turn out that way.

Chuck's parents had lost their home at the start of the Depression; they moved to another small house in south Evanston, divided it into two flats, and then a few years later that too went, to pay the back taxes. He had not done well at school (math, he said, was his best, everything else was his worst) and after a couple of years at high school dropped out to join the wartime Merchant Marine. When the War was over, he came back to the high school to work for his diploma. I remembered a rotund young man with an air of having outgrown the rest of us under the discipline of service in wartime, as indeed he had: one of the twenty or thirty early veterans who appeared in the school in our last year—in the 1946 yearbook there was a picture of the group, in their uniforms, to publicize the new vocational testing program the school encouraged them to go through. But like others coming out of school at that time, he found that jobs were scarce even for veterans, waited around for a while, and then joined the Army. After three years as an MP, he was back in Evanston, looking for work again, and was able to get taken on as an apprentice mason, laying brick. Apprenticeship, mastering the trade—it was the first in the series of definite, realizable goals, each leading to the next, that had given his life its orderly shape. At each stage, Chuck and his wife, a silent, dark-haired, attractive woman with an air of decisiveness, had worked out carefully what they would commit themselves to next. Each decision, it seemed, was rooted in the anxieties of those earliest years. After six years as a bricklayer—

—Now what worried me the most, Chuck said, was, what do I do in the wintertime now, laying brick, when I have the wife to support and a couple of kids eventually to support? So this is one of the reasons I got on the fire department.

With his fireman's schedule—twenty-four hours on duty, forty-eight hours off—he was able to go on laying brick on his own. (Several people told me about another man in the class, a fireman in Evanston, who started by using his free time putting up aluminum storm-windows and screens, another novelty of the postwar years, and now owned a big house in Evanston, rental property all over town, a resort motel in northern Illinois—in effect, a rich man.) They bought the house, worked at paying off the mortgage, still anxious; a house was something that could be taken away from you.

—Another thing that worried me, Chuck continued, was when we bought this house, now what happens if we lose this place? This gave me an incentive to work a little bit harder, and after we got better on our feet I says, well, we've always wanted a farm. . . .

His parents were against the idea ("You know, if you've got that money, put it in an apartment building or just leave it in the bank"). And with the house paid off, there was the worry about another mortgage, but they bought the farm.

—We didn't want to mortgage the farm, we wanted it outright, so rather than mortgage the farm we remortgaged this house. . . .

There was a color photograph of the land, the farmhouse, framed, on the wall of the family room, and I got up to look at it: 113 acres two hundred miles north, in the lovely rolling hills of central Wisconsin, where the hardwoods go gold and crimson in the fall as they do in New England. Twenty head of cattle, hay, a trout stream. His doubting parents had gone up there to live, and Chuck and his family made the long drive often, for weekends. It was another form of security: the worst you could think of could happen, you could lose your job, house, but—

—This gives us confidence, we've got this to go out there. And I can still lay brick. . . .

Ten years earlier, when the fallout shelter panic had come and then gone again—

—I'm one of these, Chuck said, that if we don't do it now and something did happen, well, what are we going to do? Well, I built a shelter, it's right under here—he pointed to the basement below us—it's all concrete and that. As a matter of fact, after building this one, I built five more, for different people. . . . I at least want to do everything possible to save—well, everyone wants to *save* themselves, and naturally I don't hope that anything like that ever *happens*. . . .

While we talked, the open radio connection with the firehouse crackled from time to time in the living room, but it was a quiet night, apparently. Chuck refilled my glass. His son and daughter came in and were introduced. Both were in high school at Evanston's affluent rival, New Trier, the boy a year or two younger than his sister; they seemed indistinguishable from the other young people of the new generation that I had been meeting on the well-to-do North Shore. (Chuck worried about the boy's grades and the blond nimbus of hair surrounding his head, but at least, he said with satisfaction, it was clean—his son wouldn't go to school in the morning until he'd washed it.)

—We are hoping and are pretty sure they will go to college. . . . We even want the daughter to go. . . .

How did his son feel about bricklaying? Did they work together? Chuck was planning to teach his son the work that summer—

—He doesn't have that much of an interest—to him it means money in the summertime. If nothing else, it's a knowledge, a craft. I don't care whether he *does* it or not. . . . We want him to go to college for four years and we don't care what he does after that, but he'll have the knowledge —he can go on the fire department for all I care.

Had his son reached an age where his ideas were beginning to take shape?

—The boy hasn't really settled down yet—he says O.K. to college.

It had been sixteen years now in the fire department; in another four years Chuck would be able to retire with a pension. And then? After all the years of building things brick by brick, he had thought about building in a larger sense and had wanted seriously to become an architect—he talked appreciatively about the several important houses in the area from Frank Lloyd Wright's Chicago years, he had studied them. He had gone into the possibilities thoroughly, the two years of university extension courses that it would take, the year of resident study—and then he and his wife talked it over and decided it was beyond reach. Instead, after twenty-five years of building bungalows, garages, small apartment buildings, he wanted to try large-scale construction, "something big," for a few years. And finally, with the children through their four years of college—

—We want a ranch, now. We decided on Texas for that, when I'm fifty. We don't want a big ranch. . . .

Other men that summer, in the uneasiness of middle age, were talking about making some radical change in their lives—they would quit their jobs, emigrate, go into politics, take up school teaching, write a book—but the impulse was vague. In Chuck's case, one shared his confidence that it really would happen as he intended. It seemed an enviable prospect for a man to look forward to at fifty.

—We've hit every goal that the wife and I aimed for. You don't give up when you get to the top of the ladder; if you do, you're sliding down and you're decaying. So we have to set our sights higher again and keep climbing, until— well, just keep up until the day you die.

9

※※※

Lives: Leaving It Behind

—I've never been out of work a day, Jim said, but I've had a hell of a lot of jobs since we got out of high school, I've done a million things. I seem to be awfully discontent, I can't stand a job more than two or three years. . . . Florida and Albuquerque and Chicago and Evanston and Wisconsin and so forth: I just get restless after two or three years. . . .

Jim Crandall was the man in the Class of 1946 who had missed graduation by a quarter of a credit (a typing course) and then in that first summer after the War hitchhiked to California to look for work, only to find that there were jobs for veterans but not for a boy fresh out of high school;

he hitchhiked home again to enlist but at the last minute changed his mind and walked away from the swearing-in. His life had been a succession of such turning points: there would come a time when there was nothing he could do but turn his back and walk away, starting with Evanston itself, the high school, the Evanston way of looking at things. But it was still an Evanston standard that he judged himself by, and, looking back, he was embarrassed by the impulse that had led him to all the jobs, the moves around the country, uncomfortable talking about it even though it was not something he could have changed.

Physically, Jim was still much as I remembered him except for the dark hair getting thin above the forehead: a tall, muscular man with a gentle face, an individual way of putting words together. I asked him why he hadn't gone to the reunion.

—I was a little against the place they chose, Jim said. Chevy Chase is quite an exclusive country club—and expensive—and I thought for me to spend twenty-five dollars plus drinks to go out there. . . . I had the feeling that the ones who did go back were probably the more successful ones, I may make more than some of the successful ones, but I still am a little embarrassed about being with successful businessmen, I feel a little ill at ease. I don't like to put up a front, I don't know quite how to put it. . . .

It was mid-afternoon. In three or four hours Jim would have an early dinner with his wife and daughter, leave for work on the night shift. He lived in one of the new small suburbs on the remote southwest fringe of Chicago, surrounded by big roads, an expressway. At night there was so much noise from the roads that you could not sleep with the windows open, but the apartment was air-conditioned. Immediately west, there was a belt of the forest preserve that borders Chicago with immense first-growth woodland, beyond that, the ancient prairie cut up into cornfields and towns, stretching west to the Mississippi. The apartment was in one of a small group of three-story buildings set around an inner plot of grass like a wagon train drawn up in a defensive circle for the night; crushed stone had been laid down around the outside for the cars.

Jim ran a bridge crane at a dock on the marshy Calumet River, Chicago's deep-water port; besides the bridge crane, there were two Manitowak cranes with long booms, a couple of mechanics to keep the fleet of fork-lifts running, the big gang of longshoremen, nearly all black now where a few years ago they would have been Irish. In the winter, when ice closed the port, he would work at repairing the equipment, teaching himself welding in the process—not, he said, because he was really a mechanic, but it was something he was good at, he enjoyed being able to do it. Running the crane was tense work.

—When you're unloading, these ships are so big you can't see down in the hold, so you have a signalman on the deck. You're working through another man's eyes, with no idea what's going on and half the time the signalman is drunk and you have this constant fear, any moment you might kill someone or destroy some valuable property. . . .

Sometimes the equipment failed and a whole load let go; men had been killed on other docks but not on his.

In Albuquerque, he had reached another limit of patience—working in the parts department of a Ford agency, then a car-rental business, then selling campers for a small local manufacturer—when a friend had written about the crane operator's job in Chicago and after the years in the Southwest desert with the red dust, the dry, ceaseless winds, they moved back with the Midwesterner's joy in returning to a moist green land ("You suffer through a winter and then spring comes and it seems so beautiful— you have to suffer a little bit to appreciate something"). The job had not materialized immediately; for a year and a half he had worked on the unloading dock of one of the huge truck terminals I had passed on my way to see him and had enjoyed the work ("And you can make a good buck if you want to put in a few extra hours"). Now, running the crane, he could afford a vacation in Acapulco during the slack winter months.

We talked about some of the jobs. Before going to New Mexico, Jim had worked in an auto-parts store in Evanston, gone into partnership in a service station, driven a fuel-oil truck, traveled northern Illinois as a salesman for an auto-parts wholesaler, worked as a claim adjuster for an insurance company. The selling jobs, he thought, had been best, he seemed to have a knack for that, but he had had bad luck: the owner of one parts wholesaler had gotten too interested in his secretary, gone bankrupt, and paid him off with worthless checks; the camper manufacturer in Albuquerque had folded up about the time he came back from the road with a thirty-six-thousand-dollar order and a firm deadline for delivery. He would not have changed his life. He mentioned a friend who started as a claims adjuster when he did, was now a manager, well paid—and miserable, with no way out because that was all he knew how to do; it was the way he would be if he had stuck it out.

—If all else fails, Jim said, apparently there's still a mechanic shortage in the country and I think I could go into a garage and work as a mechanic. I hate getting my hands greasy . . . but those guys make awful good money. . . .

Jim had thought a lot about his restlessness and largely understood it even if it was not something he could change. In the 30s there had been a succession of grade schools as his parents moved in pursuit of jobs. During the War, while he was in high school, they had been able to stay put in Evanston, but to do it his father worked two jobs and Jim hardly saw him. His natural intelligence was vitiated in resistance—skipping school, finding other rules that could be broken, drinking beer at the shabby bars dotted across the undeveloped land west of Evanston. Of his friends at the time, he remembered one boy who stole cars "for fun," another who specialized in stealing parts.

—I think mainly my problem then was recognition. My father—we still don't get along too well. There was no relationship at all between he and I and still is very little. ... We talk like a couple of strangers, we carry on conversations. . . . Thinking back, I think it was just a lack of any close relationship with a man that probably caused me to go wrong, because I definitely went wrong . . . and I've definitely straightened out. . . .

Jim and his father had tried repeatedly over the years to get together again—in the service station partnership, the fuel-oil business, the car-rental business in Albuquerque—but it had never worked. From very far back there had been not only the restlessness, the compulsive resistance to authority, but a fierce striving for independence.

—When I was ten years old I was running paper routes and collecting junk and taking it to the junkyard for money. I was always a worker—I couldn't wait to leave home. I left home when I was seventeen—lived in the same town, in a rooming house. . . .

I asked how his wife felt about the various moves, the changing jobs. It did not seem to be a life women cared much for.

—I'm happy—we both are happy. We had some times during the early years of our marriage that it caused some trouble between us—changing jobs all the time and the moving—which originally gave my wife kind of a feeling of insecurity. And I can see why, he added.

His wife had made the difference in his life. Jim told me the story.

—I married a girl who graduated from high school, from

Evanston, a year before we did. We went together in high
school and then she went off to college . . . and she wound
up marrying a fellow. . . . A real bad one, he left her and
there was no support or anything—he went and joined the
Army. She came back to Evanston and finally got a divorce.
I wound up marrying her. She had a baby who was fifteen
months old . . . a boy. He's twenty-three now. . . . I raised
him as if he were my own son. We adopted him right after
we were married and he knows no other father—we're
very close. . . .

Thinking of what he'd said about his own father, of the
conflicts that seem to be inseparable from a boy's growing
up, I asked him how he and his son got along.

—He's an entirely different type of person than I am.
He's a bookworm and reads an awful lot . . . not a doer. I
do love to read but I am very mechanically inclined, I can
fix anything, I can take care of my own cars and appliances
. . . and he is totally helpless and we had nothing in common. I tried to be a good father and play ball with him and
all these things that a father should do—it just generally
didn't work out too good. But all through it he knew that
he was loved and wanted. . . .

The boy had stayed in New Mexico, going to college
there and coming back to Chicago for the summer to work.
There came a time when, like most sons of the middle
generation, he let his hair grow, long and curly, to his
shoulders, and Jim, like most fathers of our generation, had
issued a paternal ultimatum: when you're self-supporting,
you can cut your hair any way you want, but as long as you
sit at my table and eat my food, you're going to cut it the
way I say. The boy, like Jim himself, accepted the challenge
and moved out, to a rented apartment. (A month later,
however, he came quietly home, with his hair, for the time
being, cut.) The word *love*, I noticed, was often on Jim's
lips, not only about his wife, their son, their daughter, but

about the old friends who had drawn them back to Chicago, the camping trips into the New Mexico desert, the coming home again: as if every part of his life were touched by love. The boy was working on a master's degree, had taken a job in a bank while he waited out the scarcity of teaching jobs (his hair cut short again for the purpose), and now he too was planning to get married.

—I got a letter from him Father's Day that made everybody cry, Jim said. Telling that he's about to marry a girl that has a baby. . . . He's been going with her for two years. Been married before: he wrote, saying that my marriage had been so successful and I'd been so successful in raising him that he feels this is not an obstacle. . . .

It seemed an admirable and accurate tribute.

To get to Chuck Head's farm, I drove south from Chicago, then straight across the state from near the Indiana line almost to the Mississippi, following the worn, narrow, cement secondary roads laid out in the rectangular geometry of Illinois counties and townships. I remembered the Illinois earth that you see freshly plowed at the end of winter, rhythmically furrowed like the waves of a sea, with the black shine of fresh-pumped crude oil: the inexhaustible prairie loam still five or six feet deep. Now, in early July, the fields were thick with the region's two crops: knee-deep in dark green, big-leaved soybeans, the field corn lighter in color and already shoulder-high, head-high; twenty-five years ago, there would have been grain as well, oats and wheat, but now it is the corn and soybeans that bring the money. There had been no rain for three weeks. In the small towns the grass around the houses was already yellow and dry, the soil under it turning to dust, but women were out cutting it anyway with power mowers because it was Saturday. At Peoria you cross the Illinois

River, part of Chicago's water link to New Orleans and the Gulf: a mile wide between bluffs, seeming at that point as big as the Mississippi. From there, the route slants northwest again toward Galesburg, where Carl Sandburg was born. Everywhere now the land is deeply slashed and hummocked by rivers flowing urgently southeast to the Illinois, southwest to the Mississippi. One of them is the Spoon River; you remember that there really was a Spoon River, that Edgar Lee Masters was educated, like Sandburg, at Galesburg. Finally I was heading south again, toward a country town too small to be indexed on most road maps; then past a white clapboard country church, along a succession of graveled roads with the yellow dust in billowing clouds behind the car, and at last I was at the gate of Chuck's farm, climbing the lane past old trees and a couple of ponies lounging in an unused field to a white farmhouse with the narrow weathered look of the 90s about it, set on a rise, with a wide porch running around three sunny sides.

A red tractor was parked beside the house, a pickup truck, the family station wagon. Behind the house, with roses planted around it, was a fenced vegetable garden wilting in the dry July heat, a fenced patch of bare earth holding a couple of sleek black steers, a 4H project of Chuck's older girls. The barn behind the vegetable garden, as old as the house, was falling down; that year he had built a new one beside it of green corrugated steel, a type I had noticed at several farms along the way. It is not a country of big barns, the climate is mild enough, 175 miles southwest of Chicago, for the cattle to forage outdoors all winter. There were a few white chickens bobbing and pecking beside the house, a swarm of kittens playing on the porch. A sleepy-looking black-and-white collie roused himself and came in when I knocked at the door.

It was a little after noon, and Chuck was just back from the morning's work. His hands were hard, with dirt ingrained in the grooves of calluses (later he mentioned having to give up their cow because his fingers had grown too stiff with muscle to milk it). Physically he seemed unchanged since high school, with hard muscles all over his burly body. His wife, a dark motherly woman, was in the kitchen finishing the meal.

We ate on the porch outside the kitchen, Chuck and I and his wife, with the older children, the youngest at a small table off to one side: beef from the farm, peas from the garden, a salad, iced tea. They did not consider this dinner, Chuck explained, the main meal was in the evening. The big mid-day meal of the past, with farm hands and family gathered around a trestle table, has vanished into American folklore; with the proliferation of machines, a man like Chuck can now run a family-size farm almost single-handed.

After lunch, we sat at the table and talked. Chuck's father had been a quite well known Evanston surgeon, his brothers had become doctors and still lived in the area. How had he happened to choose so different a life?

—I don't like city life, that's for sure, Chuck said in his rather bluff voice. I mean, being brought up in Evanston —that's one of the reasons I chose farming. That sixteen years of school was just—you know.... I like the outdoors, being outside, and all it entails. Being in an office building or a hospital like my father or brothers just wasn't appealing.

Did he remember Evanston as cold, remote, aloof?

—This is the thing about Evanston—and any town, really—that we had next-door neighbors that we didn't even get to know.

With the new self-sufficiency of the machines, life here was no longer as close as it must once have been, and yet —

—The neighbors will get together to vaccinate hogs, the

men will, there's still that element. And we'll get together to load cattle. . . . I'll borrow a neighbor's implement if I think I need it at the time—like I don't have a rotary hoe but you don't need a rotary hoe every year. So I'll borrow my neighbor's rotary hoe. And I have a drill—grain drill, for planting wheat—and he doesn't have a drill, so he'll come in and borrow my drill. We'll trade implements like that. . . .

It seemed an attractive kind of life, but it was also a business, a word Chuck used, with its own problems of capital, production, marketing (selling the beef and pork had recently been complicated by the closing of the Chicago stockyards).

—I like it out here but you have your anxieties just like any other person. It appeals to a city person but then when you get here it has problems, they're just different problems. . . .

But a wonderful life for one's children, I suggested, thinking of my anxieties over my own.

—My father always says that he thinks our family has the best upbringing, but that gets my brothers mad because they have their lives in town and think their lives are pretty rewarding too. . . .

Evanston had been only part of his family's life. They had owned a farm near Chicago—the home farm, Chuck called it—and went there often.

—Our family was the main—you know, we were always together, and with the farm—something going on out there. We'd go out there and ski on the weekends or sled —there were good hills to go down.

In 1940, when a man from Indiana named Wendell Willkie had run for President, they had gone to a huge political rally at Evansville that sounded in retrospect like a nineteenth-century camp meeting.

—The whole family went and camped out in a tent. To

hear Wendell Willkie. . . . They came from all over and camped out on the parkside or in the woods, pitched a tent. . . . All the hoopla and flag-waving—seeing him, in person, that was the big thing, you had to get right up there. And I was on my father's shoulders. . . .

Chuck spoke with admiration of his father, who had taught Latin before going into medicine; now in retirement he was writing, painting, studying philosophy. In effect, as a farmer Chuck had modeled his life on one side of his father's life, his brothers on another. After high school and college in the East, Chuck had studied agriculture at a state university in the Midwest and then for six years had worked his family's farm near Chicago; nearly ten years ago they had moved to the larger place south of Galesburg, and over the years he had added to it—some of his fields now were five miles down the gravel roads by tractor.

While we sat at the lunch table on the porch and talked, his wife cleared away the dishes and the children dispersed. Presently the oldest girl, fourteen, came back insisting on driving the truck a mile down the road to a cousin's. Why couldn't she ride her bicycle? The girl persisted; in front of a guest, her father could not be quite as firm as he wished. Finally as a great privilege he let her try the truck, but only in the pasture below the house and only in low gear. We listened a little anxiously while the truck started up and moved slowly down the lane.

With the pickup truck whining in the distance and occasionally visible, we talked about the life of the past twenty-five years. How had it changed? What had seemed important?

—In my own business, farming, the technical end of it has certainly been changed tremendously. Chemicals and horsepower. . . .

There had been much talk that year about chemical fertilizers, insecticides, organic gardening if not farming. Did he worry about that sort of thing?

—Fertilizer—it's been there ever since I started farming —it's becoming more prevalent. I've always used it but neighbors haven't . . . and there are still a few neighbors that don't. But it's been on the increase. But what I've noticed is the horsepower revolution on the farm. I can run five hundred acres now where I had a heck of a time running a hundred and eighty when I started out—or a hundred and twenty really, cropland. And now I'm doing twice as much work or more than twice as much as when I started out. . . . The equipment has gotten bigger and more powerful. . . .

What did that mean in practical terms, for him personally?

—Number of plows you could pull. In farming, when we went up on our home farm, there was horses still used at times, in the thrashing rings and hauling manure . . . for general chores around, they always had the horses. And it was only after the War that the tractor came in and the horses were put to pasture. Literally. Our neighbor was a big farmer and had horses right up to the end. And after the War, he put his horses out to pasture on our farm and never used them again. They were just there because he loved them so and didn't want to get rid of 'em. Great big Percherons. And he was proud of 'em. . . . It's a whole nother way of life.

Inevitably too we talked about the war in Indochina and the wars that in our memories had preceded it. We both retained clear images of the Japanese in China in the 30s, the atrocities in Shanghai and Nanking, the women and babies slashed by bayonets. One of Chuck's brothers had been shot down over Yugoslavia during World War II, lost for months, finally spirited out by Tito's Partisans. As we talked, we remembered the brainwashing of the American prisoners in the Korean War, the betrayals of Americans by Americans.

—They gave in to get a square meal, Chuck said. They weren't, you might say, indoctrinated enough in our way of life, in what they were fighting for, to have that override —as a religious person would be. With a person with religious convictions, you can do anything to them physically and they can come through it and bear up with it. . . .

Like a few others in the Class of 1946, Chuck in middle age had gone through a deepening of his religious life, a reaching out from the center of family and home to the world our children were growing into. The Vietnam War?

—I think it was necessary—all the way: we had to do *something*. I like the idea of Vietnamization, where they do their own fighting. This is the Russians' attitude . . . people fighting for them all over the world, and we're just naive enough to throw our own men in—and honest enough, is what it comes down to. . . .

What about the stories of atrocities that had been coming out, of whole units absorbed in marijuana and heroin? Didn't that change one's feelings about the war?

—To me the whole thing is that people in this country are trying to discredit America and the military and our position as the power that is. And if it isn't drugs, it's something else.

His wife called down from upstairs about the girl driving the truck in circles in the pasture. He called up that he would do something about it. We stood up. I had noticed the shotgun leaning near the side door of the house. Did he hunt? No, he said, he might, if he had to, shoot a raccoon that was stealing his chickens, but he did not like to kill things for pleasure. We shook hands again and I went down the porch steps to my car. Chuck set off down the lane in pursuit of the wandering truck, a gentle man, firm in his certainties.

—Very good causes can wreck people and make them ugly, Eunice said. Inside and out.

We were sitting across from each other at a table on the terrace behind her house, drinking coffee. A Maryland suburb of Washington. Behind the house the ground sloped up, half in shade from big trees beyond. Along one side of the back yard there was a strip of vegetable garden. That summer, repulsive photographs of protest leaders—Women's Lib, antiwar—has been turning up in the news magazines and I had assumed that was why they were published. Eunice—or Eunice Luccock Corfman, to give Eunice her full name, the married name under which she writes—had seen the same look in people she knew and thought she understood it: rage, "the black rage that just *spews* and you've got to let it spew for a while." She reminded me of the man who had burned himself, in Washington, as a kind of protest at the war in Vietnam—

—Two or three years ago, you remember when Norman Morrison immolated himself in front of the Pentagon—he was a Quake that set fire to himself with his child. . . . That culminated a period of time in which a lot of people that I had known looked the same way. . . . I saw really damaged psyches that did the same sort of draining, they looked really odd. One of them, his face got all misshapen, one side of his face slid down. . . .

Quake, I noticed she said, with a certain diffidence, because she had become a Quaker herself: the fact and the diffidence are part of the remove from Evanston. The public tensions—the Quaker vigils in front of the White House, the mass demonstrations in Washington for peace—had come in the midst of three years of intensive work toward a doctorate in philosophy. At her university—

—First we had a takeover. . . . Last year the university was occupied for three weeks . . . tear gas and stuff. It escalated into war protest and then there were so many things being protested you didn't know what stood for what. . . . I'm an old lady and I guess I can't take it.

Suddenly also there were no jobs to be had for a teacher with a new Ph.D. and the degree, the dissertation which was to be on civil disobedience, had become futile. Not only that: why had she felt the need in the first place for anyone's arbitrary stamp of approval on the value of what she had learned, the dissertation she was writing? It would be a weakness to go on with the degree. She had given it up.

To become middle-aged is to have learned to exclude certain kinds of experience, especially, perhaps, if one is of the middle generation, formed by Evanston and the Midwest. One of the things that had made Eunice a writer was her ability to go on experiencing things, intensely. Because she had been able to write about it, she had lived more of the life of our generation than most of us.

Eunice and her husband had met at college and married in their senior year. Living near Boston while her husband went to medical school they had begun having the four children that at the time seemed to most of us the proper and dutiful thing to do, the healthy thing. And there too, while earning a master's degree at Radcliffe, she had begun to teach herself to write. That had been the beginning of the television years, when people invited each other to their homes to watch; when you left a party early and hurried back to see a new play by Paddy Chayevsky or Tad Mosel on the seven-inch screen. Eunice wrote three scripts herself, submitted them to a network: after months of waiting, one was accepted.

With medical school finished, her husband had joined a group practice in New York State and they had built a modern house looking out on the Catskills. In the mornings she could work at a novel; on hot afternoons there was a natural pond at the foot of a waterfall to walk to across a

field of their land. It seemed to her, looking back, a supremely, luxuriously, private life. It was at this time that
she and her husband had begun going to Quaker meetings
and gradually had become Quakers themselves. That life,
but not—to use the old-fashioned Quaker phrase—the concerns that began with it, ended when the clinic broke up
and Eunice's husband moved from practice to research and
a job with the National Institutes of Health near Washington.

In Washington, the novel written and published, there
was a steady march of short stories in literary quarterlies
and monthlies, occasionally in one of the slicks. She had
become fully a writer in the sense that the things most
deeply on her mind took natural shape in written words,
as a short story, an article, a planned book. In Washington,
Eunice had been ordering her ideas of prison reform,
which had become articles published locally; she was thinking now about city housing. Like others going back to
college, she had adopted something of the outlook, language, dress of the graduate students; athletic, intense, she
would fit in. If she differed from the young, it was in seeming so physically happy ("pathologically happy," she described herself at the time of the crisis over the doctoral
degree).

Inside the house while we talked, one of the younger
boys had come into the living room and was playing
"Chopsticks" on the harpsichord Eunice and her husband
had built.

I asked her, as I had asked others, about politics, leadership. Most of us had not even gotten as far as the current
forms of activism—the demonstrations, the sit-ins, the
vigils. Could she imagine herself going farther, into something like formal politics in any traditional sense?

—I think we are not a leading generation.

What was it? The time? The special set of opportunities,

exclusions, responsibilities that Evanston had taught us?

—It's one of my feelings about our generation: we're kind of a sandwich generation, towed by followers of those that came before. . . . I have always had the feeling, it's not my turn, wherever I am. The War wasn't ours, even the people who'd done the fighting weren't us. . . .

A writer can hardly avoid thinking about his natural audience and his natural subject—his own generation—and as you get older it becomes more important. Did she remember the stupid phrase of fifteen years ago: the silent generation?

—There's no one our age as I think of it that was ever a culture-setter. For whatever reasons, it does seem that people before and after were the drummers—I don't know why. It wasn't that we were silent so much as nobody ever listened—not even us. Nobody thought it important to listen to us—our novels, our poetry, our feelings, our sensibilities weren't something interesting—the way we listen avidly to a youth culture now. . . .

Or as avidly refuse to listen, I thought later, but it comes to the same thing. You grow middle-aged, then old, and youth crashes over you like a wave, whether you listen or not.

—I went to college, Janet Warren told me, I finished college, I said, "What can you do about being a Socialist in the United States in 1950?" There isn't very much you can do—you can try to be useful to the working people. So I went off to be a union organizer. . . .

I had gone to Janet's office on the top floor of an old building overlooking Union Square in New York, the headquarters of the union for which she was now chief counsel. It was a twilight Friday afternoon and she had cleared her desk of all but emergencies so that we could talk. I had remembered a tall rather thin girl with an intellectual stoop, an air of mental quickness. She had filled out a little, becomingly, she seemed taller, athletically erect, her face serene and unlined. The mind still seemed immensely quick but with the sense of good will there was also now a lawyer's careful exactitude as she spoke that could, one imagined, be formidable. Our time had somehow not encouraged women to pursue careers and in the Class of 1946 there were few women professionals of any kind, no others who were lawyers. I had asked how it had come about.

—If you are an organizer in the South, Janet continued, you are inevitably confronted by the law.

There was a foot-and-a-half length of three-inch pipe on her desk, mounted on a handsome piece of mahogany. Janet explained it—

—The lead pipe on my desk is from the day I got kidnapped. And of course it was me that got arrested, not the people that had kidnapped me.

What charge had they used?

—Incitement to riot! You get annoyed and figure maybe it's more useful to practice law. And so I went to law school specifically and only with the notion of practicing labor law.

The decision itself was unlike any other I had encountered, but the way it had come about was characteristic of the middle generation: having perceived the problem, you set about acquiring the specific skills needed to solve it. I was still astonished that she had thought of herself as a Socialist. Had that come about in college, as it did for so many in the previous generation?

—I became a Socialist in the eighth grade, I think. I came home from school one day and said, "I found out what I am." And my parents were quite taken aback. I never heard an advocate of Socialism until after I was in college. I certainly never read any propagandistic literature until the same time. . . .

The law, labor law, had other roots in Janet's life. She had gone South in 1951, a young white woman with a master's degree, working sometimes with white, sometimes with black, workers in a still largely unorganized industry. The Supreme Court decision desegregating the schools would not come till 1954, and Martin Luther King's revolution on the buses of Montgomery, Alabama, did not begin till the year after that. That it took courage to be a union organizer in the South in 1951 seems obvious enough. It also needed an unshakable stubbornness about principles.

—I had the feeling in the South that I would by God ride in the back of the bus. Because I did not like the notion of being told I couldn't. . . .

Today, it seems hard to imagine that the obsession with segregation could have produced not only separate schools but separate swimming pools, toilets, seats on buses. At the time, it helped if you had a mind that could perceive and appreciate the absurdity—

—In addition to feeling outraged by the system, one of the saving graces of coping with it was that you could always laugh at it. When I first went South, the first segregation sign I saw was on a highway—a pulloff—and it said: "Viewing Area—White." . . . It broke me up. . . .

Although like most of us she recoiled from the abrasions of politics, Janet missed being able to get out to the local union in Mobile, the picket line in Chattanooga, where life seemed "more interesting and three-dimensional." Instead, now, there were the complexities of the law moving laboriously across her desk.

—My industry, you see, is about twenty-five years behind the times. Most industries are basically organized. This industry is eighty-five percent unorganized. We live in 1937.

That was the year, I remembered, of the bloody heads and faces at the sit-in strikes in Detroit. Was that what she meant?

—In Louisiana we had our shop activist beat the hell up two months ago. But that was unusual enough that we noticed it. It was an imported goon who had been flown out as soon as the job was over. The local DA said it's not a felony and therefore it's not an extraditable offense and therefore we won't go after him. We are presently considering bringing civil rights action against the employer, the police department, the mayor. . . .

That seemed to have been the pattern in the South. Did it work?

—We wrote to the Attorney General in connection with this. By and large nothing comes of it. One goes through certain motions. . . .

Like the others I talked to, I asked Janet what her feelings had been about "the assassinations," meaning John Kennedy's and those that followed. Janet alone thought first of a death that had preceded that one.

—The day Medgar Evers was killed, I was with an English friend who . . . reacted by saying that this struck her as being an unbelievably typical reflection of the American nature. Had it happened when she first came to this country, she would have thought that the killing and the by-and-large acceptance of it was enough to cause one to go away . . . and that whereas now she wouldn't react in that fashion, she wasn't sure but that her first reaction had been the healthy one. I think by and large I concur with that. . . .

We talked about the future as it had looked to our crop of eighteen-year-olds twenty-five years ago, graduating from high school: a world radiant with peace, of rebuilt societies and reasonable institutions for preventing misery. Not much of that had happened. What *had* become of our optimism, our self-assurance? What had been most important in her life?

—The American South, I guess—the whole package. Southern workers are, God knows, tremendously brave people. I've been in strike situations with people whom I couldn't respect more. And the other side of the coin of that bravery very often is a kind of mindless will to violence . . . a real reminder of what kind of animals we are. . . .
We would hardly have set out, it seemed to me, if we had known what was ahead. Was that all our hopes amounted to?

—I think, Janet said slowly, that one of the almost universal differences between older people and younger people is that older people are more concerned with immediacies, with personalnesses, and less concerned with ideologies and truth. I get much more satisfaction now from climbing a mountain or watching the dog or from pruning a tree than I would have expected twenty-five years ago that I could. Therefore it is not so catastrophic to confront the fact that the world has indeed not turned into Utopia.

Was it justice? I asked, still puzzled over the motives that led her from Evanston to the Southern picket lines, from there to law school and the practice of labor law. Through the years of the civil rights movement and all the other debates of our time, we had heard many passionate arguments, but justice, it seemed to me, had rarely been among them. I had not met many people in my life for whom it was supremely important.

For answer, Janet talked about a dispute she had been trying to resolve, turning on an apparently technical question of seniority. But it was justice, not law or the complex provisions of a union contract, that both sides appealed to: for all, the idea was important, whatever they might mean by it

—I think that one may be more or less lucky as to how wide-ranging a view of what constitutes justice one may have. . . .

Then was it justice, finally, that moved her?

—I don't suppose it's the only thing, Janet answered with a final precision. But certainly it moves me very much.

10

In the Time Machine

In our lifetime, the ancient human dream of travel through space has become a reality limited only by manufacturing techniques, engineering competence, and fuel capacity: the backdrop to the reunion of the Class of 1946 included the plans for the latest moon exploration, which in the summer that followed became merely another living-room wonder of an age of television. Travel through time, however, remains a fantasy, as it was in the childhood of the middle generation, its only vehicle imagination and memory.

If in that summer of our graduation I had been able to travel twenty-five years into the future, I would have found a world in some ways not so very different from the one I knew. The cities would be sprawled farther into the countryside. The suburbs surrounding the cities would be increasingly dense, increasingly remote from open land, but the houses themselves, though often spread in relentless files across the hundreds or thousands of acres of a development, would mostly come in familiar shapes; you would have to live there for weeks or months before you recognized what was new—the building materials inside and out that had not existed, the almost universal clothes washers and dryers, dishwashers and television sets—and by then they would no longer seem strange, life itself would not seem much different. If you traveled into a city, you would find it thickly rebuilt at the center in glass and metal instead of stone and brick, but that too one had already anticipated in 1946, broadly if not in detail. Around that core, however, if you stayed long enough, you would indeed find something unimaginable, inexplicable: the blocks and blocks of houses and apartment buildings with their windows smashed and their insides ripped out, falling in rubble into the basements. Thinking of the long rows of leveled houses in the London of 1946, you might say that there had been a war, and in a sense you would be right.

If you could linger in that future 1971 and read its newspapers, you would discover something else: that most of the political and social ideas that were glowing with hope in that first year after the War—that you accepted as reasonable, necessary, inevitable—had come to nothing or been changed out of recognition; that much of what seemed to be beginning in 1946 was already ending. You would find that the United Nations and its intertwining systems of alliances had become something less effectual, less noticeable, than the League of Nations. You might observe that the diary of the man who flew the bomber over Hiroshima was no longer secret but had been auctioned (to a collector who bid thirty thousand dollars) and its words at last made public—"My God, what have we done?" But the bomb itself and its descendants had never prevented one people from conquering another for reasons of ideology, religion, race, or mere power, just as in the old days; and the notion that uranium might slake the unquenchable thirst for energy seemed even more remote than it did in 1946. You might also notice some symbolic deaths: of a man named Sarnoff who more than any other had made of television a billion-dollar commercial opiate (but never a medium for ideas, for the enhancement of life); or of a white lawyer named Spingarn, a co-founder of the NAACP and its self-effacing president for most of its life, who after the sit-ins and the demonstrations, the court decisions and the deaths, had lived into cherubic old age and an era when self-respecting younger blacks found his leadership intolerable because he was white. And you could not help but notice that a revolutionary civil war that was beginning in the fall of 1946 in a French colony called Indo-China was yet again changing into something other and perhaps even coming to an end.

The time machine does not give you a very clear picture of what the people you know will become twenty-five years into the future, at the beginning of middle age. At eighteen you can imagine old age clearly or death itself, perhaps even a kind of overall pattern to your life as you would wish it to be, but you have not much sense of the reality: of yourself and your contemporaries living out your lives according to the inexorable choices and accidents of twenty-five years; of your children growing into adults who will unpredictably accept and reject what they have seen in your own life, as you did with your parents' lives. Each generation defines itself against the generation that precedes and the generation that follows, accepting part, rejecting part, but the middle generation was remarkable for how largely it accepted the immediate past and the ideas that grew out of it—and now for how readily it accepts a history and a new generation, our children, that have rejected that past and the ideas that went with it. We were reasonable people. We believed what we were told. But to find out what that means in the twenty-five-year future that has become the present, you must abandon the time machine of imagination. You must wait out the years and go there in fact.

On my way there—to the reunion—I stopped off in Pittsburgh to talk to a man who a few years back was known for his work on one of the television interview shows that were popular then. He had learned the knack of uncovering whatever pain or humiliation was hidden in quite ordinary lives and converting it into images for the show. Meaning to go on to dinner, we went to a bar where it was still quiet enough to talk, but hours later we were still there, still talking, and Chuck was ready to assemble a crew and head for the reunion himself. He knew from experience what he could make of it.

—We are now the fuckin' parental side, Chuck said. What's it all about? Where the fuck are we going? We're not old, but we're not young anymore . . . frustrated, discouraged. . . . And *this* is the story you wanta do. . . .

At the time, I was almost convinced, but what I found when I got there and saw for myself was much quieter. It was not rage or despair that we felt, looking out on the world from the privacy of our lives: we are reasonable people. The world we had grown up in and had inhabited into middle age seemed in 1971 on the point of changing into something painfully different: a world we had accepted on its own terms, whose ideas had seemed to us unquestionable—and now those values were being cast aside, and we accepted that too.

What you accept you do not hope to change. In that summer of 1971 a new and unhopeful spirit seemed to be taking possession of the country's decent majority. After twenty-five years of public clichés endlessly repeated about national power, about the nation's moral and material supremacy, there was suddenly a sense that the national life was in decline and nothing any of us could do could turn it back from ruin. The feeling seemed more serious than the old American habit of anxiety and self-doubt; nor was it simply a reflection of the defeat of every viewpoint on the war in Vietnam, of those who favored it as well as those who were against. That summer, a carefully constructed opinion survey found that a majority of Americans believed that the nation's conflicts between black and white, young and old, had reached a level of irreconcilable violence that could destroy social and political life; and the mere material comforts—home, food, job—that we had always taken for granted had assumed a new importance now that we realized they could be lost. Writers at several levels of seriousness were pointing to the disintegration of the communities we all belong to, from the small community of the family to the larger one of the cities and, finally, to the international community of nations. In that summer even the man we had chosen as President made a speech declaring that the nation now exhibited the classic signs of the decline of a civilization (he said also that if the nation could be saved from final degeneration, it was the Midwestern heartland, where values remained, that would have to do it). One thought of Rome and its decline.

In that summer, therefore, the middle generation also was beginning to feel the chill of history. In our lifetime we had seen the nation rise to a high point; now it seemed that we were coming down on the other side.

—If I had to look at our country in a historical perspective, Allen Kerr had said, I would have to say that we've passed the zenith. . . . There are so many problems. There's a sense of bewilderment that people have because they just throw up their hands, they don't know what to do, it's so complex. . . .

Others had the same perception. For a few, if it was an end of one kind of life that we were seeing, it was also a beginning, though not for us but for a new generation; it is a middle-aged feeling, and if aging itself does not give it to you, your children will.

—In the traditional framework, Spence said, we're declining as a nation. When you become sexually permissive and turn inward—this is . . . a declining society. But I think what's happened is that this is no longer *seen* as a decline. In a human sense . . . I think the world is getting better. . . .

Perhaps this new sense of a nation beginning to die that we had believed all-powerful was easier to endure—or to welcome—because for us the turning point had already come on that day in November 1963 when a couple of lucky rifle shots destroyed the leader who was peculiarly of our generation, for no reason that anyone would ever establish. About Kennedy himself—or the deaths that preceded and came after his—there were varied feelings eight years later: from conventional and only remembered regret to a still fresh hostility ("If I saw a bumper sticker that said 'Kennedy had it coming,'" one man told me without a blush, "I'd laugh"). For most of us, though, the grief had been real and had remained so, compounded with larger feelings than you can have for an individual—the sense that it was not one man but our youth and its aspirations, our generation, that ended at Dallas and that we had somehow *allowed* it to happen, had lacked the wisdom or the strength to prevent it. But for all of us that death demonstrated forever that grace and wit and good will and competence have no more weight in the nightmare of history than the beady-eyed envy that fired the gun; that if you could slaughter one man chosen out of a nation, then you could still slaughter an entire people as the Nazis had slaughtered the Jews, with no more excuse than an infantile mixture of hatred and bestial ideology, and nothing had changed, reason still had not entered men's lives. The men and women of the middle generation made up various explanations for that death: we said the man had courted death, that such a death was merely one of the risks of high office; we called the thing that had happened violence, we said that we were after all a violent people, and when the other deaths followed it was no longer necessary or even possible to grieve. We knew already that they would happen.

And so, with all of these diverse, half-formed, conflicting feelings—the sense of participating in a nation that no longer knew its direction, the memory of the assassinations, of violence and corruption—there was linked another: a yearning for a *leader*, for one man who would be able to express the feelings we could only grope at, who could bring back to us a vision of the national life so clear, so certain, so persuasive that it would bring us together again. These were, of course, qualities that have been conspicuously scarce in the middle generation, and they seemed, perhaps, all the more desirable because of that. Chuck Heimsath, in the perspective of a scholar of politics and history, rejecting our generation's past, made the connection between the lost President and the longed-for rescuer—

—I think the kind of society that we have rigged up here is to blame for the assassinations, if you take them all together. One, I suppose, might be considered an accident of history, but the fact that one led to the other— . . . I think something is emerging but I don't think that we have found a definition of it and a leader that can express it—I think John Kennedy might have been that leader—sufficient to make us all aware of what's happening. . . .

For an old-fashioned, middle-aged liberal who can

remember with what idealism and joy the disheartened Europeans of the 20s and 30s turned to the certainties of *their* leaders, it was hardly an appealing state of mind. It began to seem, in those months of renewing old acquaintances, of looking into past, present, future, as if the young with their chatter of revolution had indeed found a truth as the young Nazis and the young Communists in Berlin in 1932 had found a truth: a self-fulfilling prophecy. Suddenly for the middle generation actual revolution had become possible to imagine. Again, the thought was connected with the lost and hoped-for leadership.

—One thing that I never thought about before, Allen told me, thinking of the young men he talked to in schools, taught at church, interviewed for his college, the young he deeply *liked*—it never even occurred to me, is the possibility that we could have a revolution, or a dictatorship. . . . I've seen young people lately in a very radical form, they're pushing and government is reacting. I can see for the first time the possibility of a real strong guy coming in . . . a very basic change . . . for the first time. . . .

Even anxieties as general as these did not seem to have disturbed the lives of the middle generation, however. *Real* life remained personal and private—lived within home, family, job—and objectively it had yielded most of us a reasonable share of the satisfactions the twenty-five years have had to offer. In many of these lives at the beginning of middle age you could begin to discern a shape; you could see that events of ten or fifteen or twenty years ago that had seemed merely accidental at the time were in fact parts of a meaningful whole, with a connected beginning, middle, and end—as if your life itself were predetermined and you could observe its unfolding but not change it much. If that is the thing you discover about life in middle age, then it is also natural that you should cry out against it: *Is that all there is? Is there nothing I can do?* And many of the people I talked to over the summer were indeed crying out, though mostly in the quiet ways of the middle generation. *Crisis* would of course be too strong a word, yet many of us in our various ways had reached a turning point, a time when life had abruptly assumed a new form or seemed that it might, and we were groping toward whatever was to come. For several of the men this had simply meant changing one job for another very different one, or setting up a small business with the exhilaration of independence and the risk of loss. One man, a research scientist, had apparently abandoned the hope of ever succeeding his distinguished father and that summer was joining an institution utterly different from the one in which he had spent fifteen years of his working life. Another had turned his back on an equal number of years in advertising in order to spend a year writing a novel, and whatever happened next, he was certain he would not go back. For several of the Navy men, the adolescent dream of flying had come to an end with retirement at the age of forty or forty-one and the necessity of starting over. For others, what had happened was not a change of job or style of life but an astonishing and joyous new religious intensity that had seized them after years of merely going—or not going—to church. A number of the women in the Class of 1946 were sharing in similarly drastic changes in their husbands' careers—or simply, perhaps, discovering that children were nearly grown and would soon have no need of them. For some of them, that had meant finding the kind of job a middle-aged woman can get without having any special skills; others had gone back to college to work for a graduate degree, though not so much with the idea that it would lead to conventional college teaching as that the learning, the writing of a dissertation, would give them a chance to express something in themselves that would otherwise remain silent. Among both the men and the women it was a fairly small number whose lives had not reached a critical point of some kind, even if only the sort that jobs or children sooner or later compel you to face.

For Frank Carlborg, adult life had been a series of long-term goals defined with care, worked for, achieved: a doctorate in mathematics made possible by a fellowship that came after several years of teaching; a three-year job afterward of writing a textbook in time left over from teaching; setting up on his own as a business consultant in statistics and making a success of it. Now he was looking for another goal and the search was colored by his sense of life in the nation at large where—

—Things are very, very bad . . . the whole system is falling apart. . . . I think we're not able to solve our problems. Look at the convention of 1968—if you believe this is a democracy, then how can you explain that? Every single open primary was won by a peace candidate. The people's mandate was totally ignored. Those poor kids who wanted to exert their influence in the streets were beaten up and dragged into jail. . . .

While that bitterness was still fresh, Frank had wanted to put it all behind him, and thinking of his Swedish grandparents—

—I was very interested in emigrating, even on a trial basis. . . . I started taking Swedish, I thought it would be possible to go over there. . . .

Then why hadn't he in fact gone to the Scandinavian Utopia?

—It was so consuming it was hurting my business. . . . I'm still interested in going somewhere for a while and seeing if somebody else has figured out what to do. . . .

And yet life seemed comfortable and free, there were friends, family, home. With his growing sense of American life as exploitative and oppressive, there had come a time for him in the 60s when as a teacher he had been confronted with one of those holdovers from the Joe McCarthy years, a written declaration that one upheld the Constitution and was not a Communist or any other form of subversive. Had he resisted?

—I had to sign a loyalty oath—once, when you got your employment. It was part of the job—you take it or leave it.

· In those years, of course, teachers *did* sign such documents with hardly a thought. The alternative was a gesture for which you paid by no longer teaching, perhaps by not working at all; it was a luxury not many thought they could afford.

Jack Stauffer's turning point was nearly the opposite of Frank's, and the two careers together can be taken as the poles—pacifism and force—of American life since 1946. As a mathematician, Frank had been one of a select group of young men the Army sought out and assigned to the Redstone Arsenal in the early 50s, when the first American guided missiles were being built there from the designs of rehabilitated German scientists. The stimulation of being among so much intelligence, so much diversity, had awakened in him a rejection of the purpose he was there for and, in time, of much else in our common lives, past or still to come. (Frank had gone back to Alabama to visit the mathematicians and engineers who started with him and stayed among the weapons-systems people for whom the missiles had provided a way of life that in 1971 was coming to an end. Their thinking, he noticed, had been fixed in 1951 and he was shocked; it was a part of life—the national life, his own —that he could not accept.) Jack, a humane man whose memory of the War was his father working himself to death making rifles, had gone from the Navy, with an engineering degree and a year's study of nuclear physics, to Los Alamos, where the various hydrogen bombs were being developed. That had led him eventually to NASA, finally to an elite community in Maryland and the management of a weapon-development project too secret and too urgent to be named. (He had started out as an aeronautical engineer but had had the luck or wisdom to see, sooner than most, that the country was not going to have great interest in that particular skill.) Throughout, although he felt his children's disapproval, he had done the work not only because it was what he was good at but from conviction.

—We have adversaries around the world who would love to squash this country—for a purely economic reason. The only thing is, can our economy afford to prohibit them from doing it? . . . I have always felt that weapons are . . . a necessary evil . . . unless you can convince me that the whole world is made up of good guys. . . .

And now what, for him, when as he said, "People seem to prefer pacification to power"?

—I've been almost convinced for the last year and a half that the general trend is to minimize the weapons budget —it's fairly obvious that you're on a street that is coming to a dead end. . . .

Jack was, of course, already thinking of what he could do when the dead end finally came. Characteristically for a man of the middle generation, he understood the next step as a technical one: directing the skills he had been mastering for the past twenty-five years—systems management— to a new set of problems. There was, for a start, the spiraling consumption of limited sources of energy, the terrifying discrepancy between American use of world resources and American population.

—The United States, Jack reminded me, has six percent of the world's population—and yet of the exploited resources, we consume eighty-three percent of the world's total. If the other ninety-four percent wanted to enjoy our standard of living, we'd already be at the point of exhaustion. . . . There's only so much here and if you're going to spread it to each individual then you have to limit the number of individuals. . . .

Population, energy, the sharing of limited resources among diverse and antagonistic peoples: if that is indeed what the next twenty-five years are about, then perhaps in Midwestern Evanston—where a compact, fully-developed society has found public ways of expressing its passion without the violence that makes civilized actions impossible—the future is already taking place. There, as it does elsewhere, the future turns on the peculiarly American question of race: the question, simply, of whether blacks and whites will continue to talk and listen to each other, with whatever incomprehension, exasperation, and rage, or whether they will withdraw. And perhaps the answer to that question is what the middle generation—with its distaste for strong feeling, its exaltation of whatever is private, its impersonal and reasonable virtues—will turn out to be for.

A couple of days before visiting Jack, I had spent the evening with a man I had known particularly well in school. We had kept in touch during college and for a while afterward, when we lived within driving distance of each other in Connecticut. That had been years back. In the meantime, he had been divorced and had married an Indian woman I had never met. In the fall, he and his wife would be going to India again to work on a research project spread over several years.

Chuck's wife when I met her turned out to be strikingly dark, a woman that in a crowd an American eye would pass over as yet another variant on black—except for the sari; her speech had the precise intonations of a highly educated Indian that an American hears as British. The two small children had their mother's coloring and straight, ebony hair and were called by Hindi names; looking closely, you could see that their features were in fact like their father's. Because the joy of the very young has long since vanished into adolescence in my own family, I found myself picking the little boy up in my arms and hugging him—and then doubting the gesture, as if it had been compelled.

Presently the children went up to brush their teeth and go to bed and their mother followed them. Chuck and I sat in the living room sipping brandy. It was Chuck who as a child had had nightmares about whether he would be able to follow his father through Yale—and then had been able to imagine nothing beyond it. But he had gone there after all, graduated, earned a doctorate, and for several years had taught there—and finally had put it all behind him and begun elsewhere to gather a reputation as a scholar. And now, a teacher entering into the concerns of his students, though still in abstract, lecture-room terms—

—I find myself shifting in my values along with them and I've been influenced to an extent I would never have thought possible. I feel much better for it because I knew there was something missing in . . . the largely vacuous social ethic that I swallowed in my college years. . . . The War and the Depression made us nonthinking—we could not, as individuals, cope—we had to do so collectively and therefore in a certain degree unthinkingly. . . . After the War, we immediately had the Communist menace foisted on us . . . and we swallowed that line completely. . . .

Like teachers at many other American colleges in these last years, Chuck had faced political riots, police actions, arson, window smashings—*trashing* was the harmless-sounding word the students that year were using for such acts. (A woman in the class at a branch of Kent State had faced the possibility, in the aftermath of the shootings, that the whole enterprise of teaching and learning she was committed to would simply cease to exist—and of course for a time it *did* cease.) At Chuck's university in Washington, at the time of the Laos invasion a riot—a *minor* riot, he called it—had been—

—Caused by the police—I was there, I saw it happen. The students were taking on a procession . . . blocked traffic

... very upset. The university handled it beautifully ... but the police were absolutely abominable ... the most aggressive, provocative bunch of people I've ever seen ... insisted that the roads be kept open ... and eventually tear gas was thrown ... and a lot of innocent people were thrown into jail. ... Admittedly, there was a small group of students who prepared in advance, it seemed to me—they had lots of rocks in their pockets. ...

I thought of the Evanston police chief I had talked to earlier in the summer, holding back in the face of a similar provocation at about the same time and over the same issue; and after a week of restraining all his fierce policeman's instinct for order, discovering that he had been right—the riot had not occurred and no one had been beaten, gassed, or shot. In Washington, while the riot grew and ran its course in the streets, most of the faculty had been safely inside at a meeting discussing what to do about it; it is easy to imagine the eloquence, wit, and passion expended in the search for a sentiment that would magically make the violence go away without the need for courage, wisdom, or strength. Chuck, however, had not attended—his sympathies had led him outside.

—I was gassed several times. ... I was trying to keep the kids out of trouble. ...

It is an image nicely expressive of the middle generation: one youthful-looking, middle-aged professor with his unheeded faculty armband and the mob of students with rocks in their pockets, the burly police with helmets, plastic face masks, clubs, tear gas, all swirling around him. Whatever your sympathies, *you will not be either side's leader* even if they would have you. You remain, as you began, a reasonable man in a world that is not reasonable: a world that may praise reason or turn it to profit or power but in its heart still mostly despises it.

Afterword

The reader will have noticed that about a third of the people who speak in this book do so under fictitious names. There is a good reason for this inconsistency. As I've indicated at various points, I've drawn on several kinds of material in addition to my own recollections and observations: data supplied by members of the committee that organized the reunion of the Class of 1946, including the addresses of all members of the class who were actually found; a questionnaire sent to every fourth person on a geographically organized class mailing list; the kind of historical and statistical information about Evanston in which the Evanston Public Library abounds; and lengthy taped interviews (and a few letters) with about fifty members of the class as well as assorted Evanston town and school officials and a few representatives of the current crop at Evanston High School. (I should observe in passing and without rancor—it is another sign of the times—that the old-fashioned, pre-1946 custom of answering letters seems to have fallen off rather sharply in these twenty-five years.)

Since I had no wish to embarrass anyone by publishing their unconsidered words, however harmless, I assured the people I interviewed that I would let them correct the transcripts of the tapes and be quoted anonymously if they wanted to. Hence, for several months I was locked up with the voices of our conversations in my head while I transcribed them and produced clean copies; the process was less tedious than it may sound since I had mostly enjoyed the interviews in the first place and, apart from the mere labor of listening and typing accurately, enjoyed them again the second time around. The result of my promise, however, was not entirely predictable. A few people reacted to seeing their words on paper with the kind of dismay one feels at hearing a recording of one's voice for the first time: that can't possibly be *me*, that doesn't *sound* like me. One or two, perhaps for the same reason, revised their words beyond recognition and in the process extracted whatever meaning they had had. Others simply displayed the middle generation's normal squeamishness about saying anything that might give remote offense to a parent, wife, husband, child, friend, or colleague, and they retreated into anonymity. They would not, of course, have been the middle generation without that highly developed sense of privacy, and I was grateful for even such guarded candor. The words, at any rate, are as actual as I could make them, even if some of the names they go with are not.

One thing I discovered was that the still-vivid Midwestern proprieties did not always know what to make of my odd role of interviewer. Was I, well, The Press, and was a drink still what you were supposed to do with The Press?

Or, since it was something to do with a book, was I more like, say, a nice-mannered encyclopedia salesman and would coffee or tea be the right thing to offer? The farther I got from Evanston itself, the easier the relationship became; perhaps it was simply that I was learning my job.

To all the people who gave this work of mine, in whatever circumstances and for whatever reasons, their testimony and their time—sometimes an hour snatched from between appointments, more often an unstinted afternoon or evening—I owe more than thanks. The reader will have decided for himself, by now, whether with their help I have indeed written the collective biography of our generation that I set out to write. We have now, at any rate, a record of these lives that we have lived, for there *must be* some record saved against the anonymity of history and time.

There are some more specific thanks owed: to Jackie Butow Wieder, the reunion chairman, whose energy and courage in the face of actual pain provided the motive force that made the reunion possible and who was, I think, as warmly helpful to everyone in the class as she was to me; to Chuck Leffel, the class president (or the last, at any rate, we had a chance to elect), who helped in other ways; to the publishers of this book, who were able to recognize some value in it before I had done the work and who provided the money and the encouragement that made the work possible; to my father and mother, who in my very earliest memories were able to sympathize with whatever I was attempting to do, even when they did not understand it any better than I did myself; and finally to my wife Thulia and our four sons who for nearly a year have borne patiently with my more than usual preoccupation—with the past and a body of men and women they have heard of often enough but will know chiefly through these written words.

Robert Douglas Mead
MARCH 1972